booksonline

Read SAP PRESS online also

With booksonline we offer you online access to leading SAP experts' knowledge. Whether you use it as a beneficial supplement or as an alternative to the printed book – with booksonline you can:

- Access any book at any time
- Quickly look up and find what you need
- Compile your own SAP library

Your advantage as the reader of this book

Register your book on our website and obtain an exclusive and free test access to its online version. You're convinced you like the online book? Then you can purchase it at a preferential price!

And here's how to make use of your advantage

1. Visit www.sap-press.com
2. Click on the link for SAP PRESS booksonline
3. Enter your free trial license key
4. Test-drive your online book with full access for a limited time!

Your personal **license key** for your test access including the preferential offer

9zkf-dnsj-5tgv-wq68

Welcome to the Galileo Press *Discover SAP* series. This series was developed as part of our official SAP PRESS imprint to help you discover what SAP is all about and how you can use the wide array of applications and tools to make your organization much more efficient and cost effective.

Each book in the series is written in a friendly, easy-to-follow style that guides you through the intricacies of the software and its core components. Beginning with "Discover SAP," the first book in the series, you'll find a detailed overview of the core components of SAP, what they are, how they can benefit your company, and the technology requirements and costs of implementation. Once you have a foundational knowledge of SAP, you can explore the other books in the series covering CRM, Financials, HCM, BusinessObjects, and more. In these books you'll delve into the fundamental business concepts and principles behind the tool, discover why it's important for your business, and evaluate the technology and implementation costs for each.

Whether you are a decision maker who needs to determine if SAP is the right enterprise solution for your company, you are just starting to work in a firm that uses SAP, or you're already familiar with SAP but need to learn about a specific component, you are sure to find what you need in the *Discover SAP* series. Then when you're ready to implement SAP, you'll find what you need in the SAP PRESS series at *www.sap-press.com*.

Thank you for your interest in the series. We look forward to hearing how the series helps you get started with SAP.

Jenifer Niles
Vice President
Galileo Press America

 **PRESS**

Brian M. Carter, Frank-Peter Bauer, Joerg Lange, Christoph Persich
Extended Warehouse Management with SAP SCM
2010, app. 600 pp.
978-1-59299-304-9

Christopher Foti, Jessie Chimni
Demand Management with SAP
2009, 398 pp.
978-1-59299-267-7

Varun Uppuleti
Customizing Extended Warehouse Management with SAP ERP
2009, 226 pp.
978-1-59299-286-8

Martin Murray
SAP MM – Functionality and Technical Configuration
2007, 588 pp.
978-1-59299-134-2

Shaun Snapp

Discover SAP® SCM

Galileo Press

Bonn • Boston

Galileo Press is named after the Italian physicist, mathematician and philosopher Galileo Galilei (1564–1642). He is known as one of the founders of modern science and an advocate of our contemporary, heliocentric worldview. His words *Eppur se muove* (And yet it moves) have become legendary. The Galileo Press logo depicts Jupiter orbited by the four Galilean moons, which were discovered by Galileo in 1610.

Editor Erik Herman
Copyeditor Julie McNamee
Cover Design Jill Winitzer
Photo Credit Image Copyright GoodMood Photo. Used under license from Shutterstock.com.
Layout Design Vera Brauner
Production Editor Kelly O'Callaghan
Assistant Production Editor Graham Geary
Typesetting Publishers' Design and Production Services, Inc.
Printed and bound in Canada

ISBN 978-1-59229-305-6

© 2010 by Galileo Press Inc., Boston (MA)
1st Edition 2010

Library of Congress Cataloging-in-Publication Data
Snapp, Shaun.
  Discover SAP SCM / Shaun Snapp. — 1st ed.
      p. cm.
  ISBN-13: 978-1-59229-305-6 (alk. paper)
  ISBN-10: 1-59229-305-0 (alk. paper)
  1. SAP SCM.   2. Business logistics — Computer programs.   3. Production management —
Computer programs.   I. Title.
  HD38.5.S625 2010
  658.4'01028553 — dc22

                                                2009042512

Contents at a Glance

Contents

5   Production Planning and Detailed Scheduling (PP/DS) 99

7   SAP Transportation Management (TM) 139

9 Core Interface (CIF) 183

10 SAP Service Parts Planning (SPP) 201

11 SAP Extended Warehouse Management (EWM) ... 217

Acknowledgments

I would like to acknowledge some assistance I received in different areas of the book. For the chapter on ROI, I turned to Toly Novik at Hitachi Consulting, who has been performing value estimations on projects for years. He provided information that I complemented with my opinions on the process management of value estimation.

I would also like to thank Seal Consulting, which leads the way in providing transparency to previous SCM clients by publishing case studies. Several of these were used in this book.

Preface

This book is written to give you an insightful, practical introduction to the SAP Supply Chain Management (SCM) application. Because SAP SCM is an advanced planning product, there is a lot of depth to cover. SAP SCM was introduced as SAP Advanced Planning & Optimization (SAP APO) in 1998, and over the past 11 years each new release has included added or enhanced applications. The objective of this book is to bring the deep complexity and broad scope of SAP SCM down to a manageable level to help you truly understand what it has to offer.

Who Should Read This Book

This book is written with the following readers in mind:

> **Executive and business decision makers**
> If you're considering SAP SCM for the first time or considering implementing new applications or new functionality within already implemented applications, this book will help you become familiar with the terminology, concepts, components, and technology you'll encounter.

> **Project managers beginning an SAP SCM implementation**
> If you're a manager dealing with a new SAP SCM implementation or new components, and you want to help your people succeed and become more productive, this book explains the overall solution architecture and provides some important tips taken from work on real-world projects about how to manage SAP SCM to get good value from the software.

> **Consultants working on SAP SCM projects**
> If you're a consultant considering entering the world of supporting SAP SCM, this book provides a full solution overview of every application in SAP SCM. SAP SCM is vast, and no one can consult in all areas of the software; however, if you work in one or two applications, this book can help you understand the overall solution at a medium level of detail.

> **IT Administrators new to SAP SCM**
> If you're an IT person who has never worked with SAP SCM and you're coming from the SAP ERP side, this book can be used to get you up to speed quickly on how SAP SCM needs to be supported. We don't delve into hardware or Basis setup, but we provide an introduction to the software that can be used by IT administrators to quickly ascertain the solution they will be called on to support.

> **Workers new to SAP SCM**
> If you're coming on board a new SAP SCM implementation or are presently on an SAP SCM project that is implementing a new application, this book helps you to quickly understand the applications, and some of the broader-themed chapters explain the logic and flow of an SAP SCM project.

What You'll Discover

Two types of books are written on SAP SCM: those that cover one or just a few applications and those that attempt to cover the entire suite. As part of the Discover series, however, this book takes the broadest possible approach to give you an introduction to all of the applications. The book also helps you answer the following questions:

> Which applications best fit your business needs?
> What is the high-level functionality of each application?
> How do the applications interact with one another?
> How do the applications interact with SAP ERP?

The book can also serve as a refresher or an introduction to the functionality added to some of the more mature SAP SCM applications. And, can be a primer on the newer applications in SAP SCM that may not have been introduced the last time you looked at it. Each chapter has a listing of some of the most relevant new functionality as well as the enhancements that have been made to existing functionality.

Throughout the book, I've been careful to define business and SAP-relevant terms so anyone from an SAP specialist unfamiliar with business terms to a business person unfamiliar with SAP terms can understand the information provided. I've also made every attempt to give you examples and case studies where possible to make SAP and its products relevant to you, your business, and your industry.

Navigational Tools for This Book

Throughout the book, I've provided several elements that will help you access useful information:

> Notes provide other resources to explore, or things you should keep in mind.

> Tips call out useful information about related ideas or helpful suggestions.

> Marginal texts provide a useful way to scan the book to locate topics of interest for you, or provide insightful highlights.

This is a marginal note

> Examples provide you with real-world illustrations of functions at work.

> ▶ Warnings draw your attention to areas of concern or pieces of information that you should be aware of while evaluating specific functionality.

> ▶ TechTalk examples provide a look into the technology behind the functions being discussed.

What's in This Book?

We'll begin with a brief look at the historical origins of SAP SCM, and we'll discuss advanced planning versus supply chain planning. We'll also provide a history of the advanced planning market, which is important to understanding the market pressures that caused SAP SCM to develop in ways that have resulted in the current product. From there, we'll move on to the individual application chapters and detail how these applications can help improve your supply chain management processes and your overall efficiency. We'll wrap up the book with a look at how to get a solid return on your investment and look at examples of real-world supply chain modeling.

The following is an overview of what you'll discover throughout the book:

Read the book in sequence or go to specific chapters or sections as needed

Chapter 1 SAP SCM Basics
In this introductory chapter, we discuss who will benefit from this book and any prerequisite knowledge needed, as well as the coverage level of the book. The chapter introduces components of SAP SCM that apply to all of the applications.

Chapter 2 SAP SCM Applications
SAP SCM has 10 applications and 1 integration component. In this book, each of these has its own chapter. This chapter provides an overview of the suite as well as the common interactions between the applications.

Chapter 3 SAP Demand Planning (DP)
The first application we cover is Demand Planning (DP), which is both the most popular application in SAP SCM and also the beginning of

the supply chain planning process. The chapter breaks SAP DP down into its two components: the Data Administration Warehouse and the forecasting component. Understanding the terminology is key to DP, so this chapter describes the basic DP terminology.

Chapter 4 Supply Network Planning (SNP)
Supply Network Planning (SNP) is the heart of SAP SCM. This chapter explains SNP by explaining the different modalities of running SNP as well as going in to some detail regarding deployment and resources and safety stock.

Chapter 5 Production Planning and Detailed Scheduling (PP/DS)
Like Chapter 4, this chapter focuses on the modalities of running Production Planning and Detailed Scheduling (PP/DS). It discusses manufacturing strategies that can be employed in PP/DS as well as how the lot size functionality controls the output of the application. It also compares and contrasts the central master data component of PP/DS, which is the PPM and PDS.

Chapter 6 Global Available to Promise (GATP)
This chapter begins by drawing a parallel between Global Available to Promise (GATP) and a modality of running SNP called Capable to Match (CTM) to make it easier to understand a complex application. It then goes on to explain the different modalities of running GATP and discusses what obtaining GATP functionality can mean for a company. The chapter concludes by explaining the scope of checking, how the ATP structure works, and the ATP tree structure.

Chapter 7 SAP Transportation Management (TM)
In this chapter, we discuss the general and specific processes supported in SAP Transportation Management (SAP TM), previously known as Planning and Vehicle Scheduling (TP/VS). We also cover the interaction with transportation lanes and transportation resources.

Chapter 8 SAP Event Management (SAP EM)
In this chapter, we describe the highly flexible event monitoring software called SAP Event Management (SAP EM). SAP EM isn't so much planning software as it is monitoring software for the supply chain. This chapter discusses the types of sources from which SAP EM can

receive information. Also discussed are the processes supported and the major components that make up SAP EM.

Chapter 9 Core Interface (CIF)
In this chapter, we describe the integration component of SAP SCM called the Core Interface (CIF). We discuss the types of data transferred with the CIF as well as the data sequence. We also cover the integration model, which is the object configured in the CIF, as well as how to manage the movement of these models between the systems.

Chapter 10 SAP Service Parts Planning (SPP)
The SAP Service Parts Planning (SPP) packages are some of the newest and most interesting SAP SCM applications. This chapter covers SPP package's most prominent capabilities, including supersession, repair versus buy, inventory rebalancing, and leading indicator forecasting.

Chapter 11 SAP Extended Warehouse Management (SAP EWM)
In this chapter, we describe the organizational units in SAP Extended Warehouse Management (SAP EWM) that allow the system to be set up. Also covered is the functionality of slotting, rearrangement, and kitting, among other SAP EWM capabilities.

Chapter 12 SAP Supplier Network Collaboration (SNC)
This chapter begins by discussing the business conditions that must pre-exist prior to an SAP Supply Network Collaboration (SAP SNC) project. It then goes on to discuss the different types of collaboration as well as the objects that are shared during each. This chapter also covers how business partners enter inputs into the collaboration.

Chapter 13 SAP Forecasting and Replenishment (F&R)
This chapter communicates the integration between SAP Forecasting and Replenishment (F&R) and SAP for Retail solutions, and how SAP F&R enables the CPFR (Collaborative Planning, Forecasting, and Replenishment) process. Also discussed is how forecasting is performed in the application and how it differs from the rest of SAP SCM.

Chapter 14 SAP SCM's Direction as of Release 7.0
This chapter focuses on how SAP SCM has developed over the past few releases. This is important for those new to SAP SCM or those

familiar with the earlier designs of SAP SCM because the changes have been quite significant. Areas discussed include the DRP Matrix, Planning Services Manager, Service Level Planning (a.k.a. Inventory Optimization), cross enterprise capabilities such as cross enterprise monitoring and collaboration, as well as the addition of the warehouse and the retail store to the SAP SCM space.

Chapter 15 Getting More from SAP SCM

In this chapter, we describe how to get more from SAP SCM. This can include how to recover SAP SCM implementations that don't meet expectations, enforcing accountability, and looking for new areas of functionality within SAP SCM to leverage on currently successful SAP SCM implementations. Finally the chapter finishes by discussing ways to attain SAP SCM acceptance as well as how to most effectively maintain SAP SCM implementations for the long term.

Chapter 16 SAP SCM and ROI

Return on investment (ROI) is a proven method for evaluating software implementations. In this chapter, we discuss the components that make up ROI, as well as who should perform the ROI calculation. Overall, the way in which the ROI process is managed is at least as important as the actual technical estimation itself. The chapter points to things to look out for to make sure the process is solid and as devoid as possible of bias and influence.

Chapter 17 Conclusion

Rather than reiterating the previous chapters, the conclusion focuses on important concepts that are not addressed in the other chapters of the book. Examples include real-world supply chain modeling, such as changing constraints, a topic not often discussed in material on planning. Also discussed are under-applied solutions such as SAP TM and SPP. In addition, we look at how SAP SCM fits into the larger trends around supply chain management as well as broader topics such as environmental issues. The chapter concludes by discussing the new concept of manufacturing in which networked production facilities are treated as super factories and supported by SAP SCM.

SAP SCM Basics

In this chapter, we'll describe SAP SCM and how it's used in today's economy, the SAP approaches to supply chain management, and how companies can use and benefit from SAP SCM. A large amount of functionality has been introduced since the last time many people looked into SAP SCM, so even if you've seen it before, you'll find a lot of new information. Each chapter has a listing of some of the most relevant new functionality as well as the enhancements that have been made to existing functionality.

What Is SAP SCM?

SAP SCM is an umbrella term for a set of applications that provide advanced planning capabilities. This set of applications is fed by standard SAP integration technologies, which include the Core Interface (CIF) and BAdIs, among others, that connect the system to SAP ERP. SAP SCM is used to improve and optimize the supply chain by enabling automated decision making, providing improved analytical

SAP SCM includes applications that provide advanced planning tools to users, and sharing information with internal system customers and external business partners.

SAP SCM Origins

Although dominant in advanced planning today, in 1998, SAP wasn't yet a strong player in the supply chain management area

SAP SCM was introduced as SAP Advanced Planning & Optimization (SAP APO) at the height of the advanced planning trend back in 1998. This was a period where i2 Technologies was the number one advanced planning vendor, and Manugistics was close on its heels. It's hard to believe because SAP SCM is so dominant in the advanced planning space today, but at that time SAP wasn't seen as a factor and wasn't even predicted to become one.

 Note: Supply Chain Planning Versus Advanced Planning

It's important to draw the distinction between supply chain planning and advanced planning. *Supply chain planning* is covered by the applications and functions of SAP ERP Sales and Distribution (SD), Materials Management (MM), and Production Planning (PP). These applications provide supply chain execution functionality along with some basic planning functionality (safety stock and MRP, basic forecasting, availability checking, and production planning among a few others), but none of these applications cover advanced planning. *Advanced planning* is future based and deals in different scenarios that are presented to planners, who then pick the best alternative. In advanced planning, the plan may be recreated several times before it's firmed and sent to the execution system. True advanced planning systems can't execute recommendations; they can only make recommendations. So, while SAP had supply chain applications for some time before SAP APO, SAP APO was SAP's first venture into advanced planning.

But SAP needed to create a separate set of applications, rather than incorporate advanced planning within SAP ERP because planning systems and transaction processing systems work differently. At one point, SAP felt that advanced planning was overly esoteric and would only be desired by a small fraction of its customer base. Somewhere along the line though, SAP changed its view and developed its own advanced planning suite. This was probably largely market driven, as we'll explain later in this chapter.

SAP's Approach to Supply Chain Management

SAP has a relatively, standard solution architecture for supply chain management that has grown through time to reflect the trends of advanced planning. While SAP SCM began its life as SAP APO and was originally intended to perform advanced planning only, it has since evolved to essentially be a repository for all advanced supply chain functionality not covered in SAP ERP. As an example, while the SAP warehouse management functionality in SAP ERP has essentially been stabilized, the more advanced functionality has and will continue to migrate to the SAP SCM application known as SAP Extended Warehouse Management (SAP EWM). Both applications cover warehousing, but their capabilities are different (Figure 1.1).

SAP SCM has developed along with the trends in advanced planning

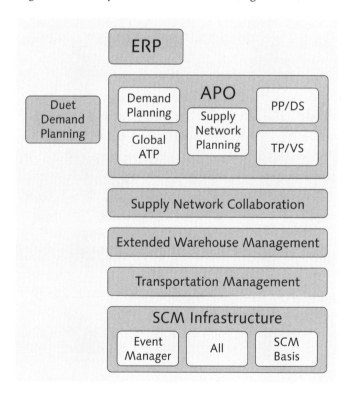

Figure 1.1 SAP SCM Solution Map

Optimization

The goal of optimization is to ensure the "optimal" operation of your supply chain

In its early years, SAP APO was sold on its ability to perform optimization. This is primarily because it was an industry-wide practice to market advanced planning software in this way. In fact, SAP APO, or SAP Advanced Planning & Optimization, had the term directly in its name.

Optimization has two general meanings. One is more of a business nature, which basically means to produce the best outcomes. The other has to do with the area of operations research, from where the supply chain optimization originates. For this book, we'll define optimization as the use of software tools and processes to ensure the optimal operation of a supply chain, including the optimal location of inventory within the supply chain and the minimizing of operating costs (including manufacturing costs, transportation costs, and distribution costs).

Linear Versus Discrete Optimization

The step function is one of the most commonly used input functions

Optimization works best in situations that are perfectly "linear," so that inputs can be increased or decreased in a continuous fashion. An example of a linear input is an order quantity. In a perfectly linear optimization, any order quantity from zero to infinity can be placed and fulfilled. But in reality, supply chains are not perfectly linear problems. For example, the lot size is a discrete value that limits the flexibility of the order quantity. One item may be ordered in units of 50, but if 135 units are desired, and the current inventory is less than 35, then 150 must be ordered to meet this demand. SAP SCM has a number of techniques, such as lot size, that alter the problem being solved from perfectly linear to discrete, or what is known as a *step function*. This is very important for making the resulting recommendation realistic (Figure 1.2).

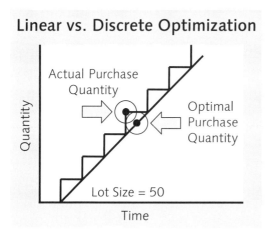

Linear vs. Discrete Optimization

Actual Purchase Quantity

Optimal Purchase Quantity

Quantity

Lot Size = 50

Time

Figure 1.2 Linear Optimization in Supply Chain Must Be Moderated by Constraints

Reduced Focus on Optimization

Although optimization drove development in SAP SCM at one time, it no longer does. The evidence for this is that optimization is an option in three of the older applications (Supply Network Planning [SNP], Production Planning and Detailed Scheduling [PP/DS], and SAP Transportation Management [SAP TM], formerly known as Transportation Planning and Vehicle Scheduling [TP/VS]), but isn't an option in any of the newer applications (SAP Extended Warehouse Management [SAP EWM], SAP Supply Network Collaboration [SAP SNC], SAP Event Management, SAP Service Parts Planning [SAP SPP], and SAP Forecasting and Replenishment). In addition, the core optimization functionality in SAP SCM has been stabilized for some time. This shift is partly due to the fact that optimization didn't meet its originally envisioned potential. So, the newer applications in SAP SCM have tended to downplay optimization in favor of other functionality.

If optimization didn't "change the world" of supply chain, the question naturally becomes "Why not?" There are a number of reasons, but one of the most prominent was the implementation and maintenance difficulty combined with the lack of company knowledge.

Ex Example

There is a story about an advanced planning vendor that was running the optimizer engine in the background, but when the engine actually went down for a few days, no one even noticed. This was because the planning was primarily being performed by heuristics that had been custom coded with scripts, and the solution was not using the optimizer at all. Whether the client knew the optimizer was not being used is unknown. This is more common than reading press releases and industry periodicals in the area would make you think. While optimization sold a lot of supply chain software, it wasn't necessarily what the customers went live with, as evidenced from this example.

Implementing and maintaining optimization methods requires much effort and long-term investment. Secondly, optimization requires a great deal of discipline and knowledge on the part of the implementing company. Many companies want the benefit of advanced planning but are not culturally, financially, or skills-wise prepared to make the sacrifices required to get the outcomes they desire.

More often than not, companies want simple solutions that deliver value quickly. That isn't how optimization works. And this is partly because the software has historically been designed to be more complex than is necessary (Figure 1.3).

Figure 1.3 Costs Versus Benefits in Planning Solutions for SNP

Which Companies Are Right for SAP SCM?

Some companies are better suited to undertaking an SAP SCM implementation than others, and Table 1.1 shows the typical characteristics that allow a company to be successful with SAP SCM.

Current users of SAP ERP are good candidates for SAP SCM

Company Characteristics	Description
Current SAP ERP users	A few SAP SCM implementations have been performed on accounts without SAP ERP, but, in general, this is a major precondition.
Already have effective planning processes	SAP SCM is very flexible and can adjust to most planning processes, but it can't fix a broken process. As with other planning software, the best successes typically come from companies that are already good at planning.
Make planning a priority	If the commitment isn't there in terms of management support and finance, it's better not to begin an SAP SCM implementation. SAP SCM implementations are complex affairs, so companies must be ready for this complexity. Part of this is content knowledge of planning, but another component is open mindedness to new approaches. This is because there are a number of best practices inherent to the SAP SCM processes.
Focused on improvement	Transaction processing systems such as SAP ERP are a necessity, but a business can still run without a planning system. SAP SCM implementations cause companies to evaluate their priorities. Some applications request the estimation of a cost of a lost sale, so those successful with SAP SCM are effective at asking these questions and getting answers.

One way of looking at whether your company is appropriate for SAP SCM is to determine if it has maximized the planning functionality within SAP ERP. And in some cases, requirements will naturally lead to the consideration of SAP SCM. In Chapter 2, SAP SCM Applications, we'll cover the specific needs that often drive the decision to implement different applications. However, more generally, SAP SCM is most beneficial to companies that are dedicated to improving their planning processes and that already have good planning processes to begin with.

This statement isn't only true of SAP SCM but of advanced planning tools generally. While we're not able to find specific research to back this up, our anecdotal evidence from our experience on projects indicates that the better the company is at planning before it implements an advanced planning system, the more the company gets from the implementation. Being effective at planning helps the company know how to design the system and also allows the company to better leverage what it ends up implementing.

Cross Application Components

As mentioned earlier, this book is broken into a format of one chapter per application. However, there are some important concepts and components that cut across the applications, so even though all of the components will be addressed in the same form in individual chapters, they may also be covered in other chapters.

Product Location Master

SAP SCM is based upon a supply chain network, which is a combination of locations, products, and transportation lanes (Figure 1.4).

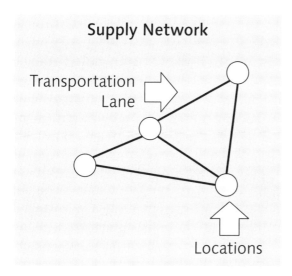

Figure 1.4 Combination of Transportation Lanes and Locations Is Referred to as the Supply Network

SAP SCM, as with the plant and material master in SAP ERP, stores a large amount of configuration information in the *product master*, *location master*, and the *product location master*. We refer to these masters throughout the book, so it's important to know the differences between them.

Product master, location master, and product location store data in SAP SCM

1. The *product master* contains the information and attributes that relate to the product across all locations. Data elements such as the product number, the material group, and the gross weight and volume are all attributes of the product master. The product master is set up once per product.

2. The *location master* deals with the attributes of the location. This includes the location name, address, any calendars associated with the location, and specific settings that apply to a few of the different applications, such as SNP, TM, SAP Forecasting and Replenishment, and SAP SPP.

3. The *product location master* is essentially the product master with added fields and added tabs to hold these fields that modify the product per location.

For instance, in SAP SCM, safety stock isn't set at the product or location level but at the product location level, so there's no field for safety stock control on the location master or on the product master, but there are safety stock control fields on the product location master. This not only holds true for safety stock but also for many other attributes that only come into play at the product location master.

Planning Areas and Planning Object Structures

Planning areas are containers for key figures

Planning areas and planning object structures are important cross application items. They are high-level data groupings that control the entire supply chain model. They have a central administration that allows the areas and structures to be copied, maintained, and deleted.

 Note

> Planning areas are the central data structures of Demand Planning (DP) and Supply Network Planning (SNP). A planning area is a container for key figures. Planning areas feed an interface object called a planning book, which is a spreadsheet view with a number of aggregation and macro capabilities. At the most basic level, key figures are the numerical values in the spreadsheet.

Planning Object Structure

Just as a planning area is a container for key figures, a planning object structure (POS) is a container for characteristics. The combination of characteristics is called characteristic value combinations (CVCs). The POS stores every unique combination of CVCs, which is then used to help control disaggregation when data is manipulated at summary levels. In the previous analogy, we stated that key figures are the numerical values in the planning book spreadsheet. Characteristics are like the textural column and row headings, with the time characteristic on the horizontal axis, and the product characteristics on the vertical axis.

Planning Versions

The planning versions set up the data that are available for use. A model with the same supply network can have slight alterations in terms of control fields on, say, the product location master, making the version create different planning results than a different version of the same model that has the original product location master settings. Multiple versions can be kept over time and run to see how the results change. Because only the active version planning results are communicated back to SAP ERP, multiple versions can be run in perpetuity along with a live active version, without ever impacting the active version. If the changes are deemed desirable, then the settings from the inactive version can be migrated over to the active version.

Planning versions are variations of the planning models

However, it's important to remember that this all takes maintenance effort. It's one thing to talk about the benefits of simulation and say that SAP SCM supports it, but it's another thing to support simulation modeling with the resources necessary to make it happen.

Planning Versions and Mass Maintenance

Planning versions can be particularly effective when used with the MASSD or the mass maintenance transaction. This allows the person performing the configuration to make wholesale changes in the master data; however, this transaction should not be used on the active version. Instead, by using the simulation planning version and then mass maintenance to make changes, the changes can be fully tested before mass maintenance to make the tested changes on the active version.

Planning Book

DP and SNP are two SAP SCM applications that use the planning book intensively. The planning book is the window into the planning data for most planners and other users. Planning books consist of the following areas:

> Characteristics

> Key figures

> Data views

> Macros

> Forecasting functionality

> Promotional functionality

> Interactive graphics

Planning books provide views of various levels of aggregation as well as ad-hoc viewing of planning data. Planning books allow you to combine characteristics and key figures in a flexible way for presentation to the planners. In fact, the planning book is the main user interface into SAP, and SAP SNP also uses it, but it uses other views as well.

Creating the planning books is a significant part of the implementation because there are many different combinations of planning books that can be created. Here are some of the important characteristics of planning books:

Planners can be assigned to as many planning books as you like

> Different planners are responsible for different products and geographies, so the planning book can be customized for each planner or for groups of planners.

> As planners become more familiar with the planning book, they can be trained to create planning books for themselves.

> The act of creating a planning book doesn't change or affect the underlying data that the planning book displays.

> The planning book is provided with the capability to perform complex calculations through its own macro builders. The results of the macro calculation are displayed through extra rows in the planning book.

Tip

> SAP SCM comes with some standard macros, but they aren't sufficient to cover all of the implementation needs. Unfortunately, creating macros in a planning book is nothing like creating calculations and formulas in Excel. So, because of the substantial learning curve, planners typically can't create their own macros.

Conclusion

This book is designed to provide an introduction to the entire SAP SCM suite by providing the broadest possible exposure to SAP SCM with the lowest possible effort on your part. Areas of detail that are not covered in the book can be found from the many references included in the Bibliography of other SAP SCM books that go into more detail on the different topics. For the older applications such as SNP, DP, and PP/DS, this will be relatively simple. For the newer applications such as SAP EM, SAP SNC, and SAP EWM, this will be a bit more challenging. Of course, SAP training offers courses in all of these topics.

But let's move on to the next chapter and get a broad overview of all of the applications offered in SAP SCM.

SAP SCM Applications

In this chapter, you'll get a high-level overview of the entire SAP SCM suite. SAP SCM is made up of a series of applications that address the supply chain planning areas of most companies. One area of great interest to companies is how SAP ERP supply chain planning is different from the advanced planning that is available in SAP SCM. While a point-by-point comparison could be its own book, generally speaking, SAP ERP contains a simplified version of some of the functionality in SAP SCM, so an application from SAP ERP can be substituted, at a lower level of functionality, for an application in SAP SCM. To show you how this works, let's look at one area that is well understood by many people, Supply Network Planning (SNP).

In SAP ERP, the forecasts and sales orders are taken into account, and reorder point methodologies are used to develop the in-stock positions at the various locations. However, SAP SCM can do much more than this. For instance, not only does it have more methods to apply to develop the supply network plan (such as the ability to prioritize demands with Capable to Match [CTM] as well as the ability to optimize against cost), it also has many more settings that lead to a more

SAP ERP offers much of the same functionality as SAP SCM, but at a reduced level nuanced and sophisticated supply plan than SAP ERP. Additionally, as a planning system, SAP SCM can have different planning approaches tested without ever affecting the transactions that are managed in SAP ERP. This simulated capability is one of the significant advantages of planning systems generally. But it's important to note that the vast majority of companies that purchase and implement SAP SCM also have SAP ERP. Therefore, an important project objective is to determine which areas will be handled in SAP ERP versus which will be managed by SAP SCM. Unfortunately, there is no easy answer to this, so it must be solved on a project-by- project basis.

Most companies that implement SAP SCM also have SAP ERP

But because no company has implemented the entire SAP SCM suite as of this writing, it's common for a company to use only one application from SAP SCM. Implementing two makes the company a serious user of SAP SCM, and implementing three to four applications makes that company an intense user. What this means is that companies that decide to implement SAP SCM select the areas of supply chain management that are most important for them and implement the SAP SCM application or applications for that area, leaving the rest of their supply chain controlled by a combination of SAP ERP and other legacy or best-of-breed solutions.

Find experienced consultants, and keep an open mind when planning your implementation

Determining which applications are the best to implement isn't as straightforward as it sounds, however. Many companies are currently attempting to move toward service level planning (a.k.a. inventory optimization); however, this functionality is contained within an application that many customers don't look at unless they're considering service parts planning. Fortunately, the service level planning capability in SAP Services Parts Planning (SPP) can be applied to finished goods businesses just as easily as it can be applied to service parts businesses. For this reason, it's important to find resources and consulting partners who have deep knowledge and broad experience in the various applications. It's very difficult for one resource to be both, however. In addition to resources, it's important for your company to keep an open mind, because there may be functionality that is accessed from applications that weren't originally thought to be part of your initial implementation, but they could add value to the company.

This is just one side of the story, of course. The other side is that SAP SCM is now such a broad suite of products that there are applications that cover areas of the supply chain for which companies don't have business processes. For instance, many companies don't have manufacturing operations, so they don't need Production Planning and Detailed Scheduling (PP/DS). And, not every company does supplier collaboration, so obviously they wouldn't need SAP Supplier Network Collaboration (SNC).

Customize your implementation to include the applications for the areas important to your company

In addition to limiting the implementation of different applications, companies also don't implement all of the functionality within a given application. In fact, when performing SAP SCM diagnostics on accounts, the amount of functionality implemented within an SAP SCM application is usually surprisingly small. For example, we've seen SAP Demand Planning (DP) implemented in a way that has it acting as a container for the forecasts from other systems, but it performs no forecasting itself. And we've seen PP/DS used only to level production output and nothing else. There's nothing wrong with this, and implementing even small areas of functionality can be beneficial to a company because each of the applications can be used for narrow or broad implementations.

 Tip

Because Transportation Management (TM), and Production Planning and Detailed Scheduling (PP/DS), can be implemented with constraints, they add more reality to the planning process.

But we're getting ahead of ourselves a little. For now, just keep in mind that, in most cases, companies can benefit by implementing more SAP SCM applications than they do, but every company has a finite amount of resources to apply to planning.

There's no one
correct way
to implement
SAP SCM

So there's no one right answer and no one right way to implement SAP SCM, but there are approaches to implementing the software that have proven to be more successful than others, and we'll highlight many of them throughout the book. For now, let's look at an overview of the different SAP SCM applications.

SAP SCM Applications

SAP SCM is an umbrella term for a number of applications that address specific areas of the supply chain. Table 2.1 lists the applications that make up SAP SCM:

Application	Full Name
DP	Demand Planning
SNP	Supply Network Planning
PP/DS	Production Planning and Detailed Scheduling
GATP	Global Available to Promise
TM	Transportation Management (formerly known as Transportation Planning and Vehicle Scheduling (TP/VS)
SPP	SAP Service Parts Planning
EWM	SAP Extended Warehouse Management
EM	SAP Event Management
SNC	SAP Supplier Network Collaboration
F&R	SAP Forecasting and Replenishment

Table 2.1 SAP SCM Applications

The CIF integration
component enables
SAP SCM to run.

Another component that comes with SAP SCM is called the *Core Interface* (CIF), which is used for integration. Some people consider CIF an application; however, we don't list it as an application here because it's an integration component that is necessary for SAP SCM to run but doesn't provide supply chain functionality.

SAP SCM Configuration Folders

The SAP Easy Access configuration screen organizes the applications by folder. The Implementation Guide (IMG), which is where the more basic configuration items are set up, also organizes the applications by folder. The SAP Easy Access screen incorporates settings from the IMG into its configuration (see Figure 2.1).

SAP segments its configuration into two different areas: IMG and Easy Access Menu

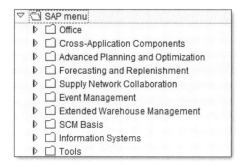

Figure 2.1 The SAP Configuration Menu

The SAP configuration menu is now broken into folders with older SAP SCM applications in the Advanced Planning and Optimization folder. APO was the original name of SAP SCM, and the term still applies to the suite. For applications such as SNP and DP, these are listed under the Advanced Planning and Optimization folder. Newer applications such as SAP SNC and SAP EWM are not purely planning applications, and, therefore, they are listed under the overall SAP SCM folder, but not under the Advanced Planning and Optimization subfolder. When we refer to menu paths in this book, we'll refer to this path as simply APO in order to save space. So when the APO folder is opened, all of the application folders within SAP SCM become visible (Figure 2.2).

SAP APO helps improve customer service while lowering costs and increasing profits

Figure 2.2 The Only New Application Under the APO Folder Is SAP SPP

Roughly one half of the applications (DP, SNP, PP/DS, GATP, and TM) are older and more established, so they have a large number of implementations behind them. The other half (SAP SPP, SAP EWM, SAP EM, SAP SNC, and F&R) is more recent additions that have received the bulk of the development work in the past few SAP SCM releases. One in particular, F&R are really just getting started as an application, and this book is one of the first to cover it in any detail.

SAP SCM as a Visionary Application

The SAP SCM suite is developing rapidly and is adopting many supply chain practices that are on the leading edge and even somewhat beyond what the industry is doing. Much of the functionality around supply chain management is becoming stabilized in SAP ERP, and the advanced supply chain capabilities are increasingly released in SAP SCM.

This means more companies that haven't considered SAP SCM in the past will likely be analyzing it in the future. Understanding the capabilities of the new applications and how they can be used with the older applications as well as with the rest of SAP is a challenge for many companies and consultants. But that's where this book comes in and why it focuses on clearly explaining topics that may be confusing, including the various SAP SCM application interactions.

New functionalities in SAP SCM integrate well with the rest of SAP ERP

 Tip

Being visionary can be good, however, it's important that companies pick a level of functionality that is realistic for them, especially because there are many different levels a company can implement with SAP SCM, some of which are advanced. And some of the more advanced levels are not appropriate for every company.

SAP SCM Application Interactions

Understanding how each application operates is one part of understanding SAP SCM. However, another equally important component is knowing how the applications interact with one another and with other systems. Because we'll cover each application in its own chapter, we'll spend the rest of this chapter discussing interactions. But keep in mind that although there are strong tendencies for certain applications to work together, SAP SCM doesn't have a singular workflow between the applications.

There isn't one singular workflow between applications

 Example

One of the most common workflows in SAP SCM is for DP to produce the demand plan and for it to be sent to SNP.

However, this example is only one of a few possible workflows between the systems. The supply plan, which is created by SNP, can also be sent from SNP to SAP ERP, and it can also be sent to DP as you can see in Figure 2.3.

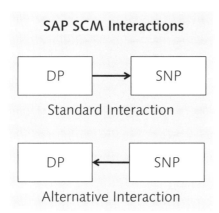

Figure 2.3 SAP SCM Interactions

It's also true that different systems can be placed between applications. So your company could implement SAP TM but use a non-SAP warehouse system (instead of SAP EWM) and use SAP Event Mangement (EM) to monitor both the non-SAP warehouse system as well as SAP TM.

 Tip

Throughout this book, we'll frequently use the term "100% SAP solution," but this is merely a hypothetical term used to explain what the SAP alternatives are because this is a book focused on SAP. In reality, at the majority of companies, a mixed application strategy will be in place. Therefore, it's important to remember that in the real world, the architecture implemented by companies is much more complex and varied and includes many non-SAP applications.

Common Application Interactions

Most SAP SCM implementations include non-SAP applications

Although there is flexibility in SAP SCM applications interactions, there are some application interactions that are common, and some that will very rarely, or never, be implemented. One of the most common is the interaction described earlier between SAP DP and SNP. This is a very established process (sending the demand plan to supply planning) within SAP SCM. On the other hand, it's unlikely that very many implementations have integrated SAP DP with SAP TM, although even this integration is possible (DP could be used to forecast transportation volumes). Figure 2.4 highlights which applications tend to work with which for the most common application interactions or co-implementations.

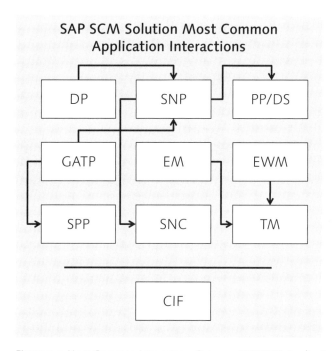

Figure 2.4 Most Common Interactions Between SAP SCM Applications

The Core Interface (CIF) is an integration harness with pre-built adapters that transfer both master and transactional data between SAP ERP and SAP SCM. CIF supports all of the applications for integration, although to different degrees, which is why we've placed it in Figure 2.4 as unassociated with the SAP SCM applications. This way, it represents CIF as a platform component. The one caveat to Figure 2.4 is in reference to F&R and EWM. Both of these applications are just getting started in the marketplace as of this writing, so there isn't a lot of integration to date. In Figure 2.5, you'll see the second types of most common integrations.

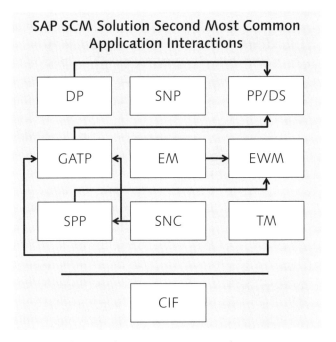

Figure 2.5 The Second Most Common Types of Interactions

SAP ERP to SAP SCM

SAP SCM and SAP ERP integration is highly effective and well defined

SAP SCM can be implemented without SAP ERP, but it's extremely uncommon, and we've never heard of a single case of SAP SCM being implemented this way (this isn't to say it doesn't exist). The integration between the systems is a primary reason SAP became the number one advanced planning vendor in the world. Today, SAP ERP's interaction with SAP SCM is more defined than the interactions between the SAP SCM applications. The most common SAP SCM to SAP ERP interactions are shown in Figure 2.6 and 2.7.

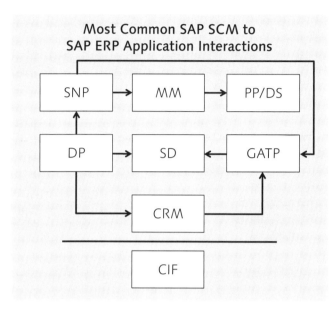

Figure 2.6 Most Widely Installed SAP SCM Applications' Interaction with SAP ERP Applications

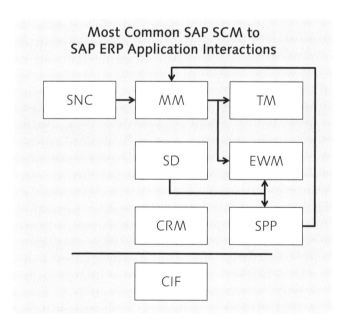

Figure 2.7 Lesser Installed SAP SCM Applications' Interaction with SAP ERP Applications

In addition to how SAP SCM applications can interact with SAP ERP, there are other key drivers to consider.

Implementation Key Drivers

If you have maximized the planning in SAP ERP, you're a candidate for SAP SCM

In Chapter 1, SAP SCM Basics, we said that one way of looking at whether your company is appropriate for SAP SCM is if it has maximized the planning functionality within SAP ERP.

In addition to this, there are often key business drivers that lead a company to implement one of the SAP SCM applications. Table 2.2 summarizes a list of the business drivers that have inspired companies to turn to SAP SCM. This list is by no means comprehensive but it gives you an idea of some of the reasons.

Application	Business Drivers
DP	› Improving forecast accuracy
	› Creating faster forecast analysis
SNP	› Handling reduced inventory
	› Needing more sophisticated safety stock management
	› Constraining the supply plan (i.e., making it more realistic)
PP/DS	› Enhancing production asset use
	› Constraining the production plan (i.e., making it more realistic)
GATP	› Providing an available-to-promise commitment on orders to customers.
	› Enabling more comprehensive searching for inventory to meet customer orders
TM	› Reducing transportation costs
	› Improving carrier management
	› Synchronizing transportation with factories and warehouses

Table 2.2 Key Business Drivers for SAP SCM

Application	Business Drivers
SPP	› Obtaining planning capabilities customized for service parts › Repositioning service parts › Making improved buy versus repair decisions
EWM	› Managing large-scale warehouses › Interacting with RFID › Using advanced slotting, rearrangement, and cross docking
EM	› Monitoring supply chain activities in partners › Creating a nerve center for supply chain management
SNC	› Improving communication with supply chain partners › Handling reduced inventory levels
F&R	› Improving replenishment of retail shelves › Integrating with RFID › Creating more accurate store forecasting

Table 2.2 Key Business Drivers for SAP SCM (Cont.)

Conclusion

As you learned in this chapter, the SAP SCM applications can be connected in a number of different ways to address your company needs. As SAP SCM has grown, it has added more applications to address more areas of functionality. Now that there are a large number of SAP SCM implementations, and experience with the system has become more widespread, there are more options for using SAP SCM in new and inventive ways.

This makes implementing SAP SCM more complicated but also more interesting than it was when there were only five applications. SAP SCM is no longer a specialized option but an integral part of supply chain management for SAP-oriented companies. Increasingly, having a high-level understanding of the overall architecture of SAP

SCM is critical but not sufficiently emphasized by many companies. And, while it's logical to use consulting companies to perform SAP SCM implementations, the implementing companies must eventually develop their own SAP SCM solution architects who understand the business needs, the SAP SCM design, where the product is going, and what new functionality can be leveraged to advance business interests. Deciding which applications are best for your company as well as the best areas of the application to configure requires a detailed analysis that explains how the selected applications will integrate with each other and other non-SAP systems, as well as how they will integrate with SAP ERP.

In the next chapter, we'll begin our look into the individual applications, starting with SAP Demand Planning.

SAP Demand Planning (DP)

In virtually every industry, companies are challenged by increasing customer expectations, stricter regulations, changing market dynamics, and the ongoing impact of the Web — all of which are compelling them to re-examine and refine how they forecast and manage demand. In supply chain planning, it's considered one of the more, if not the most critical processes.

For some time, the main area of differentiation between forecasting software was the algorithm used to drive the results. However, over the past few years, software companies began using more sophisticated databases that allowed fast response times for looking and forecasting at different levels in the product, location, and time dimensions.

SAP Demand Planning (DP) in SAP SCM offers both robust forecasting and database capabilities that integrate very strongly with SAP SCM Supply Network Planning (SNP). SAP DP can also be implemented at very different levels; for example, it can be used to model at a high level or at a detailed level, and it can quickly roll up forecasts at various levels in the hierarchy. Companies also find SAP DP convenient because it uses the same underlying database as SAP NetWeaver Business Warehouse (BW), which is the SAP data warehousing solution.

Demand Planning as SAP SCM's Most Popular Application

SAP DP's forecasting is more advanced than SAP ERP forecasting

SAP DP is the most widely installed of the SAP SCM applications. Along with Supply Network Planning (SNP) and Production Planning and Detailed Scheduling (PP/DS), SAP DP is one of the original applications introduced with SAP APO. SAP DP has been popular in part because many businesses are interested in forecasting and are typically striving for continued improvement in the quality of their forecasts. And, while SAP ERP has some basic forecasting functionality, SAP DP's forecasting capability is far more advanced. SAP DP fills a need for clients who are already SAP ERP customers.

For those customers who don't have SAP ERP or SAP SCM, DP offers several advantages over other offerings, including the capability to integrate the forecasting system into the rest of the enterprise. SAP ERP can be run with its internal forecasting capability, or this functionality can be disabled, and SAP DP can be used to send the demand plan directly to SAP ERP. It can also be used along with SNP, allowing SNP to perform the supply planning and communicating the purchase requisitions to SAP ERP.

 Note

Forecasting in SAP SCM is performed in SAP DP and several other places, including SAP SPP and F&R. For example, Expected Goods Receipt functionality can be seen as a forecast in SAP EWM, and SAP SNC manages forecasts.

Two Halves of Demand Planning

SAP DP has two major components that require two very different skills. One half of SAP DP is the Data Warehouse Workbench, which sets up all of the data structures and transfer rules from other systems to populate the model with data. And because SAP DP deals with large amounts of historical data, it (along with SAP Service Parts Planning [SPP], which uses the same data tools) has the greatest data emphasis of any SAP SCM application.

 Note

> Most clients use forecasting systems that are designed for finished goods systems to perform forecasting for service parts. The reason for this has to do with several factors. One is that many companies do not know that service parts have different forecasting requirements. For example, service parts are forecasted using a different probability distribution (Poisson or Negative Binomial rather than the Normal distribution used for finished goods). A second reason is that service parts planning forecasting as part of a differentiated software product is still relatively new and still gaining acceptance. SPP provides far more appropriate forecasts for service parts over SAP DP.

The second half of SAP DP is the actual forecasting portion. If you have been exposed to forecasting, SAP DP will be very familiar. All of the same forecasting techniques that you've used in the past with other tools can be found in SAP DP. Figure 3.1 illustrates how the two halves of SAP DP come together.

If you are familiar with standard forecasting techniques, the biggest adjustment using SAP DP will be to the Data Warehouse Workbench

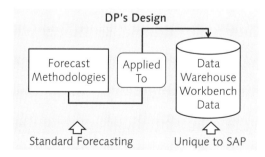

Figure 3.1 Data Applied Over Data Warehouse Workbench Data

> **▶ Note**
>
> For some time, SAP DP was the only SAP SCM application that used the Data Warehouse Workbench, but this changed with the introduction of SAP Service Parts Planning (SAP SPP), which uses the Data Warehouse Workbench the same way as SAP DP. However, SPP does this for service parts, while SAP DP is used to forecast finished goods. The forecasting methodologies for service parts benefit from a custom service solution, but if a company hasn't implemented SAP SPP or doesn't intend to, SAP DP can be used for service parts forecasting, though with a less effective and less accurate result. More specifically, with the same demand history, SAP DP tends to forecast a higher unit quantity.

Basic Functionality and Concepts of SAP DP

There is a natural, common process flow to SAP DP that many companies use as illustrated in Figure 3.2:

1. Receive data from different sources.

2. Perform forecasting.

3. Manually check the forecast.

4. Release the forecast to SNP.

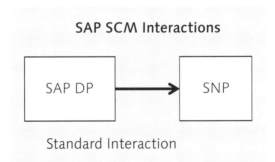

Figure 3.2 SAP DP Sending the Demand Plan to SNP

This is the most common interaction between SAP DP and any other application. However, not all implementations of SAP DP also implement SNP, so when SNP isn't used, SAP DP can pass the demand plan to another supply network application, or the demand plan can be sent to SAP ERP (Figure 3.3).

The "demand plan" is also known as planned independent requirements (see Chapter 1)

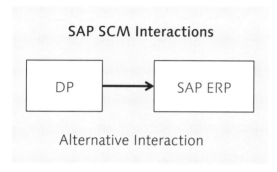

Figure 3.3 SAP DP Can Also Be Connected to SAP ERP

You can then use this demand plan to create planned independent requirements in SAP ERP. However, this isn't the only alternative way to set up SAP DP to run in a process workflow. Another option is to send the forecast to Production Planning and Detailed Scheduling (PP/DS) to procure or produce individual components based upon the characteristic-based forecast.

But the most common way of running SAP DP is in the background. It's also the most efficient from a processing perspective. However, when a planner is trying to see how the forecast reacts to changes or is trying to break in a new forecast method, interactive planning is more desirable because interactive planning allows the planner to quickly observe how changes they make affect the forecast.

Interactive Demand Planning

Sending the forecast to PP/DS is covered later in the, Forecasting section

Interactive planning works best when the planner is working with a more narrow set of data, so the planner can apply the necessary analysis to understand the impact for forecast changes. Interactive SAP DP has its own view, which allows forecast comparison and aggregation and disaggregation. The Data Warehouse Workbench supports the flexibility in aggregation along the dimensions of product, location, and time.

Data Warehouse Workbench

The Data Warehouse Workbench is the configuration interface for the SAP DP Data Mart, which is the data environment that supports SAP DP. The Data Warehouse Workbench is also the identical data-modeling tool available with SAP NetWeaver BW (previously known as SAP NetWeaver Business Intelligence). Data is manipulated in the Data Warehouse Workbench in preparation for having the forecasting methodologies that are selected applied to the data. This can be the most challenging area of SAP DP because of the complexity of setting up the workbench. The workbench is where data objects are set up, where objects are related to other objects, and where the loading from different sources is configured. In the workbench, the most basic objects are the InfoObjects, which are either key figures or characteristics.

 Tip

A person with a good background in forecasting can understand the forecasting methodologies in SAP DP quickly. However, using the Data Warehouse Workbench is a specialized skill that takes time to acquire and a good deal of time to master.

InfoObjects

Several types of InfoObjects are used, but the two most important are *characteristics* and *key figures* as described in Table 3.1 and illustrated in Figure 3.4.

Characteristics and key figures are the new names for data elements used in spreadsheets

InfoObject Types	Description
Characteristics	Best thought of as the rows and columns of spreadsheets. Characteristics can be things such as time or sales units. Characteristics are text or date values.
Key figures	The actual values of the intersections of the row and column headings. Key figures are numerical values.

Table 3.1

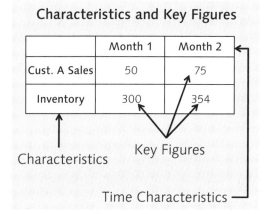

Figure 3.4 Characteristics and Key Figures

 TechTalk

Key figures are numerical values because they represent the actual values to be forecasted. Characteristics, on the other hand, are the text headings for what is forecasted.

In SAP DP, because the key figures are numerical values, you edit them in the Data Warehouse Workbench (Figure 3.5).

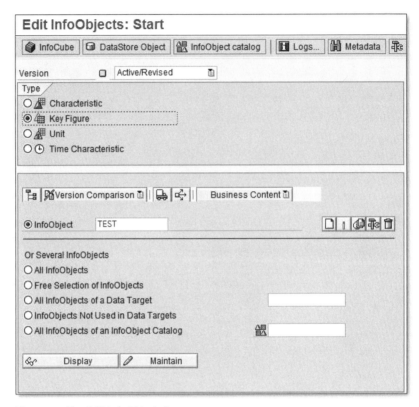

Figure 3.5 The Edit InfoObjects Screen

Data types are all numerical for InfoObjects

Figure 3.6 shows the different data types that can be selected for creating key figures: Amount, Quantity, Number, Integer, Date, or Time. You'll notice that all of the alternatives are numerical values. The actual process of setting up the InfoObjects is easy, and can be set up very flexibly. The main issue is how to get the InfoObjects to represent the business.

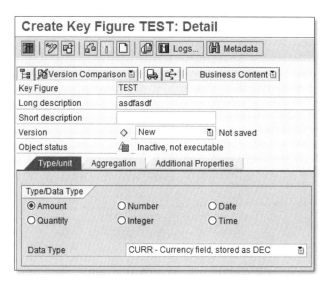

Figure 3.6 Selecting Key Figures Type/Unit Type in One of the InfoObject Create Screens

All of the InfoObjects that are used for forecasting must be configured in the Data Warehouse Workbench; however, the actual data to populate the InfoObjects are fed from other systems, such as from the history of sales orders in SAP ERP. Characteristic InfoObjects are placed in another container called a planning object structure (POS) (covered in Chapter 1). POS is one of the two main planning structures within SAP SCM; the other is the planning area. POS contains the characteristics, while the planning area contains the key figures. These two structures work in conjunction with one another to support SAP SCM.

Configure InfoObjects in the Data Warehouse Workbench

Sometimes, it seems the SAP DP objects are much like a Russian nested or Matryoshka doll, where one layer simply hides another, which reveals another. Similarly, there are many containers in SAP DP, and a significant part of understanding SAP DP is simply learning

To understand SAP DP, you need to understand containers

which containers do what and which containers reside inside of other containers. Table 3.2 provides a brief list of the most prominent SAP DP containers.

Container	Description
Planning area	Contains the units of measure, aggregation level, and key figures.
Planning object structure (POS)	Contains all characteristics. They are assigned to planning areas. POSs are assigned to planning areas and can be assigned to more than one.
InfoProvider	An SAP NetWeaver BW object which data can be loaded into. Some InfoProviders are actual containers for data, and others are virtual InfoProviders. This includes InfoCubes and InfoObjects.
DataSource	Loads an InfoProvider. DataSource examples include flat files and SAP ERP. They load data targets, which are InfoCubes and InfoObjects.
InfoCube	Star schema structure, which forecasting methods are run on.
InfoObject	Characteristics and key figures. The lowest level of data in SAP DP.

Table 3.2 SAP DP Containers

Many of the objects listed in Table 3.1 may be viewed in the Data Warehouse Workbench, which is where the objects are built and manipulated (Figure 3.7).

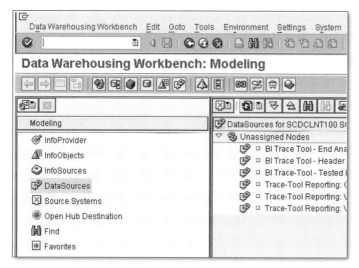

Figure 3.7 Data Warehouse Workbench Showing the Modeling Objects (left) and the Nodes (right).

InfoCubes are built from several intermediate objects but incorporate the InfoObjects described in the previous paragraphs.

In addition to InfoCubes and InfoObjects, DataSources load DataStore objects

InfoCubes

InfoCubes are multidimensional structures that provide analytical capabilities such as drill-up and drill-down navigation. They are "multidimensional" because the product, geography, and time dimensions are combined in an interrelated manner in the database.

A number of activities must happen to InfoObjects before they become InfoCubes, and most of the activity in the Data Warehouse Workbench is intended to eventually move data into InfoCubes. However, the SAP InfoCube is actually a misnomer. InfoCubes aren't "data cubes" but instead star schemas. The distinction goes beyond simple nomenclature and has important implications.

Data cubes versus star schemas

TechTalk: Data Cubes Versus Star Schemas

Data cubes are very specific multidimensional data objects. One of the main features of data cubes is that they take time to build. While being built, the data cube isn't accessible. However, the advantage of multidimensional data objects is their speed of query or report generation. Star schemas, on the other hand, are relational structures that are slower to query but have the advantage of a higher uptime percentage than data cubes. One mechanism isn't better than the other; they simply have different advantages and disadvantages. However, the SAP InfoCube is a star schema.

A star schema is a relational structure that has a fact table surrounded by dimension tables. Figure 3.8 shows the structure of an InfoCube, and Figure 3.9 shows how they appear in the Data Warehouse Workbench.

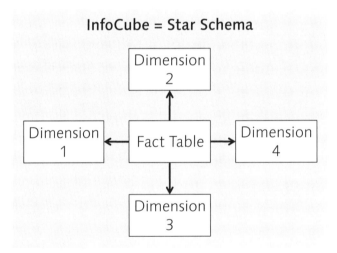

Figure 3.8 An InfoCube Diagram

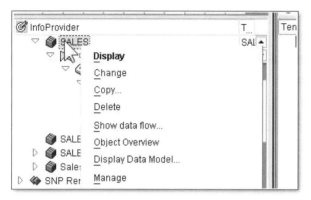

Figure 3.9 InfoCubes in the Data Warehouse Workbench

Now that we've covered the data side of SAP DP, let's move on to its forecasting functionality.

Forecasting

If you are familiar with forecasting, this should be easy to understand because forecasting methods for supply chains have been standardized for some time now. SAP DP's forecasting methods can be selected from the Model tab of the planning book, which was discussed in detail in Chapter 1.

SAP DP can choose from different forecasting methods to find the best fit

However, the methods don't necessarily have to be selected manually. SAP DP also provides best-fit functionality that allows it to choose from the different forecasting methodologies to pick the one that "best fits" with the historical trend line. This is a very useful feature for automating the forecasting selection process and is activated by selecting Auto Model Sel 1 or 2 from the Model tab of the planning book. However, when SAP DP is implemented, it often, although not always as the case study in this chapter demonstrates, replaces the existing software-forecasting solution, so any new results provided by SAP DP's best-fit calculations must be reconciled with what has been done up to the time of the new implementation.

This is part of the normal migration process and particularly true if the system that is being replaced doesn't have best-fit functionality or the best-fit functionality was not accessed or used. Use of the best-fit functionality may result in an extremely similar or identical inventory forecasting method to what has historically been used. However, either way, running the best-fit functionality can provide beneficial observations, and the best-fit functionality can be run repetitively. Additionally, there are factors in terms of running the best-fit functionality that must be performed appropriately and fully documented to understand the best-fit selection.

Forecasting Methods

The methods available within SAP DP and their descriptions are listed in Table 3.3.

Forecast Type	Description
Univariate	Using a single variable to perform forecasting.
Causal	Using the assumption that it's possible to identify the underlying factors that might influence the variable that is being forecast.
Composite	A combination of univariate and causal.
Forecasting with BOM	Essentially aggregated forecasting, which forecasts at a high level and then forecasts the subcomponents as derived demand. Uses SAP DP-PPMs (production process models) or PDSs (production data structures).
Characteristic-based forecasting	Forecast integrated with SAP PP/DS to allow the production or procurement of the individual components. Uses the iPPE (integrated Product and Process Engineering) or the products' versions from SAP ERP.

Table 3.3 Forecast Methods

Next, let's discuss *what* SAP DP forecasts.

Characteristic Value Combinations

Characteristic value combinations (CVCs) are one of the most impor- | CVCs are key to
tant features of SAP DP — they are the master data of SAP DP. CVCs | SAP DP and must
are used to create relationships between fields. For instance, the com- | be consistently
bination of the characteristic of *sales* with the characteristic of *region* | realigned with
allows the model to show sales by region. And because forecasts are | your business
performed for all sold units (except at the highest levels, e.g., a financial forecast), CVCs are critical to creating complex multidimensional
forecasts.

CVCs are the combinations that are eventually displayed in the planning books to users. CVCs in an InfoCube can be as small as just two
characteristics or as large as hundreds of CVCs. The ability to see
more relationships is desirable but only up to a certain point. A large
number of CVCs will negatively affect performance, so they must be
added with a view toward economy.

 Example

Several questions must be answered on SAP APO projects, including
what is the right level of detail to model and how many CVCs to model.
SAP DP provides significant capabilities in terms of the number of CVCs;
however, each CVC takes up resources to manage. Again, the deciding
factor is what is appropriate for the specific business need.

Realignment

CVCs aren't stagnant because they represent business activities that
aren't stagnant. So CVCs must reflect the current configuration of the
business and must change through time with the business. As new

products are brought out, and the organizational structure is altered, the CVCs must change as well because they are representations of the products. For instance, if an item is offered in new regions, this must be reflected in SAP DP. Some CVCs must be deleted, and some new CVCs added, as well as copying planning data between the CVCs. The procedure for doing this in SAP DP is called *realignment*. If you are experienced with data warehousing, this term will be familiar because the same term is used in other data warehousing solutions. Because you need to continually update the CVCs with the business, realignment is a critical housekeeping function for SAP DP.

 Note

There is another process connected to realignment called the *copy function*. Realignment for this process is complex and detailed, but for the purposes of this book, you just need to understand that realignment is the main activity to adjust the SAP DP data to changes in the business.

This concludes our look at some of the underpinnings of SAP DP, so now we'll move on to a discussion of the more business-oriented functionalities of SAP DP.

Promotion Forecasting

Business-oriented functions

Promotions forecasting is actually closely related to collaborative forecasting (which is discussed in Chapter 13, SAP Forecasting and Replenishment [F&R]) because when companies focus on promoting specific items, the forecasting system must reflect this, or the forecast will be in significant error. This adjustment to both the promoted item, and items whose demand is related to the promoted item, is called promotion forecasting.

The promotion functionality in SAP DP allows historical sales data to be adjusted for the timing of previous promotions so the promotion doesn't erroneously influence future forecasts. There are a number of settings for promotional forecasting in interactive planning; however, some of the more interesting are listed in Table 3.4.

Setting	Description
Number of periods	The periods to apply the promotion factor (along with the start and end date)
Key figure where promotional data is to be saved	A key figure created in anticipation of performing promotional forecasting and called something to identify it with promotions
Promotion base	Characteristics used as the basis for promotions

Table 3.4 Promotional Forecasting Options

Releasing the Plan

Managing aggregation in SAP DP is a significant issue because forecasting at the right level has important implications for system performance. Forecasts are often aggregated both by product group and duration.

Plan Release and liveCache

SAP DP data are stored in liveCache, which is a combination of hardware memory and memory management software that allows planning calculations to be performed to meet the performance needs of SAP SCM. LiveCache is one the components that allows users to interact with the data in memory through the planning book interface. After manual review and approval, the forecast is released from liveCache.

liveCache allows users to interact with the data in memory

Plan Destination

When the demand plan is released to SNP or SAP ERP, the plan is most often disaggregated because SAP DP has the longest time horizon and is the most aggregated planning application in the SAP SCM suite. So while this is necessary and works for SAP DP, the other applications aren't aggregated in this way, in which case a disaggregation process is necessary. This disaggregation is controllable by users and can be performed based on equal measure, manual adjustment, or the averages of the level below the higher aggregation level. This is necessary for making the forecasting performed at a higher level usable for subsequent planning processes.

This concludes our look at the core functionality of SAP DP. If you've used SAP DP in the past, you may recognize a few of the changes, but for those of you who are new, we'll summarize the main improvements, and wrap up with a real-world case study.

SAP DP Release History

Recent improvements to SAP DP include the following:

> Point of sale data to create short-term statistical forecasting

> Re-initialization of forecast parameters and trend depending (placing limits on the values of the forecast)

> Configuration relevance for characteristic-dependent planning

> Customer forecast management (where customers regularly send forecasts data to the vendor, and where this is used as the basis for replenishment planning)

These improvements provide extra functionality at the margin of SAP DP and extend existing functionality by improving its maintainability.

Now let's look at a case study of a company using SAP DP.

Case Study

Company

This global entertainment company is focused on the production and distribution of entertainment products.

Challenge

Having many forecasting systems, the company wanted to integrate its forecasts from various systems in a way that allowed many different groups to have access to the forecasts, to compare the forecasts, and finally to incorporate the combined demand plan into the supply plan and to SNP, which the company had also implemented.

Solution

This company opted to use SAP DP, but not for its forecasting, and instead decided to accept and display the forecasts from various systems with the planning book. Adjustments were made in SAP DP, and the combined demand plan was released to SNP.

Value Achieved

SAP DP can be implemented in many different ways. One forecasting issue many people don't think of is what happens when SAP DP or any other forecasting software is implemented at an account that already has other forecasting systems implemented. In some cases, it's more inconvenient and difficult to normalize on a single forecasting system. However, it's important that the forecasts end up in SAP SCM to drive the supply plan. The solution that several companies have come up with is to use SAP DP as a "container" that incorporates the forecasts of other forecasting systems.

After the systems are brought onto the same time buckets, different divisions may keep their existing forecasting system, or some departments may decide to use SAP DP, which is a mixed approach. This allows different users to access the overall forecasts (from all departments) by viewing the data in SAP DP using the planning books. In addition, high-level finance forecasts for all departments can be obtained by simply extracting data, or viewing the data in SAP DP. Next, the combined demand plan can be released to SNP. This is an excellent way to integrate multiple forecasting systems into SAP DP, which then integrates to the rest of SAP SCM.

Conclusion

SAP DP uses a complex data infrastructure to support standard forecasting techniques. This infrastructure is controlled through the Data Warehouse Workbench. SAP DP can send its demand plan to other SAP SCM applications such as SNP or to SAP ERP. As the most implemented SAP SCM application, SAP DP has a large number of implementations behind it. Because companies tend to place significant resources in forecasting, SAP DP is one of the most desirable of the SAP SCM applications to implement and is often the first application implemented.

In the next chapter, we'll cover Supply Network Planning (SNP).

Supply Network Planning (SNP)

Having a responsive supply network that can seamlessly integrate with your own systems is critical in a demand-driven market. With Supply Network Planning (SNP) in SAP SCM, you can achieve this goal. SNP manages your supply network and the planned inventory positions at all of your product locations. The common outputs of SNP drive the procurement and production processes with requirements that have been filtered through SNP and managed in a way to provide systematic procurement and production signals that are, in some cases, constrained and realistic. SNP is important in matching supply with demand. When both SNP and Global Available to Promise (GATP) are implemented, the supply plan from SNP is used to commit on requests, and when allocation is performed, the inventory from SNP is allocated by GATP.

SNP comes with predefined key figures and characteristics

SNP is often considered the heart of SAP SCM because it ties together many of the other SAP SCM applications. Those implementing SNP must be keenly aware of the interrelationships with other SAP SCM applications. SNP is about managing the inventory at all of the locations that make up the supply network, which is all of the stock holding locations (warehouses, manufacturing plants, regional distribution centers, even retail stores, in some cases).

Although there are several ways to achieve your supply network plan objectives, the end result of your supply plan should be to have the best possible inventory position per location along with the necessary transactions being sent to the execution system to make this happen. At the highest level, your demand plan, which is a time bucketed forecast that either begins as or is eventually disaggregated to a product level, is compared with the stock on hand and in-transit to determine your production, procurement, and inventory repositioning decisions. This demand plan can come from SAP DP or other demand planning applications.

Manage your inventory at all locations so you have the best inventory position per location possible

The strength of the system is its capability to look out to the edge of the planning horizon (which is set as a parameter); incorporate all of the planned inbound and outbound material movements, along with the future expected demand; and make decisions that put the company in the best position to meet demand at the lowest possible cost. A 100% SAP solution looks like Figure 4.1.

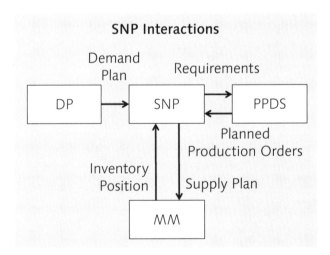

Figure 4.1 SNP Interactions

Many other SNP interactions are possible besides the one we just described, such as performing inventory collaboration with SAP SNC.

 Tip

SNP is a highly flexible application that has a high number of interactions with different application. This is because supply planning sits at the center of planning and interacts with the most planning processes of any of the SAP SCM applications. These different interactions could fill another book, but the important thing to take away is that SNP has many interactions that can support different processes.

Basic Functionality and Concepts of SNP

SNP is designed to plan the movement of material through a supply network. The supply network is made up of locations, connected by transportation lanes.

Methods of Running SNP

SNP can be run in three ways: heuristics, Capable to Match (CTM), or the SAP Optimizer. The method you select will have a great effect on the implementation and on the resulting output. The decision to select one method or another is often due to company characteristics such as the following:

You can run SNP via heuristics, CTM, or the SNP optimizer

1. Whether the company is generally supply constrained

2. Whether the company maintains good cost data and can agree on how these costs are to be applied

3. The effort the company is willing to place in both the implementation and in the maintenance of the solution

Table 4.1 compares these three methods.

SNP Method	Description
Heuristic	Used for unconstrained planning and requires capacity leveling. Designed for companies that either cannot or aren't interested in modeling their constraints. Of the three methods, heuristics are the closest to MRP (Material Requirements Planning), and so this method is the easiest transition for planners.
Capable to Match (CTM)	Used for capacity-constrained clients that need to allocate inventory to a set of prioritized customers.
SNP optimizer	This creates different plans and then selects the plan that minimizes costs. These costs include production and procurement. Perfect for companies with a good understanding of their costs and that want to plan their business around these costs.

Table 4.1 SNP Methods

SNP Optimizer

The methods differ along a number of dimensions. For instance, optimization is the most time consuming of the methods for running SNP. The time it takes is understandable when you consider what the optimizer is doing. SAP Help describes this in detail:

> *The SNP optimizer takes into account all model constraints simultaneously. This means that the optimizer takes into account the available capacity of all resources at the same time. Thus, during multilevel production, for example, all the manufacturing levels are incorporated simultaneously into planning.*

It's much easier to create software to perform something complex, than to actually run the software and consistently do that complex thing well

The optimizer is designed to result in the best possible plan with respect to constraints such as transportation lane capacity and warehouse capacity. However, "best" is subjective and based on assumptions. So if "best" to your company means meeting requirements at the lowest possible operational (not implementation) costs, then the optimizer is the "best" of the three methods. However, the optimizer has the highest implementation and maintenance cost. This is primarily because the detailed cost information required to set up and run the SNP optimizer takes a great deal of effort to build, agree upon, and maintain. Many companies find that they simply don't have this level of detail and can't commit to develop it. In our experience, optimization is beyond most companies.

To run the optimizer, you need to quantify the following costs:

> Production

> Storage

> Transportation

> Procurement

The SNP optimizer runs through a routine that creates a number of different plans that each result in a different cost calculation. It then selects the plan that produces the lowest overall costs. The optimizer also attempts to minimize costs while meeting the demands placed upon the system. It performs this optimization against constraints that are the natural limitations of the supply network, such as transportation and storage capacity.

Optimization models maintain both soft and hard constraints

 Tip

Soft constraints can be violated but at a cost. Hard constraints can't be violated.

Heuristics

On the opposite site of the complexity and implementation effort continuum from optimization is the heuristic method. Because they are less precise, heuristics, or "rules of thumb" as they are colloquially known, are the fastest way to arrive at a solution. The use of heuristics shares some similarities to using Materials Requirements Planning (MRP) in SAP ERP, but they provide far more flexibility than MRP. Heuristics are also the easiest to implement, and planners can usually understand what heuristics are doing most easily of the three methods. Furthermore, a number of heuristics are designed for specific problems, so combining heuristics can lead to a solution that is customized to a given planning situation.

Unlike CTM or optimization, heuristics require a multistep planning process. After heuristics are run, capacity leveling is performed to move loads off of overcapacity periods and resources. Because the process is so close to MRP, if you want the most incremental change possible from MRP, heuristics are a good alternative.

 Tip

> One of the first decisions to be made with regard to SNP is which method should be used. Each has their advantages and disadvantages, and one isn't "better" than the others. The question is appropriateness. Because every implementation is based on the knowledge and capability of what the companies and planners have done previously, and because heuristics are so similar to MRP, it can be considered the lowest risk of the methods to implement.

Capable to Match

Pegging is the link between receipts and issues

Capable to Match (CTM) is the third way of running SNP. CTM is suitable for clients that are resource constrained and that have a number of customers that they need to allocate inventory to in a prioritized manner. A simplified way of thinking about this planning approach is that the end result of a CTM plan is that higher priority customers take inventory from lower priority customers. For example, between two customers of different priority that place their orders on the same day, the higher priority customer receives a full allocation, and the lower priority customer receives whatever is left over. Depending on whether fixed or dynamic pegging is used, a day later a higher priority customer can place an order and possibly take all of the inventory from both of the previous customers.

Note

Fixed pegging means assignments are permanent; dynamic means the assignments can change on each successive planning run.

Capable to Match Configuration

Let's look at some of the configuration details for CTM. CTM is primarily configured through CTM profiles defined in Table 4.2.

CTM Profile Control	Description
The Master Data Selection	Includes which product and locations the CTM profile should apply to.
Demand Selection	Determines which orders or forecasts are included. This is a very important configuration detail that completely changes the scale of the implementation. With forecasts commitment, CTM looks as far out into the future as is defined in the planning horizon.
Supply Selection	Includes different categories of stocks

Table 4.2 CTM Profile Control

The important things to know about configuring the CTM profile are that you can set multiple parameters differently between the profiles; there's no limit to the number of profiles you can create, and they can be copied over providing a high degree of flexibility in terms of how CTM is run and how the parameter data for CTM is maintained.

SNP optimizer is also controlled by a profile

Figure 4.2 shows the CTM Planning Scope tab, which is where the Master Data Selection of the CTM Profile is selected. This determines what will be included and what will be excluded from the planning run.

Figure 4.2 The Planning Scope Tab of the CTM Profile

Figure 4.3 shows the Strategies tab of the profile, which controls critical settings such as whether CTM should use fixed pegging or dynamic pegging. The pegging type has important implications for system performance as well as for which companies receive allocations. Fixed Pegging assigns the requirement to the supply once, and Dynamic Pegging reassigns requirements that were assigned to supply in previous runs again, and during every new planning run. Another important setting is the scheduling direction that directs CTM to schedule before or after the lead date minus the total lead time.

Figure 4.3 The Planning Strategies Tab of the Strategy Tab of the CTM Profile

While prioritizing customers is the most implemented prioritization method in CTM, CTM can prioritize requirements a number of ways:

> Location

> Delivery priority

> Product number

> Desired quantity

 Note: CTM and Capacity Constraints

The entire CTM logic is based on the idea that the implementing company is capacity constrained. However, companies don't stay constrained, or at the same level of constraint as time passes. In some years, for instance, during recessions, companies that were previously capacity constrained can find themselves with overcapacity, so you need to discuss this topic during the implementation. Technically, CTM can be run without capacity constraints, and although this undermines the concept, companies do model this way.

CTM is covered in great detail by Balaji Gaddam in *Capable to Match with SAP APO*, SAP PRESS.

SNP Resources

Resources are used to model constraints in the supply chain

Resources are used in multiple applications in SAP SCM to model constraints in the supply chain. Of all the SAP SCM applications, resources are used most in PP/DS. However, SNP, TM, and SAP EWM all use resources. SNP resources come in more of a variety than the resources in the other applications because SNP is modeling more types of activities, though at a higher level. For instance, SNP uses transportation resources, which are similar, although used differently than vehicle resources used by TM. There are different types of resources because there are many types of constraints in the supply chain. The resources in SAP SCM that apply to SNP are listed in Table 4.3.

SNP Resource Type	Definition
Single-mixed resources	These can be used for continual and exact time scheduling. Exact time scheduling is the most detailed form of scheduling. These are used when one activity can be carried out at a time. Because they are simple, they are easier to set up and maintain.
Multi-mixed resources	Essentially the opposite of single-mixed resources. Used when several activities are carried out concurrently.
Production line resources	These are resources that can be scheduled to the exact time for an activity.
Bucket resources	These are higher level resources expressed as a quantity or a rate. However, they can only plan down to the level of a day.
Transportation resources	Same as the bucket resource but with the distinction that it may apply to consumption or production capacity.
Production line mixed resources	Used for task-based scheduling where the resource determines working times and rates.
Calendar mixed resources	These are only time-oriented resources and not capacity oriented.

Table 4.3 SAP SCM Resources for SNP

Note

Resources can be constrained or unconstrained; using unconstrained resources is called infinite planning.

Common SNP Objects

SNP has a number of the same elements as SAP DP, so if you just read Chapter 3, these will be familiar (Table 4.4).

SNP and SAP DP Elements	Description
Key figures	The numerical values to be planned
Characteristics	The row values to be planned
Planning areas	Container that defines the key figures, the aggregation of key figures, and the currency planned, among others
Master planning object structures	Groups together characteristics that can be planned in SAP DP and SNP

Table 4.4 SNP and SAP DP Elements

Capacity Leveling

Capacity leveling is performed as part of the heuristic planning process and for specific bottleneck resources (resources that restrict the capacity of the operations). Under heuristic planning, constraints aren't set, and the plan is allowed to place an unlimited amount of capacity on resources. This is the first step of the planning process when using heuristics. The second step is called capacity leveling. Capacity leveling moves loads that are too high for the resources to before or after the period of time of the request date. This results in either excess inventory being held (if moved prior to the request date) or an order delay (if moved after the request date). But if customers can know this far in advance, they can either accept or reject the schedule

Use capacity leveling for bottleneck resources

adjustment. Rejecting it usually means you'll have to search for other suppliers. However, even when you have to turn away customers, your credibility could be enhanced because the customer has ample time to make alternative arrangements.

Capacity Leveling Profiles

Profiles are used to control the capacity leveling process. This allows for the reuse of the same capacity leveling profile options, which can be configured. Table 4.5 shows several of the options in the profile.

Capacity Leveling Profile Options	Definition
Capacity Leveling Method	Heuristic, optimizer, or BAdI (Business Add-In)
Scheduling Direction	Forward, backward, or combined
Order Prioritization	Order priority for processing
Handling of Fixed Orders	Order fixing during capacity leveling
The Maximum Resource Utilization	Capacity of that resource
The Maximum Runtime for Capacity Leveling	Time allocated to the exercise

Table 4.5 Capacity Leveling Profile Options

 Note

Business Add-Ins (BAdIs) are inserted into SAP to provide for specific user requirements.

This concludes our look at the different methods for running SNP, so let's move on to other aspects of the application.

Planning Book

As with SAP DP, SNP also uses the planning book to provide planners and users with a view into the planning data. SNP comes with a number of standard planning books that enable the following functionality:

> Sales and Operations Planning

> Interactive SNP and Transport Load Builder

> DRP

> VMI

> Interactive Scheduling Agreements

> Hierarchical Planning

> Product Interchangeability

The planning books are all designed for specific processes, but planning books can be created flexibly to customize the view for the various planners. The planning books, in addition to custom reports, are important ways for planners to gain information from and interact with SAP SCM (Figure 4.4).

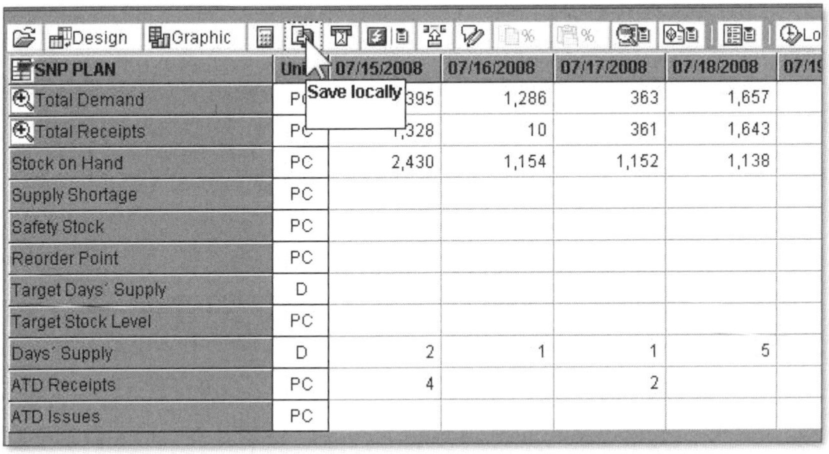

Planning books

SNP PLAN	Uni	07/15/2008	07/16/2008	07/17/2008	07/18/2008	07/19
Total Demand	P	Save locally 395	1,286	363	1,657	
Total Receipts	P	1,328	10	361	1,643	
Stock on Hand	PC	2,430	1,154	1,152	1,138	
Supply Shortage	PC					
Safety Stock	PC					
Reorder Point	PC					
Target Days' Supply	D					
Target Stock Level	PC					
Days' Supply	D	2	1	1	5	
ATD Receipts	PC	4		2		
ATD Issues	PC					

Figure 4.4 The Planning Book Provides a Spreadsheet View of the Planning Data for Users

SNP stores the data that is in the planning book in a way to support user needs, which we'll discuss next.

liveCache and Data Storage

SNP allows data to be stored in several ways:

> liveCache time series objects

> liveCache orders

> InfoCubes

liveCache stores objects in a combination of memory and database. liveCache can be contrasted with another storage technology that we discussed in Chapter 3 — InfoCubes. While InfoCubes are long-lasting structures stored in the SAP DP Data Mart and designed to be repeatedly queried, liveCache is designed to provide performance and storage for values that constantly change. The pegging, which connects demand elements to supply elements, occurs in liveCache. After pegging has been performed, the data is moved out of liveCache into the normal SAP relational database.

Safety stock mitigates variability in the supply chain.

SNP Subcontracting

SNP can plan not only the internal capacity of the company that implements and manages SNP but the capacity of subcontractors. This capacity setup data originates from SAP ERP and is imported into SAP SCM as a subcontract relationship. You'll gain significant extra functionality if you use SNP production process models (PPMs), which are the source for obtaining products that are produced internally.

PPMs allow for production planning to be modeled at a high level within SNP. These PPMs represent production capacity that resides at the subcontractor's plant. Another method of incorporating external partners is through SAP SNC.

 Tip

> The allure of being able to manage subcontractor's capacity and perform supply demand matching is powerful. It opens the possibility for companies to specialize in managing supply chain systems, and it allows others to perform fulfillment.

SNP and Supplier Network Collaboration

Planning subcontracting material is becoming increasingly common. To meet this growing need, SAP has invested significant development effort in enhancing the functionality in Supplier Network Collaboration (SAP SNC). SNP even has its own subcontracting planning book view that ships with the product. This allows SNP to incorporate the subcontracting planning process. And this is where the planners view the input from business partners that may be in far away subcontract suppliers, but which are collaborating with the company that has installed SNP.

Detailed coverage of SNC is in Chapter 12

SNP Product Location Tabs

SAP SCM has a large number of settings available for SNP on the product location master tabs, which are where the parameters are located that can significantly alter the output of the supply plan based on their configuration. Table 4.6 provides a synopsis of each of the tabs and the controls that are contained within them.

SNP Product Master Tab	Description
SNP1	Sets the penalty costs for no delivery and delays. This can be set at a product location or an overall product level.
SNP2	Contains a large number of controls related to the forecast horizon, supply and demand profile to be used, and the fair share and deployment profile.
Demand	Controls pegging and forward or backward consumption, as well as the stocks to use (stock in quality inspection, restricted use, blocked, etc.).
Lot Size	Determines whether the lot sizing procedure used is lot-for-lot, fixed lot size, or by period or reorder point. This tab also has the control field for the lot size unit.
Procurement	Sets procurement costs.
GR/GI	Sets goods issue and goods release times as well as cost and other warehouse-related functions.

Table 4.6 SNP Product Master Tabs

Now let's look at one of the most critical master data parameters in the product location master, safety stock.

Safety Stock in SNP

Safety stock is the quantity of redundant inventory that is held in stock to mitigate variability in the supply chain. Its existence is necessary to manage the lead-time variability from supplier to customers, and its use in SNP is critical to the management of the overall supply chain. SNP has strong functionality in this area, which we'll discuss in detail in Chapter 15, Getting More from SAP SCM.

You should now have a good understanding of how SNP works and its benefits, so now let's look at how to deploy it.

SNP Deployment

Deployment controls which requirements will be covered by a shortage of supply and which won't. Deployment is required where the plan doesn't pre-position sufficient inventory to meet all demands. It allows stock to be distributed among locations that are vying for the same inventory by the following alternatives:

> Three alternatives for deployment: heuristic, optimizer, and real-time

> Deployment heuristic

> Deployment optimizer

> Real-time deployment (essentially similar to the deployment heuristic)

Deployment Heuristic

Under the heuristic method, there are two ways to use deployment heuristics:

> Fair share

> Push

The applicability of each depends on whether the planning company's products are over or under supply. If a product is under supply, the method called *fair share* is used to allocate the inventory to competing locations. There are several ways to run fair share in terms of allocation:

> Fair Share method

> Proportional distribution (based upon previous demand allocation)

> Proportional fulfillment of target stock

> Quota arrangements

The push method takes care of the opposite problem, where there is too much supply that needs to be pushed out to forward locations. The following list is a sample of some of the ways that push distribution can be performed:

> Pull distribution

> Push distribution by demands

> Push/pull

> Quota arrangement

Deployment Optimizer

The optimizer can be run with a variety of rules that provide a flexible solution

Like the standard SNP optimizer, the deployment optimizer works off of costs that have been set up by the configuration team. However, it also can follow distribution rules and constraints that are set up in the SNP deployment profile.

This concludes the review of the SNP functionality, So let's wrap up the chapter with a look at the release history and then a brief case study that shows SNP in a real-world scenario.

SNP Release History

Because SNP is one of the original applications, it has received only minor updates for the past few releases. But some of the most important improvements in SAP SCM 7.0 include:

> Enhanced queue processing

> Enhanced supply demand matching

> Characteristic-dependent planning, shelf life planning

Case Study

Company

This high-tech consumer electronics manufacturing firm is in multiple consumer and business electronic markets globally with a strong focus on product lifecycle management.

Challenge

Because this company has many Asian contract manufacturers and suppliers, it needed to make fast decisions regarding the lowest cost source of supply among its many suppliers and contract manufacturers. Selecting based upon the lowest cost was important because the products were standardized and because this company had a limited ability to pass on higher costs to consumers due to the competitive nature of the market.

Solution

A textbook application for optimization, the SNP optimizer was implemented primarily to help improve the speed and accuracy of the procurement decisions. Although SNP was also used to move material through the supply network, its main benefit to the company was source of supply determination.

Value Achieved

While struggling at first, the company was eventually able to implement the optimizer in a way that greatly increased its procurement flexibility. Optimization projects with SNP can be quite interesting, although most companies have not used optimizers previously to develop the supply plan.

Conclusion

SNP is one of the most implemented applications in SAP SCM. It provides a strong combination of functionality, is highly flexible, and can incorporate both supply constraints and production constraints (with the use of PPMs and PDSs). SNP is a very good introductory application to begin using SAP SCM due to its logical design, deep functionality, and flexibility. Along with SAP Event Management, it takes the highest level view of the supply chain, and the wide variety of resources that it can use allows it to model the supply chain in many levels of detail. SNP can plan supply chain for both the internal company and for subcontractors. It also provides a strong safety stock and deployment capability.

In the next chapter, we'll cover Production Planning and Detailed Scheduling (PP/DS), which is another application that is often tightly integrated with SNP.

5

Production Planning and Detailed Scheduling (PP/DS)

Production Planning and Detailed Scheduling (PP/DS) in SAP SCM is designed for the manufacturing portion of your company's supply chain. Planning systems for production planning help you decide when to schedule production requirements in a way that matches your factory capacity.

PP/DS is part of the SAP advanced planning solution for manufacturing that supports all of the standard manufacturing methods such as make-to-stock, make-to-order, and assemble-to-order. Additionally, PP/DS allows you to create custom strategies, which are referred to as requirement strategies in PP/DS.

Additionally, PP/DS manages the portion of the supply origination associated with internal manufacturing. Although your company may have a number of contract manufacturers, PP/DS is only used for planning internal manufacturing that your company has control over and manages.

Plan internal manufacturing with PP/DS

99

Although PP/DS is one of the original SAP APO applications, it lags in implementations behind SAP DP and SNP. Part of the reason is that many product companies don't have manufacturing operations, so they procure 100% of their items. Therefore, more companies need SAP DP and SNP than need PP/DS.

PP/DS generates a production plan for the system to execute

The output of PP/DS is the *production plan* and the necessary *planned production orders* that are sent to the execution system to make this happen. At the highest level, PP/DS receives requirements that can come from SNP or other supply planning applications. This is the requirement side of the equation. The other side of the equation is the capacity of the factories. PP/DS takes these requirements and compares them to the capacity to arrive at planned production orders that either meet constraints or are capacity leveled. A 100% SAP solution would look like Figure 5.1.

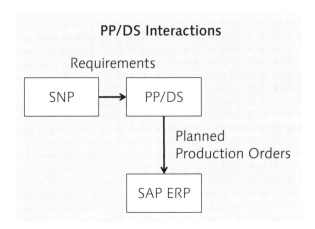

Figure 5.1 PP/DS Interactions

Basic Functionality and Concepts of PP/DS

PP/DS is two applications in one

PP/DS is really two applications in one. The production planning side performs the short- and mid-range production planning. The detailed scheduling side performs scheduling to a fine level of detail, even to the minute. PP/DS typically has one of the shorter time horizons in SAP SCM.

Methods of Running PP/DS

Unlike SNP, which can be run with three different methods, PP/DS can only be run with two different methods, either with the optimizer or with heuristics.

You can run PP/DS with the SAP Optimizer or the heuristic method

The optimizer requires the estimation of costs for different production activities and attempts to arrive at the lowest total cost. The optimization achieved with PP/DS and the constraints in PP/DS positively affect the rest of the supply chain. So, if your company sets up its production constraints properly, you can quickly find out which items you can produce in-house and, by extension, which need to be procured.

 Note

The optimizer was discussed in Chapter 4, and the principle of optimization is the same here, so we won't cover it in any depth.

The second way to run PP/DS is with heuristics, and just as with running SNP with heuristics, similar advantages and disadvantages apply to PP/DS heuristics. They are relatively simple for planners to both understand and adjust, and they typically mirror more closely what the company is currently doing. They also can be combined in unique ways to offer a customized planning solution. But they don't offer the lowest possible cost solution, as does the PP/DS optimizer.

Heuristics are similar to Material Requirements Planning (MRP) in SAP, (which is the main planning method available in SAP ERP) but they provide much more flexibility and more sophisticated problem

Heuristics give you many options for planning

Heuristics can be
combined to fit your
planning
environment
solving. And again, they can be combined to develop unique planning outputs that are customized for the planning environment. The
similarities can be demonstrated by the fact that there's a PP/DS heuristic called SAP_MRP_001, which produces the exact output of MRP
run in SAP ERP. In addition to this heuristic, there are many more to
choose from. A sampling of some of PP/DS's heuristics and their descriptions are listed in Table 5.1.

PP/DS Heuristic	Description
SAP_PP_009: Rescheduling From The Bottom Up	Applicable for the planning of assemblies and subcomponents.
SAP_PP_005: Part Period Balancing	The setup costs and storage costs are taken into consideration in the lot size calculation. Takes lot sizes parameters into account.
SAP_PP_18: Create Safety Stock in liveCache	Creates a requirement element for the safety stock, which can be used to establish dynamic pegging.
SAP_PMAN_001: Critical Path	Identifies the critical path in engineering-to-order or make-to-order production. Attempts to reduce the overall manufacturing lead time.

Table 5.1 PP/DS Heuristics

From Table 5.1, you can see the variability of the heuristics. There are
many ways to perform planning with heuristics, and SAP is always
adding new heuristics with new releases, so we can't cover them all
in this book. However, the short list in Table 5.1 demonstrates that
heuristics can do everything from taking lot size parameters into account to identifying the critical path in engineering to order.

Now that we've looked at the two methods of running PP/DS, let's
move on to how capacity is modeled in PP/DS.

Tip

You can find many details on PP/DS heuristics in *Production Planning with SAP APO PP/DS*, by Jochen Balla and Frank Layer (SAP PRESS).

Capacity Leveling Versus Capacity Constraining

As we discussed earlier, there are two sides to the equation of production planning. On one side are the requirements or what needs to be produced, and on the other is capacity, which is the ability of the factory to produce. Capacity is a broad term that can be segmented into resources (physical work stations where work is performed) as well as materials. In production planning, constraining capacity means putting limits on capacities, so that during a production planning run, the capacity is "capped" or constrained so that each capacity factor can only accept its real requirement. Requirements are then moved to periods where there is capacity available, and some of the requirements that can't be assigned to a capacity factor are unfulfilled.

> Capacity leveling is also available in SNP, and SNP and PP/DS use similar methods to reconcile requirements with capacity

Capacity constraining performs this process during the optimization run, while, with capacity leveling, the process of moving requirements is more interactive. And while this may seem confusing, capacity leveling uses heuristics as well. The commonly used heuristics for capacity planning, move-in and move-out demand, essentially reposition demand to a period where there is excess capacity. Capacity leveling exists in SAP ERP; however, between SAP ERP and SAP SCM, only SAP SCM has the ability to constrain capacity.

Settings for PP/DS in the Product Location Master

As with the other applications, many of the control parameters for PP/DS are located in the product location master. The product location master holds a very high number of settings, some of which apply to

PP/DS, but most of which are controls for the other applications in SAP SCM. The areas that can be set up for PP/DS on the product location master are detailed in Table 5.2.

Product Location Master Settings for PP/DS	Description
Requirements Strategy	What strategy PP/DS will use (i.e., Make to Stock, Make to Order, etc.).
Pegging	How the pegging between requirements capacity will be managed.
Lot Size Procedure	How lot sizing will be managed, for both procurement and production (this value is used by both SNP and PP/DS).
Time Settings	How far out PP/DS will look and perform its planning.
Conversion	How planned procurement orders and planned production orders will be converted in SAP ERP.

Table 5.2 PP/DS Product Location Master Settings

Manufacturing Strategies

Create custom strategies

As mentioned earlier, PP/DS is an advanced planning solution for manufacturing that supports all of the standard manufacturing methods, including make-to-stock, make-to-order, and assemble-to-order. Additionally, PP/DS allows you to create custom strategies, which are referred to as requirement strategies in PP/DS. Because most companies have settled on their manufacturing strategy, it's really just a matter of setting the PP/DS fields to match this strategy (Figure 5.2).

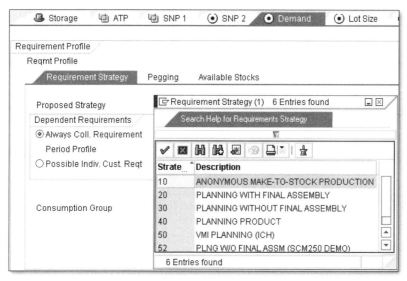

Figure 5.2 Product Location Master Requirements Strategy Tab from Within Demand

Pegging

As with SNP, PP/DS can be run with dynamic or fixed pegging. As mentioned in Chapter 4, Pegging is an important setting in SAP SCM that impacts the plan, as well as the system processing time and the system performance. Under a fixed pegging selection, production order or capacity is assigned once to a requirement (i.e., a sales order or forecast). There's a "peg" between the requirement and the resource, which doesn't require a re-pegging because each successive planning run only attempts to peg the unpegged requirements.

Pegging is also known as the creation of a relationship between demand and capacity

Example

> Beyond the decision of fixed or dynamic pegging, there are many other selection fields on the Pegging subtab of the product location master. For example, you can define how late or early a receipt can be scheduled. This increases or decreases the flexibility of the system. While more flexibility means more requirements can be accepted, it really comes down to the tolerance on the part of the customer, combined with the company's tolerance for additional inventory. For instance, if a given customer can accept an early delivery of one month prior to his need date, then the pegging earliness of receipt can be set to one month (for this particular customer, let's keep this example as simple as possible). However, if the company implementing SAP SCM is willing to build a moderate amount of inventory, the earliness of receipt can be increased a further month. A company that is willing to carry more inventory can increase the earliness of receipt. On the other side, how long customers are willing to wait often has to do with the competition and the availability of alternatives. In situations where there are few alternatives and the overall industry is capacity constrained, customers may have no choice but to wait, which would mean increasing the lateness of receipt.

Fixed pegging versus dynamic pegging

With dynamic pegging, the pegging is constantly preformed on every planning run. The requirements may or may not be re-pegged to the assigned capacity because new requirements can come in and become pegged to capacity, breaking the original pegging. The performance implication is that it's more computational work to perform dynamic pegging, so using dynamic pegging will either take more time or a higher capacity server to meet the runtime durations of a fixed pegged configuration. Finally, it's important to remember that all pegging and production orders created in SAP SCM are planned. Only SAP ERP, or another execution system, can confirm the production order.

TechTalk

The distinction between planning systems and execution systems is an important one to consider and to internalize. Aside from GATP and SAP EWM, which have transactional capabilities, the rest of SAP SCM is focused on planning. It doesn't execute actions, as much as develop recommendations. Recommendations from SAP SCM are then passed to SAP ERP for execution. Not all of the recommendations will be executed, and SAP ERP passes the information back to SAP SCM concerning what was executed. SAP SCM then goes through its planning process again and resends recommendations. This is the continual loop between planning systems and execution systems that applies to SAP SCM particularly but to planning systems generally.

Pegging is set in the Pegging tab (Figure 5.3) within the product location master.

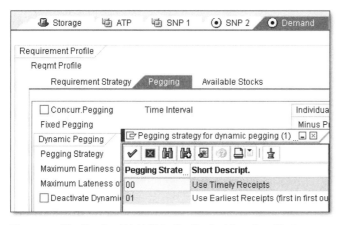

Figure 5.3 The Pegging Tab Within the Product Location Master

Lot Size Setting

The lot size setting affects both SNP and PP/DS, and it determines the quantity at which that material is either procured or manufactured. So if a requirement is for 100 units, but the lot size is 30 units (and if the future inventory is 0), then the total quantity planned to be produced would be 120 units, which would be 4 production runs of the lot size of 30. This would leave the company with an excess of 20.

The logic for lot sizes is based upon fixed costs. This can be the fixed costs of ordering or of setting up machinery, among many other types of fixed costs. Lot size is often greatly underestimated in terms of its importance on projects, even though on many projects it controls much more of the decision making than the company implementing SAP SCM realizes. See Figure 5.4 for the Lot Size Profile settings.

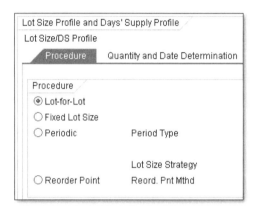

Figure 5.4 The Lot Size Profile Within the Product Location Master

It's important to estimate your lot sizes accurately

As you can see in Figure 5.4, different types of lot sizing procedures can be selected, and you can also select the Quantity and Date Determination. While most advanced planning software has lot size functionality, SAP SCM offers quite a few settings.

 TechTalk

The question has been asked as to why SAP ERP PP offers a more dynamic way of setting the lot size, if SAP SCM is supposedly the more sophisticated planning system. This is an excellent question, and the answer lies in the orientation of two systems. While in SAP ERP, reorder point methods may be used to control the planning of items that don't have a forecast, for SAP SCM, it's rare that a reorder point with lot size is the only planning method. Products that are considered critical (long lead time or capacity constrained) are typically planned in SAP SCM (as well as products that require allocation); meanwhile, noncritical materials can be planned in SAP ERP using standard reorder point methodologies. Because of this fact, reorder point methods are not very extensive in SAP SCM.

After you've set up the lot size, you can set up the demand you expect. And from there you move to the PP/DS settings (Figure 5.5).

Figure 5.5 The Product Location Master

The numerous buttons on the Product Location Master reveal relationships with other data and other views. A great variety of other data can be accessed from this one transaction, and it's one of the most useful in SAP SCM. For instance, by selecting the facility icon (next to the text "San Diego Distribution Center"), you are taken directly to the facility and to the Display Location View. This tab controls the procedure used for planning, the heuristics applied, when the BOM is to be exploded, as well as how far out the PP/DS should plan.

Numerous relationships with other data are available in the Product Location Master

The Product Heuristic selection can be found by selecting the Product Heuristic dropdown button in the middle of the screen (Figure 5.6).

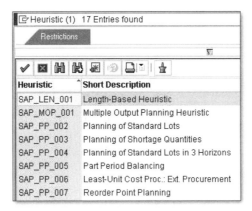

Figure 5.6 Heuristics from the Product Heuristic Selection

Heuristics can be applied per product location

If you choose to use heuristic planning, then you'll need to select the combination of Heuristics. These can be applied per product location, so not every product location needs to have the same heuristic applied. To see the details of heuristics, refer to Table 5.1with the listing of sample PP/DS heuristics.

You should now have a good understanding of how PP/DS can be run and some of its basic settings, so let's move on to a discussion of the structures that support PP/DS.

Production Process Models and Production Data Structures

There are the two main modeling structures in PP/DS; production process models (PPMs) and production data structures (PDSs). They are designed to both set the consumption rate of materials and set the constraints of production on the overall SAP SCM application. But their configuration has implications far beyond the PP/DS application. When constrained (and both PPMs and PDSs can be unconstrained), they control the capacity of the supply and production system. So, they (or more specifically their associated resources along with material constraints) determine what requirements the company can meet.

A company typically decides whether to use PPMs or PDSs, but not both, because they provide duplicate functionality. In fact, it's not recommended to use both PPMs and PDSs in the same SAP SCM system. Let's start off by discussing PPMs because they preceded PDSs and are the most common of the two structures on projects, at least at the time of this writing (Figure 5.7).

Use either PPMs or PDSs—not both

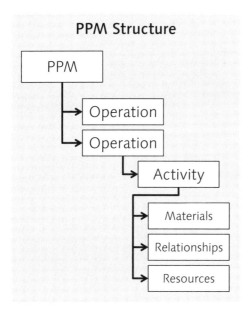

Figure 5.7 PPMs are Hierarchical Structures That Include Much of the Master Data Necessary for Production Planning

Production Process Models (PPMs)

PPMs, are used to model production activities both for your company and for subcontractors. Work centers and routings come over from Production Planning (PP) in CIF and are combined to form PPMs (Figure 5.8).

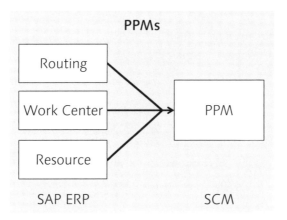

PPMs

Routing

Work Center ──────▶ PPM

Resource

SAP ERP   SCM

Figure 5.8 PPM Comes from SAP Through CIF and Is an Integrated and Nested Object

---

Ex Example

PP/DS is most frequently implemented for companies that control manufacturing facilities. However, a company doesn't have to necessarily be in this situation to use PP/DS. For example, PPMs can be used to model manufacturing capacity outside of the company performing the modeling. This can be accomplished by creating subcontract PPMs that reflect the production capacity of subcontractors. However, unless a fine level of production planning is required, most companies could probably opt for simply using PPMs in SNP to perform the modeling. The solution selected depends upon the level of detail as well as the implementing company's budget.

Production Data Structures (PDSs)

We'll discuss PDSs in more detail in Chapter 15

PDSs were introduced for several reasons. One was to allow companies to model their production processes with engineering changes and to incorporate concepts related to product lifecycle management. Another reason was to improve the performance over that of the PPM. PDSs also offer an advantage over PPMs because PPMs must be converted between SNP and PP/DS, but PDSs are essentially native to both applications and required no conversion. However, one disadvantage is that PDSs can't be maintained or altered in SAP SCM, so changes to the routing or resources must be made every time a change is desired in SAP ERP and then CIFed over.

Constraining PDS and PPM

There's generally great interest at companies to develop accurate available to promise (ATP) capability. They are also interested in the discussion of what ATP is based upon but to a lesser degree. In a 100% SAP SCM solution architecture, GATP (Global Available to Promise) is based on the results of SNP (or other supply planning software), for planned inventory on-hand and PP/DS for planned production orders, which also results in planned inventory on-hand. The accuracy of the plan is what results in an accurate ATP. This in turn is based on the accuracy of the transportation lead times, the accuracy of the inventory commitments from suppliers, and the accuracy of the resource constraints.

ATP is generated from SAP ERP GATP, and responds to requests from an order management system such as SAP SD or CRM

For the ATP quantity returned to be realistic and meaningful, it's important to have constrained PPMs and or PDSs, or fully capacity-leveled production plans for manufactured items in conjunction with confirmation from suppliers on procured items (Figure 5.9).

Noncritical materials should simply be managed with reorder point methods in SAP ERP

PPMs and PDSs vs. Resources Usage

	PPMs / PDSs	Resource
DP	YES	NO
SNP / CTM	YES	YES
PPDS	YES	YES
EWM	NO	YES
TPVS	NO	YES

Figure 5.9 As with SNP, PP/DS Is the Only Other Application That Uses Both PPMs/PDSs and Resources

Resources

Resources are varied planning objects in SAP SCM, and they make up part of every PPM or PDS. They apply to SNP, TP/VS, SAP EWM, and PP/DS, and they can be constrained (i.e., set with limits) or unconstrained. However, when resources are constrained, they bring reality to the plan. If a plan operates within resource constraints that are comprehensive and constrained in a manner that matches with the supply chain realities, then the resulting plan is referred to as "feasible." You can see the resources used by PP/DS in Table 5.3. Some are shared with SNP.

PP/DS Resource Type	Description
Single Activity	The simplest form of resource; one activity processed at a time
Single mixed	Continual and exact time scheduling; the most detailed form of scheduling
Multi-activity	Several activities carried out on a resource at once
Multi-mixed	Same as multi-activity but used by both SNP and PP/DS
Production line	Specialized resource for discrete manufacturing
Production line mixed	Identical to production line but used by both PP/DS and SNP
Calendar	Only time oriented, not capacity oriented
Calendar mixed	Identical to the calendar resource but used by both PP/DS and SNP

Table 5.3 Resources Use by PP/DS

Single and multi-resources are the only resources that come across from SAP ERP, while all others are created in SAP SCM

There are many different settings for each resource, and these settings change depending on the resource. One example is shown in Figure 5.10, where we set up a bottleneck resource. This means it's a critically constrained resource on the production line. PP/DS then makes the necessary adjustments to the plan to account for this. Of course, this is just one example, so keep in mind that the time you spend in the resource configuration transactions can result in all types of settings that cause the resources to behave in different ways.

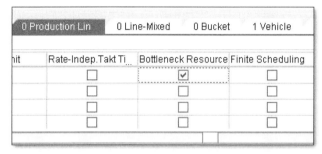

Figure 5.10 The Resource View

 Note

Although there is a finite resource selection, which would seem to set up a resource as constrained, in fact, all resources that are to be constrained must be added to the PP/DS optimization profile. This is true for the SNP and TM optimizers as well.

Now that we've discussed two of the structures that allow PP/DS to perform planning, we need to move on to a special type of planning called *process industry production planning*.

Process Industry Planning

PP/DS was originally designed for discreet manufacturing such as consumer electronics items (laptops, cell phones, hard drives, etc.). Although discreet manufacturing often has complex BOMs, after the materials are in house, the manufacturing process tends to have low variability and consistent output.

PP/DS can work for discrete or process manufacturing

Because of this, discreet manufacturing is arguably the easiest form of production to plan because it's the most stable manufacturing environment. Process manufacturing on the other hand, which applies to food, beverage, pharmaceutical, chemicals, and paints, among others, is quite different. Discrete manufacturing uses a BOM, and the closest approximation in the process industry is either referred to as a formula or a recipe. Although the process industry formula often has fewer components, each component usually has special storage and handling characteristics. But, in general, the manufacturing process is different for the process industry.

Differences between process and discrete manufacturing

For example, in milk processing, the type of milk byproducts produced, and the quantity of each varies depending on the season and the weather, among a host of different factors. This can mean different yields for the byproducts based on the time of year. Combine this with the more variable nature of the uptime and maintenance of milk processing equipment, and you end up with constantly changing constraints. Additionally, in the process industry, the formulations are stated in terms of proportions rather than in individual units, which requires a flexible unit of measure conversion engine. These are just a few of the differences between process and discrete manufacturing.

Until very recently, PP/DS was primarily designed for environments with basically stable constraints and predictable outputs from inputs. However, recent additions in SAP SCM 7.0 have made PP/DS more process industry friendly.

PP/DS Release History

PP/DS is one of the earliest models and so its development has slowed in the most recent releases as development effort has been channeled into the new areas of SAP SCM. The following is a listing of some of the important improvements:

> An enhancement for the process industry includes the ability to take recipes from SAP SCM and create a product storage definition in SAP SCM.

> A new deployment heuristic that allows the creation of stock transfers. This is essentially allowing an SNP function to be run in the background or from the product view, which means it provides more flexibility and access than in SAP SCM 5.1. This allows production planners to more easily perform an important network inventory function.

> The addition of several heuristics for cross plant planning. These include the following capabilities:

  – Allows the interactive selection of source of supply from different source procurement proposals.

  – Allows the deletion of pegged orders across all BOM levels. This includes all subassemblies and purchase requisitions that are pegged to the order.

  – Allows shelf life to be propagated across the pegging network.

Case Study

Company

This company is a specialty chemical manufacturer that makes a wide variety of chemicals and is known for the many innovative materials that it produces.

Challenge

With many recipes, and complex and sometimes difficult-to-forecast production constraints, this company needed to upgrade the production planning system so that it could perform simulations.

Solution

The company selected and implemented PP/DS and sized the hardware so that it allowed for a high number of simulation models and versions, which enabled the company to test multiple scenarios. With the great resource variety offered in PP/DS, the company was also able to model a difficult and often changing production environment. And, the company had become attached to the concept of a "product wheel," where production is scheduled to make best use of resources in view of competing products and meeting the needs of minimal inventory and maximum inventory availability at the right time for shipment to warehouses. PP/DS was able to provide the company with output that matched its product wheel.

Value Achieved

This company faced very static methods of production planning and decided to implement PP/DS to provide more intelligence and flexibility to their production planning process. One of the major needs was to move from SAP Production Planning (PP), which is the SAP ERP solution, to the more advanced methods in PP/DS that provide more flexibility regarding simulation and resources. Because this client had already implemented SNP, it was in a very good position to move the production planning process over to PP/DS. After the implementation, planned productions requirements were communicated from SNP to PP/DS instead of to PP. After go-live, PP was turned off, and the planned production orders flowed from PP/DS to SAP ERP.

Conclusion

PP/DS is one of the more commonly implemented SAP SCM applications. It provides capabilities to perform all of the different manufacturing strategies, and can be run in either heuristic or optimization mode. While still being absorbed by the industry, the PDS allows for the incorporation of engineering change management in the production planning process. PP/DS has solidified its position as a desirable choice for those clients who want to perform constraint-based planning or heuristics with capacity leveling and who want more than SAP ERP Production Planning offers. Its recent enhancements open up a larger customer base for the application and deserve a second look by processing manufacturing companies.

In the next chapter, we'll cover Global Available to Promise (GATP).

Global Available to Promise (GATP)

The need to provide commitments back to customers is called available to promise (ATP) capability. This is a capability offered by operations to sales. Strong ATP functionality is important to a company's credibility with its customers. And while this is a desired state, unfortunately, there are many cases where companies make promises to customers without knowing if they can actually meet the demand. The ability to provide a solid promise quantity can allow a company to better use its internal resources and keep its customers satisfied.

Of all of the applications in SAP SCM, Global Available to Promise (GATP) is often considered the most difficult to explain and, as a result, the most difficult to understand. This isn't because the concept behind GATP is so difficult to grasp (in fact, it's quite straightforward) but because the implementation and design of GATP is quite involved and dependent on other SAP SCM applications and SAP ERP. A few reasons for the general opaqueness of the application include the following:

GATP is challenging to implement because of its dependency on other applications

> GATP is actually a much more complex concept of availability checking, which is the background with which many people come to GATP.

> There are a number of different ways of implementing GATP and different types of ATP that can be provided by GATP.

You can implement GATP in a variety of ways

> The GATP configuration is the least straightforward of the SAP SCM applications. The configuration screens lack an inherent logic that the other applications have.

Because of these factors and the limited information available on GATP, we'll only cover the fundamentals in this chapter and provide you with as much depth about the basics as possible. To maximize your understanding, let's begin by drawing the parallel between Capable to Match (CTM) and GATP.

GATP and CTM

CTM is a much easier area of functionality to understand, and because there are a number of similarities between CTM and GATP, it's a good place to start.

 Note

If you're reading this book in sequence, you should have already learned about CTM in Chapter 4, SAP SCM Supply Network Planning (SNP). But if not, you may want to go back and read the section on Capable to Match, before reading the rest of this chapter.

Let's look at the similarities between CTM and GATP:

> Orders or planned orders are associated with inventory or production capacity.

> Supply selection is performed in both applications.

> Both can be connected to PP/DS and allocate productive capacity to customers. In both cases, this is an optional way of running the applications.

> Both use ATP categories. (ATP categories are the represent stock, requirement, forecast, and receipt categories, all of which can be turned on or turned off during an ATP check).

> ATP categories represent both sides of the supply and demand equation.

> Both processes deal in terms of allocation and priorities. CTM generates the allocations, while GATP represents these allocations to the order management system.

> As of SAP SCM 7.0 (for GATP), both CTM and GATP can schedule backwards and forwards.

 Tip

Pegging is used in SAP SCM to describe a connection between demand and *actual* inventory. Allocations are used to describe a connection between demand and *future* inventory.

However, in addition to these similarities, there are also differences, and understanding these differences will help you understand GATP.

> GATP is performed in real time and connects back to the order management system (either SAP ERP Sales and Distribution [SD] or Customer Relationship Management [SAP CRM] in a 100% SAP solution). CTM doesn't connect in real time to any order management system but instead performs its processing in batch.

> Giving priority to certain customers over other customers who have ordered earlier is the heart of CTM. GATP allocation is based upon who places a request first. CTM is based partially on who places the order first (particularly if fixed pegging is selected); however, CTM also allocates inventory on the basis of the customer priority level. So while CTM uses both time and priority to allocate, GATP works primarily on time.

When comparing these solutions it's also important to consider that they work in conjunction with one another.

So now that you have an idea of the differences and similarities of GATP and CTM, let's look at GATP within the broader umbrella term of availability checking.

Availability Checking

Availability checking is the standard functionality of SD. It provides a return date and quantity on planned sales orders, which leads to a distinction that should be understood. So, it's important to differentiate between availability checking, which is the functionality in SAP ERP, and availability to promise in GATP. This is an important distinction to draw because on projects, these terms are often used interchangeably, so being unaware of the differences can lead to confusion.

Availability checking is a broad category of obtaining information on material availability that can cover both *current on hand* as well as *planned on hand*. There are several types of availability checking available from different areas within SAP. Figure 6.1 shows both the types of availability checking and their location within SAP.

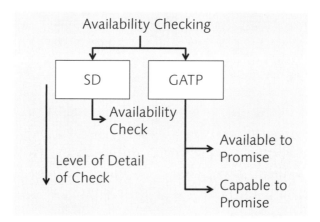

Figure 6.1 Hierarchy of Availability Checking with Distinctions Between the Different Methods

(margin notes)

Where availability checking is performed (in SAP ERP or GATP), it must be set up in CIF to communicate requests from SAP ERP to SAP SCM

Availability checking also occurs in SAP EWM, covered in Chapter 11

Available to Promise

Available to promise (ATP) is a type of availability checking offered in GATP. However, it's not the only type of availability checking provided by the GATP application. Another form of availability checking is called *capable to promise* (CTP), which we'll discuss later in this chapter. ATP provides extra functionality over SD availability checking, which makes it significantly enhanced.

GATP offers two types of availability checking: ATP and CTP

One of the major differences between availability checking in SAP SD and in GATP is that GATP looks out across many different locations, comparing forecasted inventory positions with planned demand, and returning both a promise quantity and a location that will satisfy the demand. It can continue searching until it finds a location, even a location distant from the customer, which can satisfy the demand. GATP not only returns a confirmation on requested quantities and dates but also different alternatives regarding when material might become available. It can present this to SAP ERP or SAP CRM, or other order acceptance systems, and the customer connecting to these systems then has an opportunity to accept or reject the altered proposal.

As with availability checking, after the customer provides a confirmation on the commitment, it becomes a planned order and an allocation. This has the immediate effect of reducing planned capacity or planned inventory, or both. Much like CTM, a specific customer is allocated inventory or production capacity. GATP has complex application interactions, as shown in Figure 6.2.

If you've read Chapters 3 and 4, you'll recall that liveCache is also used in DP and SNP

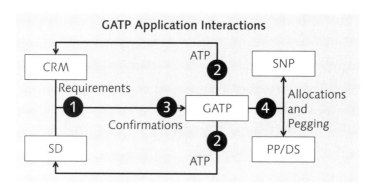

Figure 6.2 GATP Application Interactions

GATP can be seen as an intermediary between the SAP SD and SAP CRM applications and the SNP and PP/DS applications. GATP holds the planned inventory and planned orders in liveCache with GATP in a way that allows the application to provide a real-time response. For the solution designed as just described to work, GATP must be continually updated with information from SNP and GATP.

Basic Functionality and Concepts of GATP

You can select different supply and demand elements to include during configuration

The specific supply and demand elements that can be included in an ATP check are listed here:

> **Supply**
>> – Warehouse stock
>> – Planned receipts
>> – Production orders
>> – Planned orders

> **Demand**
>> – Sales orders
>> – Deliveries
>> – Reservations

Different combinations of these elements can be selected to be included in GATP during configuration.

Different Levels of ATP Checks

There are different levels of ATP checks. Each has different functionality and also different levels of configuration and maintenance effort, in addition to different levels of data update and quality requirements.

The different levels of ATP check are shown in Figure 6.3.

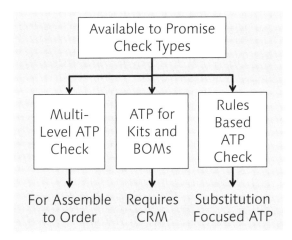

Figure 6.3 Different Levels of ATP Checks

Multilevel ATP Check (M-ATP)

Multi-level ATP is designed for assemble-to-order operations and for configurable products. Like CTP, which we discuss in a few paragraphs, this architecture connects GATP to PP/DS. The difference is that the output of this ATP check is stored in an ATP tree structure. The ATP tree structures store the ATP check output for the short term, until the ATP check output is converted to receipts in a batch process.

Assembly to order is the manufacturing strategy that Dell popularized, and which is now standard in the computer industry

Multilevel ATP checking is advantageous when the subassemblies to the prospective sales order are already manufactured or procured, and they aren't placed in final assembly until they receive a sales order. This provides maximum flexibility to the manufacturer and allows for lower inventory costs. There are two ways of running the M-ATP check:

> Automatic source determination
> Two-step process:
  – The plan for requirement is exploded
  – The sales order is entered for configured products

Availability Checking for Kits (or BOM)

This method of ATP requires integration with SAP CRM. A kit is a combination of items that are planned together, while a BOM is a series of co-planned items that result in a manufactured or assembled item. If stock for the kit or BOM is available, the extent of the interaction between ATP and SAP CRM is limited.

However, if no kit or BOM stock is available, this method of availability checking has GATP connecting to integrated Product and Process Engineering (iPPE) to schedule kit production. iPPE enables PP/DS to collect all of the data for an entire product lifecycle in one integrated model. It's particularly well suited to products with many variants and to repetitive manufacturing.

Rules-Based Availability Checking

Rules-based availability checking allows the check to be performed with either substitutes of the same product at different locations or alternate PPMs. This requires the set up of rules that control the ATP process. These rules, which control substitution such as product substitution and location substitution, are managed in integrated rule maintenance and are part of the master data of GATP.

Example

Rules-based availability checking allows a high degree of configurability for the ATP check. For instance, it could set up the system to look in the same location for a substitutable product, in a different location for only the requested product, or some other combination.

What Attaining ATP Proficiency Can Mean

GATP has a powerful set of functionality, and if implemented correctly, a company with ATP capability can gain great credibility with its customers. This is because ATP allows a company to commit on orders with credibility. By reducing the need to move around and reallocate inventory to different customers when delivery dates approach, it greatly increases execution stability. In addition, all other things being equal, a company with reliable delivery dates should pick up market share from those competitors that lack this capability and over-promise to these same customers.

Accurate ATP capabilities gain credibility with customers and position the company as a premium supplier

Capable to Promise

SAP calls this an availability check, not an ATP check. However, in other documentation, SAP shows both CTP and multilevel ATP checking as subcategories of availability checking that calls PP/DS.

Regardless of its categorization, from the supply side, not only can planned inventory be included in the analysis but also planned production capacity. SAP SCM performs this by including PP/DS in the ATP check. Incorporating production capacity in the ATP process changes the definition of what is being done from ATP to CTP. The change in terminology is clear from what is planned to be available, which is the future planned inventory position, to what is "capable" to promise, or what the factory capacity could produce.

One way to break down the different ATP methods is by defining which ones connect to PP/DS and which ones only check inventory (Figure 6.4). Using PP/DS with GATP allows for the allocation of capacity in addition to the allocation of inventory, providing a higher degree of integration between your customers.

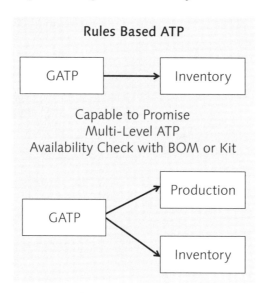

Figure 6.4 Defining ATP Methods

When using PP/DS in conjunction with GATP, the following apply:

> A PP/DS horizon must be created for the product and stored in the product location master.

> In the active version, it's important to have PP/DS set to change active planning.

> The structure link of the "Standard Planning Procedure 3" should be configured.

> There should be no order splitting or partial delivery.

> PP/DS should be called with the location determination activity.

In addition, there are specific heuristics you should run in PP/DS in conjunction with CTM:

> SAP_PP_CTM Planning Shortage Quantities

> SAP_PP_003 (this adjusts the procurement proposal for the finished product, if you've reduced the requirements quantity in the sales order)

Ex Example

Many people notice the similarities between CTP and M-ATP and naturally ask how the two compare. The best way to think of it is that M-ATP is a lighter version of CTP. M-ATP provides less time-specific results than CTP. While results are stored in the ATP tree with M-ATP, in CTP, the orders are created immediately within PP/DS. Other differences include that CTP schedules using the detailed scheduling portion of PP/DS, and M-ATP uses lead times to derive dates. Also, CTM considers lot sizes, while M-ATP doesn't. From these differences, you can see that CTP is a much more involved and feature-rich solution, but the advantage of M-ATP is that it takes far fewer computing resources. The right solution for your company depends on the accuracy required as well as the project's budget.

The topic of PPMs and PDSs was covered in Chapter 5, Production Planning and Detailed Scheduling (PP/DS), however, we wanted to mention here that if either the PPMs or PDSs aren't constrained, then the ATP value and date will be returned, but there's no guarantee that the quantity is feasible. That is, there's no guarantee that the quantity can actually be met because the planning, in this case, is being performed with the assumption of infinite capacity.

However, the main point of ATP and CTP is that the ATP value and date are realistic. If all products are procured, then GATP is only dependent upon the accuracy of the plan produced by SNP. ATP begins to get particularly complex when it takes productive capacity into account because this becomes more involved than simply checking against planned inventory. This makes perfect sense in that ATP is checking the planned inventory, or checking against what is planned

GATP is only dependent on the plan produced by SNP, if all products are procured to be available, and CTP checks against both what is available and what is *capable of being produced*.

ATP Tree Structure

GATP also has the ATP tree structure that we've referred to several times already. ATP tree structures are used for storing data not returned to the calling system (either SAP SD or SAP CRM). For instance, there is an ATP tree structure for each request schedule line in the sales order that contains the requirements data for the finished products and components. This can be thought of as a buffer for GATP that is used to enhance performance. It exists because continually creating receipts generated by GATP in PP/DS and SNP would degrade the performance of the system. This conversion with the ATP structure can be performed during off peak times when few people are on the SAP SCM system. ATP tree structures are used for the following:

› Backorder processing

› M-ATP checks (they are particularly important here because M-ATP connects to PP/DS, and this interaction is resource consuming)

› Third-party order processing

Third-Party Order Processing

Third-party order processing is one of the most interesting aspects of GATP. This is where GATP presents the availability and receives commitments on requests from a customer, while the fulfillment of the request is performed by a supplier to the owner and maintainer of the GATP system. This opens up a possible state where the information system is separated from the company actually performing the logistics functions, and it also opens up a number of alternatives for new ways of doing business. Third-party order processing is accomplished by setting up supplier profiles in GATP configuration, and then assigning products to these suppliers. By leveraging this functionality,

GATP can be run by a company that simply manages systems but has no factories or even any inventory or warehouses.

Third-Party Order Processing at Amazon.com

A good way to think of this is how Amazon.com operates. They match customers and suppliers through the website. Sometimes Amazon is selected as a vendor, but often another supplier showcased on the site is selected. Either way, Amazon manages the matching process and the customer contact, and maintains the data of the on-hand balances of different direct-to-customer suppliers.

In third party order processing GATP receives the customer order but it's fulfilled by an outside supplier

It's a similar concept to third-party order processing in GATP, but GATP is providing commitments based on both current inventory and planned inventory. Amazon is only matching demand with current supply, so the time horizons between Amazon.com and GATP are very different. GATP can look out for planned on-hand and productive capacity far into the future, providing specific commitment dates. Amazon.com also provides geographic shipping differences, which you can read more about at *http://sapplanning.org/2009/05/07/gatp.atp.trees and amazon.com*.

 Example

Amazon does allow pre-ordering, but it doesn't work the same way as its ordering for items that are currently in stock. How these pre-orders are allocated against future inventory or serves as a signal to increase production is unknown to us. However, there is no confirmed date on pre-ordered items. On the other hand, stocked items do have confirmation dates.

 Example

We can also use Amazon.com as an example of a well functioning ATP system because it's a system that many people use and can be immediately referenced simply by visiting the site and placing items in the shopping cart. The company is also a leader in connecting many vendors seamlessly into its website. Amazon could, if desired, stop fulfilling orders and simply serve as a website to match supply and demand. By understanding Amazon.com, both from the web frontend and the inventory backend, it's easier to understand GATP.

Scope of Checking

During an ATP check, the scope of the check must be defined. Table 6.1 shows some of the alternatives that the ATP check can be applied against.

GATP output is greatly affected by which stock or receipt elements are included or excluded

Scope of ATP Check	Description
Stocks	Safety stock, stock in transfer, blocked stock, restricted use stock, subcontracted stock, inspection stock
Receipt or issue elements	Purchase orders, purchase requisitions, dependent requirements, reservations, sales orders, delivery notes, shipping notifications, dependent reservations, call requirements, production orders, planned orders

Table 6.1 Scope of ATP Check

These are all optional entries, and GATP can be configured to include all of these, or any combination of them. However, inclusion or exclusion of each stock or receipt element greatly affects the GATP output, and the decision needs to be fully analyzed. A very important setting for GATP is the time horizon, which has a strong influence on system performance, as well as how far out allocations can be set. We'll move to this topic now.

The GATP Time Horizon

Checking horizon

Performing the ATP or CTP check is a computationally intensive activity. One way to help place a boundary around the problem and reduce the time spent computing a result is by limiting the time horizon. This is a common strategy throughout SAP SCM. To use this strategy, GATP is set to limit its checking to a defined horizon, beyond which requirements aren't checked. This is called the *checking horizon*. This horizon is entered in the ATP tab of the product location master. This means that different checking horizons can be set not only for a specific product but also for a product location. However, in most cases, a single product usually has one checking horizon, and groups of products usually have the same checking horizon. But it's important to know the option does exist.

To go to the ATP tab where the time horizon is set, go to product location master by choosing APO • MASTER DATA • PRODUCT • PRODUCT. Then on the introductory screen, add a Location, so the system takes you to the product location master rather than just the product master. After selecting the return key, navigate to the ATP tab (Figure 6.5).

To review the difference between the product and the project location master, refer to Chapter 1

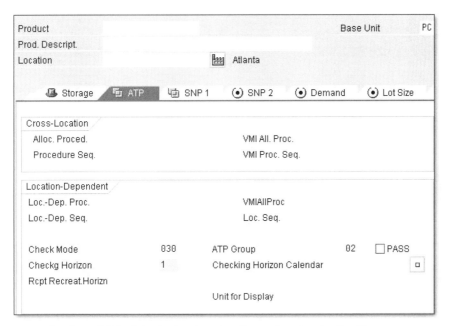

Figure 6.5 The ATP Tab of the Product Location Master Contains the Checking Horizon Field

Now that we've discussed the functionality of GATP, let's move on to the technologies that make GATP possible.

liveCache

liveCache is covered in more detail in Chapters 3 and 4

What GATP is doing as an application is impressive when you consider what's going on behind the scenes. GATP looks out across many locations, for many periods, and can also return with changed proposals. The fact that this is done in real time means that GATP is the most computationally intensive of the SAP SCM applications. Not coincidentally, it's also a key user of liveCache.

Integration

The sales process is managed in SAP ERP, however, GATP is within SAP SCM. ATP requests are communicated in real time to GATP, so the integration between SAP ERP and SAP SCM is the bottleneck to this process. We aren't aware of a more real-time interaction between SAP ERP and SAP SCM than the interaction between SAP ERP and GATP.

GATP Release History

As one of the original applications, GATP has seen fewer improvements in recent releases than many of the other applications.

SAP SCM 5.1 (SAP SCM 2007) improvements included:

> ATP check can only consider substitute products from master data for interchangeability that belong to the interchangeability supersession chain group type.
> Enhanced ATP characteristics view.
> Rules-based ATP checks can be defined to access the input products, input location product before the substitute product, substitute location, or substitute location product.

SAP SCM 7.0 improvements include the following:

> New capabilities for consignment of vendor-managed inventory such as a consignment indicator, shipment split, and consignment stock in transit.

> GATP now supports backward consumption.

The enhancement that GATP needs but hasn't had is a redesign of the configuration screens.

Case Study

Company

This multinational telecommunications equipment company has a very broad product line and a lengthy history of innovation.

Challenge

With a high amount of product "churn," in terms of new and discontinued products, the company required a solution that could support different fulfillment models. Equally important was the ability to have a rules-based availability checking engine to provide alternative sourcing.

Solution

This company needed rules-based availability checking that supported alternate sourcing. It also was a large SCM implementer with multiple applications including SNP and SNC as well as GATP. The solution called for the ability to provide visibility and alternate sourcing to multiple suppliers all by combining SNP, SNC, and GATP to provide this visibility.

Value Achieved

GATP was a complete change from how the company previously managed alternatives in order promising. Previous to GATP, the client followed a more or less manual system for allocation and supply substitution. This resulted in less satisfied customers. By implementing GATP, the company was better able to manage changes to the supply chain and systematize the ATP process. This resulted in a higher integrity planning process and better relationships with customers, even for those customers who didn't receive allocations because it allowed them sufficient lead time to find alternate sources.

Conclusion

GATP is a sophisticated application that is best considered by companies that are already at an advanced state in their supply chain planning. Applications such as SNP depend on the quality of data in SAP ERP and, in some case, the quality of data coming from other applications in SAP SCM. However, GATP depends on everything that SNP depends on, in addition to the quality of the overall supply plan from SNP. GATP is demanding in terms of data quality and the implementation quality of the applications it relies on. GATP is one of the most resource intensive of all of the SAP SCM applications. However, if implemented correctly, GATP can provide a significant advantage to your company.

In the next chapter, we'll move on to cover transportation planning and vehicle scheduling.

7

SAP Transportation Management (TM)

Transportation planning is the business function of planning your company's transportation in a way that meets quantity movements and time objectives, at a reasonable cost. Transportation tends to be separated from the other supply chain planning functions, but it really shouldn't be. And with integrated planning systems such as SAP SCM, you can keep all of the planning functions together, including transportation planning, to be more tightly connected and integrated.

As with PP/DS, which combines production planning with detailed scheduling, SAP Transportation Management (SAP TM) is also separated into two distinct areas of functionality. While typically considered for use in planning outbound shipments, SAP TM is also used to plan inbound shipments as well as inter-facility shipments. Transportation planning is the smaller section of the application, and covers areas such as transportation forecasting, strategic transportation management, and the assignment of individual deliveries to aggregated

Transportation has one of the shortest planning horizons of all supply chain functions

shipments. In addition, vehicle scheduling is focused on sequencing the deliveries and mode, carrier, and vehicle resource selection.

SAP TM was originally called Transportation Planning and Vehicle Scheduling (TP/VS), so you may see it referred to as such

SAP TM is one of the early SAP SCM applications, but it is installed less frequently than the more popular applications such as DP, SNP, and PP/DS. This may have something to do with how ancillary transportation is often viewed to the business as compared to demand or supply planning. But what is often missed in this view is the interconnection of all of the supply chain functions. Because transportation planning is not only important in terms of improving transportation management specifically, and in obtaining good transportation rates, but also in terms of supporting goals such as inventory management, retail in-stock position, and even production efficiency. In addition, trends such as increasing energy prices and smaller buffer inventories are making transportation management more important than ever. A 100% SAP solution implementation would look like Figure 7.1, and the most common form of integration will be SAP TM to SAP ERP. But SAP TM could integrate to non-SAP ERP systems.

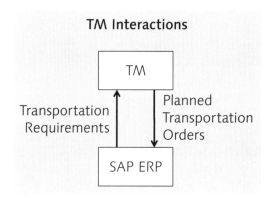

Figure 7.1 100% SAP Implementation with TM

So let's look at the general functionality offered in SAP TM and find out how it can benefit your company.

Basic Functionality and Concepts of SAP TM

SAP TM is designed to plan and schedule freight and vehicles moving across a supply network at the lowest cost while meeting the transportation needs in quantity and time based on specific requirements. You can use SAP TM to perform the actual vehicle scheduling, which is necessary if your company actually owns the transportation equipment, or you can use it to manage hired carriers, if you outsource transportation.

Use SAP TM to schedule your own vehicles or manage hired carriers

High-Level Processes

It's easy to underestimate the complexity of transportation planning unless you have firsthand experience working in the area, but even then, there are many steps to the overall transportation management process. In SAP TM, the processes are broken down into the following high-levels:

> Strategic freight management
> Transportation forecasting
> Freight order taking
> Transportation planning and execution
> Freight tracking and tendering
> Freight settlement and analysis

Within these larger overall processes, there are also specific processes that SAP TM has been designed to handle.

Specific Processes

There are many specific processes within SAP TM, but some of the most prominent are listed here:

> Shipment creation
> Carrier tendering and selection

> Contract management

> Vehicle scheduling

> Carrier cost estimation

> Transportation load building

Understanding these processes is important to understanding the scope of what SAP TM does, so let's look at each of these a little closer.

Shipment Creation

Various ways to create shipments in SAP TM

There are different ways of creating a shipment in SAP TM, including the following methods:

> From the create a shipment function

> From a planning proposal

> From the collective processing run

The create shipment function is a manual process, while the planning proposal creates shipments according to preset profiles. The collective processing run is a method of creating shipments in batch. It creates shipments automatically and can be scheduled. SAP TM uses the following documents to create shipments:

> Sales orders

> Purchase orders

> Stock transport orders

 Example

The sales order moves material to customer locations, the purchase order initiates a movement inbound to the company from a supplier, and the stock transport order initiates a movement between company locations, most often between warehouses.

Carrier Tendering and Selection

Carrier tendering is the process of the shipper putting freight out to bid and receiving confirmation on prospective freight movements from carriers. It's a form of collaborative transportation planning. This ordinarily is a very labor-intensive process if you don't use a system of some type to manage the process. The ultimate goal is to set freight out to bid automatically and have the system select the best alternative from the returned responses. According to SAP Help, "the accepted quote contains the updated terms and conditions of the transportation service and the TSP that carries out the transportation service."

Carrier Selection

SAP TM provides carrier selection functionality based upon lowest cost. However, SAP TM can also make carrier decisions with consideration for service standards. SAP TM performs this task by maintaining the past history of each of your carriers' performance. SAP TM can then use this information to make better decisions in the future regarding carrier selection. In addition, direct freight cost is one of the many costs associated with transportation that can be tracked, and using the service level selection functionality gives you a more comprehensive view of transportation activities.

Lowest cost carrier selection functionality

Contract Management

Contract management allows the system to accurately maintain a list of the transportation companies under contract in a centralized database and incorporate updated rates. It also allows you to compare and contrast carriers and then adjust contracts on the basis of this information. This functionality can have strategic decision-making implications because it records the cost to service various regions, allowing you to determine if some areas should be outsourced to another transportation provider or simply dropped from service.

In transportation contract management is the management of the contract between the shipper and carrier

Tip

> To use capabilities such as contract management, the logistics department must actually have time to perform analysis. But too many logistics departments are caught in the trap of lacking the skills, budget, or systems to perform longer-term analysis.

Vehicle Scheduling

Within SAP TM, vehicle scheduling is where most of the heavy lifting or at least a lot of the really interesting functionality is contained. The following are some examples:

> Optimization which uses a variety of costs related to transportation, delivery inside and outside of location windows, loading costs, wait time costs, and other costs associated with the transportation movement to arrive at optimal routing. Optimal routing is simply the best sequence of location combinations that results in the lowest costs while meeting all constraints and requirements.

> Selecting among multiple modes

> Selecting carriers (tactically)

> Selecting vehicle resources

Use the optimizer or manually assign vehicle resources

You can run SAP TM in two ways. You can use the optimizer, or you can perform a manual assignment of demand to vehicle resources. Vehicle scheduling, when employing the optimizer, also uses constraints to arrive at a feasible result. Constraints on vehicle scheduling include the following:

> Delivery windows

> Vehicle capacity

> Depot location

> Vehicle incompatibility

> Schedules of vehicle types

> Handling resources

> Opening hours of locations

> Maximum storage time at location

> Limits on distance, duration, and stopover

Carrier Cost Estimation

This functionality allows a cost function to be produced for every transportation movement, for each to be compared against alternatives, and for the best or lowest cost alternative to be selected. For instance, one alternative may have a cost structure that looks like this:

Cost estimations allow you to compare your alternatives

1. *$25 per mile per 1000 units*

2. *$150 per stopover*

For a transport of 2000 units over 100 miles with two stopovers, the cost would be $5600.

After these values are placed into SAP TM, the software can perform the calculation iteratively and automatically. However, this is a simplified example because SAP TM can incorporate many different costs. If you really want to understand what's happening in the optimizer, you need to consider the following:

1. All of these costs are calculated automatically for hundreds or thousands of alternatives.

2. The lowest cost alternative for each shipment is selected.

This gives you a good appreciation for the work the SAP TM Optimizer is performing.

 Example

The issues with respect to the optimizer are similar to those for the SNP and PP/DS optimizers, which comes down to quantification of costs, inputting these costs, and then allowing the optimizer to run.

Transportation Load Builder

The transportation load builder (TLB) optimizes the loading of transportation assets by reconfiguring the load to use the internal container space in the most efficient way. There is actually a 3D solver at work behind TLB. But TLB doesn't have to be part of your initial SAP TM implementation and can be separated due to its highly specialized nature.

> **Ex Example**
>
> Yard management is the management of the flow of vehicles that pick up and deliver material to the warehouse. The parking area for the trucks is where the trucks are staged. In a 100% SAP SCM solution, this isn't controlled by SAP TM but rather by SAP Extended Warehouse Management (SAP EWM). However, SAP TM does affect yard management by placing SAP EWM in a better position to manage the yard by adhering to the delivery windows that are set by facilities. These windows can be either soft or hard constraints for SAP TM. To read more about yard management, see Chapter 11, SAP Extended Warehouse Management (SAP EWM).

This concludes our review of the specific processes in SAP TM, and hopefully you've seen how effective they can be for your own business. Now let's move on to discuss the important SAP TM structures that need to be configured.

Important SAP TM Structures

Some of the more important areas of SAP TM that must be set up include the following:

> Transportation lanes

> Transportation modes

> Transportation zones

> Transportation resources

> Freight units

So as with the specific processes, let's look at each of these to help you understand SAP TM's high-level design.

Transportation Lanes

As mentioned in Chapters 1 and 4, a transportation lane is a route between two locations. Transportation lanes are prominently used in the SNP application, and they're also used by SPP and GATP. Different lanes can have different means of transport assigned to them. So for instance, a transportation lane from Long Beach to Antwerp could have an ocean carrier or air transport lane assigned to it, while a transportation lane from Long Beach to Phoenix could be assigned an air transport, rail, or truck lane. In addition, a supply network is made up of transportation lanes and locations. Transportation lanes set the legitimate material movement routes through the supply chain (Figure 7.2).

Transportation lanes are not set up for all locations because transportation isn't necessarily valid between all locations

> **Note**
>
> Transportation lanes are one layer of restriction on the supply network. Material can only move across locations that have lanes set up between them; however, there are other restrictions on the supply network, and lanes themselves can be set with maximum capacities.

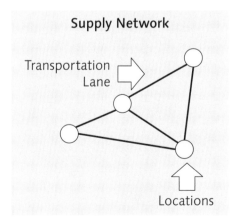

Figure 7.2 A Simple Supply Network Is Made Up of Transportation Lanes and Locations

Note

SAP TM simply plans the material movements that have been communicated to it by another application or system. However, the transportation lead times and costs that are used by SAP TM to plan transportation also affect decision making in other areas of SAP SCM.

Usually in the supply network, in most cases, the movements between different locations are not restricted explicitly; however, there is an exception to this rule. The SPP application restricts some of these location combinations to improve system performance (although inventory rebalancing in SPP removes these restrictions). You can read more about this in Chapter 10, SAP Service Parts Planning (SPP).

Create transportation lanes automatically or manually

Transportation lanes are automatically created in SAP SCM when purchasing info records and scheduling agreements are brought over from SAP ERP. However, they don't exist as transportation lanes in SAP ERP and only become transportation lanes when incorporated into SAP SCM. In addition to coming in through CIF, transportation lanes can be created within SAP SCM manually. This allows lanes to be added quickly and is especially useful when making small changes after the initial model has been created.

Location Geo-coding

Geo-coding provides for more accurate location definitions

SAP TM provides significantly more accuracy to locations and, by extension, to transportation lanes through geo-coding. Geo-coding is the assigning of longitude and latitudes values to locations. SAP TM can automatically determine the distance between locations to a precise level of detail if they are geo-coded.

Geo-coding can be entered using the location master on the General tab (Figure 7.3) or by using the Mass Maintenance transaction.

General	Address	Calendar	TP/VS	Resources

Identifier		External Location Short Te:	
GLN	0	Ext. Location	33
DUNS+4		Bus. System Group	BS

Geographical Data				
	Sgn	Deg.	Minutes	Seconds
Longitude	-	122	24	9
Latitude	+	37	47	15
Time Zone	PST	Precision		0

Figure 7.3 Geographical Data as Coded in the Location Master

In addition, transportation lanes can be created very simply within SAP SCM either manually and one by one (Figure 7.4), or in a batch using the Mass Creation of Transportation Lanes transaction (Figure 7.5).

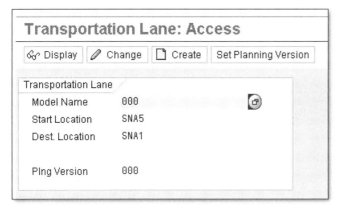

Figure 7.4 Creating Transportation Lanes Individually

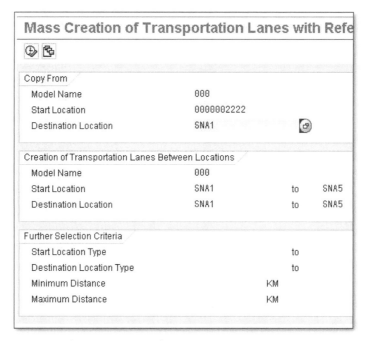

Figure 7.5 The Mass Creation of Transportation Lanes

Transportation lanes also include configuration data

While transportation lanes control the flow of material in the supply network, they also have a number of configuration data elements associated with them:

> Product procurement parameters such as validity dates, shipment lot sizes, and priorities

> Controls such as transportation calendars, distances, and duration

> Carrier capacities

This is another way you can constrain the actual transportation lane that applies for all vehicles that use that route. And because it allows the constraints to be set on the lane rather or in addition to any constraints placed on the vehicles, it's an added way to control the flow of material consistent with company objectives. You can configure these data elements in the location master as shown in Figure 7.6.

Figure 7.6 The Location Master

The Location Master has its own TM tab, which allows the entry of values for things like the Transportation Zone. This applies to the location as well as the amount of time goods can wait at the location.

Transportation Modes

SAP TM is most often used for managing truck fleets. However, less often implemented is the use of SAP TM for planning and scheduling rail, air, and ocean transportation. By simply adding the mode alternatives into the vehicle scheduling profile, SAP TM can make decisions between both modes and specific carriers as part of its normal run. However, because far fewer shippers own private fleets outside of trucking, it's something more appealing to transportation companies in these different modes.

SAP TM can be used for a variety of transportation types

Transportation Zones

One of the most important parts of master data for SAP TM is the transportation zone. Transportation zones are created from the following SAP ERP master data:

> Plants

> Customers

> Suppliers/vendors

> Transportation lanes

> Scheduling agreements

TLB is the transport load builder in SNC

You can use these transportation zones to assign multiple locations to a single zone so that all of the locations are served with one transportation lane. This allows you to reduce the number of transportation lanes that must be processed. And, in addition to its general use in planning to reduce the complexity of the transportation solution to be solved, the transportation zone is also used in TLB.

Transportation Groups

Transportation groups are used to categorize materials for the purposes of defining shipments for specific types of transportation to be scheduled. It's based on the reality that many products have unique transportation needs. A common transportation group category is refrigeration. And as you probably know, refrigerated items can only be transported on vehicle units that have refrigerated containers. By using transportation groups, SAP TM ensures that refrigerated freight is only assigned to refrigerated vehicles. Other examples of transportation groups include hazardous goods and chemicals. While SAP TM ships with a number of standard transportation groups, you also have access to an unlimited number of transportation groups that you can create manually.

SAP TM Resources

Along with SNP, PP/DS, and SAP EWM, SAP TM uses resources for planning. Both SNP and SAP TM deal in resources that transport material; however, for SNP, they are called transportation resources, while for SAP TM, they are called vehicle resources. Vehicle resources can be both different modes, as well as subcategories within a mode (Figure 7.7). For instance, less than truckload (LTL) is a subcategory within the trucking mode. And as with other resources, these are given a capacity and are scheduled. All of the resources have many uses; for example, the setting of average speed for a vehicle allows SAP TM to forecast how long a transit will take.

Vehicle resources are used when a company is planning its own fleet

 Note

You might wonder whether resources are used for outsourced transportation, but the most logical option is actually the tendering functionality that can be used to obtain commitments on loads and routes. Tendering refers freight being put out to bid by shippers and being accepted by carriers. A company can model an outsourced carrier's capacity with resources but only with significantly added complexity. It would also require that the carrier update the company frequently with its capacity, or at least the segment of its capacity that was allocated to the shipper.

Where resources are assigned capacities that are realistic, the resulting plan is considered feasible. However, transportation plans that don't use capacity-constrained resources are considered "infinite," which is a technical term in operations research for unbounded or unrealistic. SAP TM resources are designed to represent loading and transportation capacity. The following are resources that apply to SAP TM:

> Vehicle resources

> Handling resources

You can see the Resource configuration options in Figure 7.7.

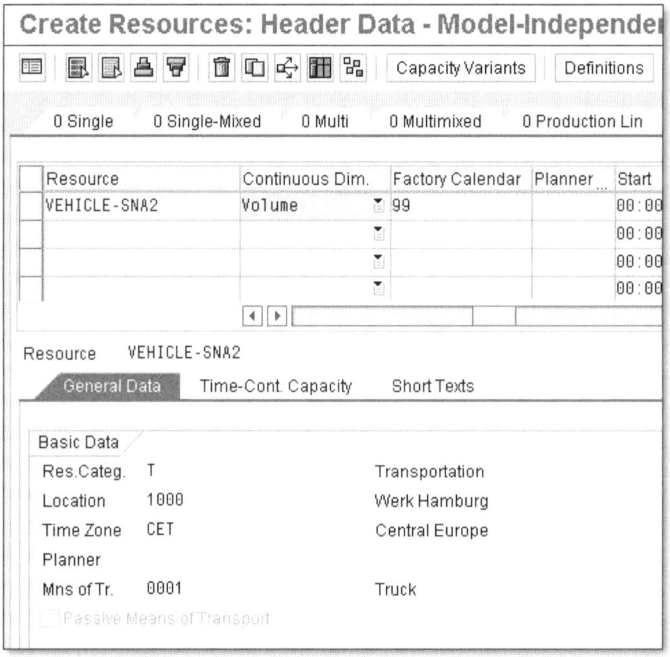

Figure 7.7   Creating a Vehicle Resource

Vehicle resources are specific to SAP TM, and the means of transportation are extremely varied. In addition, all of the resources in SAP SCM are enormously flexible in terms of what can be set as a constraint.

Vehicle Resources

Vehicle resources are only used in SAP TM, not any other part of SAP SCM

In all of SAP SCM, vehicle resources are only used in SAP TM. They are set in terms of capacity per unit or per a unit of time. By constraining these resources and then applying the projected volumes, SAP TM calculates how many of the different unit load types are necessary to meet the plan. The vehicle resource capacity is flexible and can be stated in pallets or cubic feet among many other units of measure. This can allow the system to use the unit of measure that is the actual constraint. For example, on light, but high-volume material, the cubic feet unit of measure can be used. For heavy freight, a weight unit of measure can be applied.

Transportation Versus Vehicle Resources

SNP can also be involved in transportation planning through the use of transportation resources. SNP transportation resources can hold roughly the same amount of data and constraints as a vehicle resource. Transportation resources are assigned to the transport mode in the transport lane and can be used by either CTM or SNP. The processes supported include the following:

> Outbound delivery

> Delivery

> Stock transfer

> Cross docking

> Returns

Transportation resources support a variety of processes

You can see the resource configuration of the SNP Bucket Cap. tab in Figure 7.8.

Figure 7.8 SNP Bucket Cap. Tab of the Transportation Resource

Transportation and vehicle resources share many similarities, but resources are used for vehicle scheduling in SAP TM, whereas transportation resources are only used for higher level planning in SNP.

Let's wrap up our review of the resources in SAP TM with a look at freight units.

Freight Units

Consolidation organizes freight units

Much like the SAP EWM handling units, SAP TM uses freight units to control the material to be moved. After consolidation, the freight units are loaded into the vehicle resource. The process of consolidation organizes the following into freight units:

> Order items

> Delivery items

> Order schedule items

This consolidation can occur interactively, which gives you a high degree of manual control, or it can occur in the background.

One final thing to consider about SAP TM is integration with other applications, particularly SAP Event Management (SAP EM).

Integration to SAP Event Management

As we'll discuss in the next chapter on SAP Event Management (SAP EM), SAP EM can accept data from many sources, which is how it provides an integrated view of the supply chain to the company implementing the software, and to select partners alike. SAP EM is a combination of a monitoring frontend and integration component. It can receive data from the following different categories of sources, which when combined, provide a comprehensive view of the supply chain:

> Transportation providers

> GPS

> Scanners (both facility and vehicle based)

> Vehicle computers

> Suppliers

> RF devices

Note that the majority of the listed areas are related to either warehousing or transportation, and in a 100% SAP SCM solution, that includes SAP EWM and SAP TM. However, SAP EM is most often used in conjunction with transportation (either to SAP TM or connected to other carrier-based system, receiving documents such as ASNs). This is because transportation is often outsourced, even more often than warehousing, and the planning system needs a way of knowing the location of freight in motion.

This concludes our look at the functionality of SAP TM, so let's take a brief look at what was added in the newest release.

SAP TM Release History

SAP TM is one of the older applications within SAP SCM. However, it has still seen some significant improvements as of SAP SCM 7.0:

> Enhanced ability to add users with different roles. Roles include the following:

- Transportation Booking Agent
- Transportation Charge Clerk
- Transportation Dispatcher
- Transportation Manager
- Transportation Network Admin

> Simplified Create Shipment Requests screens. These are targeted at mid-sized firms.

> Enhanced planning interface that allows for defining loading and unloading sequences, replacing resources, changing destinations and locations, and displaying detailed information about transportation charges.

> The ability to perform internal customer freight invoicing between different organizational units of your enterprise. This is important

SAP TM has improved significantly as of SAP SCM 7.0

if different organizations are responsible for paying for and executing different transportation stages.

> More flexibility in distributing freight invoices from the customer freight invoice request and the supplier freight invoice request.

> Integration with SAP BusinessObjects Global Trade Services for shipment processing.

Case Study

Company

This case study involves a gas company focusing on the industrial market and offering a number of specialized gases for industrial applications.

Challenge

Due to its short customer lead times and the fact that many products could be made in multiple plants, the company needed to combine production and transportation planning to answer the questions of where to produce and where to ship from.

Solution

Combined with SAP TM and other applications of SAP, the company was able to implement a solution that provided for more efficient sourcing and transportation decisions with significantly decreased overall costs.

Value Achieved

By using SAP TM, the company was able to greatly smooth the integration between supply planning and transportation planning. Previous to installing SAP TM the company had far less integrated systems, which exacerbated the already significant departmental separation between supply planning and transportation planning. This case study highlights the importance of considering transportation in the overall planning process (a focus of this chapter). Because transportation is the last cost in the chain, it's one of the easiest to overlook when making overall supply chain planning decisions.

Conclusion

SAP TM is a feature-rich application that deserves more attention than it gets. While many may see transportation as an afterthought to the supply chain management process, the effective planning of transportation is essential in supporting the in-stock position of companies and maintaining these stocks at a reasonable cost. As manufacturing and warehouse operations become more integrated, transportation planning and vehicle scheduling is critical to having the vehicles show up at the right time and place.

Now let's move on to look at SAP Event Management, an application that communicates the status of shipments that have been planned with SAP TM, among many other items.

8   SAP Event Management (EM)

The capability to provide alerts and engage in exception-based planning is an extremely important functionality. The capability to do this for areas of the supply chain that aren't under your company's control is also important. For years now companies have been sending EDI communications that allow business partners to know the status of different supply chain activities; however, to meet today's needs, this status information from external business partners needs to be incorporated into a comprehensive status or event application that includes both internal and external status information.

SAP Event Management (SAP EM) provides such multi-partner visibility into the supply chain. It does provide supply chain tracking, but more broadly, the integration and visibility it provides supports cross-company collaboration. SAP EM is a very timely application because of the current movement of so many companies to outsource different aspects of their supply chains (anything from manufacturing to fulfillment). This has resulted in a web of supply chain partners that although they don't share ownership, they must share data to

Multi-partner visibility into the supply chain

perform the supply chain processes. SAP EM not only allows this data sharing but also allows supply chain collaborators to monitor material movements that may only partially flow through their supply chain networks.

In addition to outsourcing, another important change to supply chains over the past decades has been that they are lengthening. According to the film, *The Future of Food*, grocery items in the United States travel an average of 1500 miles to arrive at stores, while nonperishable manufactured items typically travel even farther. This makes tracking systems more important than ever.

Many benefits from SAP EM are related to tying business partners more tightly together

In addition to tracking events and adjusting the SAP SCM applications, SAP EM can also send reminders between your partners. These reminders can be automatically generated in response to events that were scheduled to have already occurred, and multiple partners can be informed in unison so no one is left out of the loop. All of this offers you the major benefits of improving the integration across the supply chain, which according to research, is sorely needed.

 Warning

We don't want to give the impression that SAP EM can adjust SAP SCM applications out of the box. This is advanced SAP EM functionality that requires considerable implementation effort.

Because SAP EM is complex and powerful, it offers a lot of functionality, so let's take a look inside.

Basic Functionality and Concepts of SAP EM

SAP EM has three major areas of functionality: supply chain coordination, SAP Event Management Infrastructure, and analytics. SAP EM is specifically designed to widen the net of activity tracking by accepting communication from a wide variety of sources:

> RF devices

> EDI

> Portals

In this way, SAP EM can be used internally (e.g., only for the company implementing SAP SCM) and externally. SAP EM uses the SAP Event Management Infrastructure to provide messaging that supports supply chain coordination. These messages can then be exported from SAP EM to SAP NetWeaver BW for long-term trend analysis, which can in turn be used to adjust your decision making and improve supply chain outcomes.

Within SAP EM, the event is the main object, so let's look at what an event is.

The Event

Events are discreet activities in the supply chain that can be tracked, and they have expected time elements (Figure 8.1). The option of comparing an event against the current time taken helps you determine whether the event should have an alert created to notify the users to get more involved in monitoring the process. A series of events strung together in a sequence is called an expected event list, and it covers an entire process.

Expected event lists are a series of events strung together in sequence

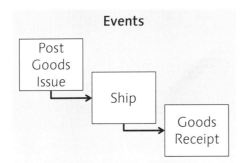

Figure 8.1 SAP EM Events

Example

> An example event list might include the following: An inbound shipment includes an advanced shipment notification (ASN) supplier, followed by a receipt confirmation from the carrier. And a series of shipment status events followed by a warehouse receipt make up the set of events for the inbound process.

Event tracking provides effective upstream and downstream monitoring

Events are simple things. When a goods issue is posted, it's an event. A series of these events models an entire process. SAP EM can tell a company where it is in the process—if it's late, on schedule, or early. And it can do this for thousands of events, which when aggregated, provide an overall picture of the supply chain status.

SAP EM event tracking can mean that events are tracked no matter in which supply chain partner they occur. And events may occur at a variety of supply chain partners, yet partners that are upstream or downstream of the current event can monitor the progress of the entire process. This knowledge of events in other companies upstream allows the companies downstream to make adjustments. Originally, event management was handled in SAP SCM using the Alert Monitor, so let's look at how it evolved and what the new, more comprehensive SAP EM has to offer.

How Event Management Is New for SAP SCM

SAP SCM has had the Alert Monitor for some time, and the concept of exception-based planning was built into SAP SCM in some of its earliest releases. However, SAP EM is much larger in scope than the Alert Monitor. Traditionally SAP SCM applications have focused on interacting with other SAP SCM applications based on data brought in through various methods, including CIF and remote function calls (RFCs).

TechTalk

The Alert Monitor is based on the monitoring architecture introduced with SAP Basis 4.0

This has changed with applications such as SAP Supplier Network Collaboration (SAP SNC) that manage various collaborative processes. However, it reaches an extremely open state with SAP EM where the application is receiving messages and monitoring the company's own SAP SCM, SAP ERP systems, as well as any number of partner systems. Some of the systems SAP EM interacts with will be SAP, but many others may not be, and they don't need to be. This point is critical because not every company uses SAP, and restricting the monitoring to only SAP software would make cross-organizational monitoring almost impossible. In fact, even companies that use no other applications of SAP SCM can use SAP EM to perform its monitoring and cross-partner coordination (Figure 8.2).

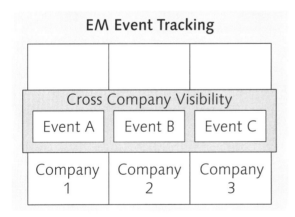

Figure 8.2 SAP EM Event Tracking Multi-Company Example

SAP EM also has a transaction for listing an "Expected Event Overdue List," which can be flexibly searched for as you can see in the fields in Figure 8.3.

Example

The Expected Event Overdue List can be used to search for any overdue event and by any number of selection criteria. This way, the event category can be directly queried.

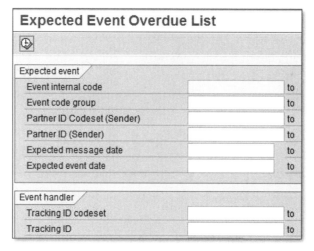

Figure 8.3 Overdue Events Search Transaction

In addition to providing monitoring and cross-partner coordination, SAP EM provides visibility into various supply chain processes.

SAP EM Processes Visibility

SAP EM provides coverage for the following supply chain processes:

> Procurement

> Manufacturing

> Transportation

> Order fulfillment

> Asset management

Procurement

Beginning with a purchase order, the notification is sent to the application system. You can then configure SAP EM to track, at any level of detail for which there are data feeds, the movement of material ending with the receipt of the material into the plant or warehouse.

Manufacturing

SAP EM notifications are created in response to a number of production activities. And because manufacturing is one of the most complex of the supply chain processes, with many events you need to consider the appropriate level of detail for the SAP EM manufacturing tracking model. You can create an event notification in manufacturing in response to the following:

> Machine breakdown

> Production order scheduled

> Malfunction and repair

Transportation

Transportation has a high degree of variability in terms of its duration and delivery performance. Transportation spans the continuum from local truck delivery to international ocean carriage. By bringing carrier data feeds into SAP EM, the implementing company can better understand its actual material delivery date, as opposed to the planned dates. This is particularly important for long lead time shipping (such as ocean freight) because it allows you to make adjustments and place new expedited orders to adjust for a pending late shipment so you aren't placed in situations of material undersupply.

Adjust orders easily to prevent material shortages

Asset Management

RFID is most prominently featured in SAP EWM of all of the SAP SCM applications, and discussed in Chapter 11

By focusing on large equipment items, SAP EM can keep track of equipment as it moves through the supply chain. Notifications can be set up when the assets come out of service, when they are transported, or when they go through their predictable lifecycle stages. There are similarities here with the SAP ERP application Plant Maintenance (PM) in that SAP EM can accept messages and display the position of equipment as is performed with normal material tracking. Therefore, materials that are purchased, transferred, and sold are tracked the same way as equipment. However, the bigger question is how this data will be originated. GPS transmitters assigned to vehicle resources is one way of doing this. But technologies such as RFID will be increasingly popular in the future for tracking equipment such as forklifts and pallets. Of course, manual methods (manual entry and recording of equipment at certain process steps such as goods receipt) should not be discounted.

Along with the general processes we just covered, SAP EM provides functionality for other specific areas.

SAP EM Specific Areas

SAP EM supports the following specific areas of supply chain management:

> Fulfillment
> Transportation tendering
> Sales order processing
> International sea transportation
> Automotive returns processing
> Handling units in outbound shipments

> Service parts delivery and tool management

> Rail car management

And in addition to the specific areas supported by SAP EM, there are a number of major components within SAP EM.

Major Components of SAP EM

The following are major components within SAP EM:

> Event handlers

> Event notifications

> Reactions to event

> User interface

> Analytics

Please note that the user interface is simply the way users observe and interact with the events, so we won't be covering that in detail. As for the rest of the preceding list, those components are detailed in the following sections.

Event Handlers

The integration component is made up of *event handlers* that interpret and manage SAP NetWeaver Process Integration (SAP NetWeaver PI, formerly SAP NetWeaver XI), BAPIs, IDocs, and other feeds. The relationship is that every time a new event occurs, a new event handler is created in the system. These events are predefined, so there is a list of predicted events called the *expected events,* which have dates associated with them.

SAP NetWeaver PI serves as the integration engine for SAP's implementation of SOA middleware

You need to set up the expected events during configuration (Figure 8.4).

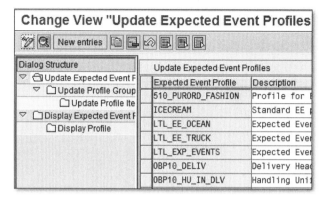

Figure 8.4 Expected Events Must Be Defined in Configuration

Additionally, each event handler has status attributes defined for it, and these status attributes are for the different degrees of completion for the event (Figure 8.5).

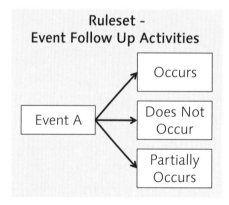

Figure 8.5 Event Follow Up Activities

Events must have a decision matrix

The events must have a decision matrix, which defines what occurs after an event, and what occurs if an event either doesn't complete or only partially completes. Another way of thinking of this is as a decision workflow.

Event Handler Questions to Ask

One of the first things you should do on any SAP EM project is identify which events should be tracked. This also means deciding which events to leave out. There may be events that your company considers important, but there may be no reasonable method for attaining them. So, those events will have to wait for future rollouts. And because many of these events have to be provided by supply chain partners, the list of events must be readily available for these partners to provide their feedback on in the early stages of the implementation and planning, and of course, to provide feedback on as the implementation proceeds. There are a variety of methods for collaborating on this information; however, we've created a sample entry on our supply chain blog to demonstrate how this information can be shared. The design is essentially to use blogging software to share information between business partners. Our solution has been to create one entry per event in a password-protected blog, such as the following:

> SAP EM Event Description: Item Scan At 3PL Warehouse

> SAP EM Event Location: San Jose, California

> SAP EM Event Projected Frequency: Daily

> SAP EM Event Providing System: Penske Logistics Warehouse System

> SAP EM Event Message Format: XML

> SAP EM Event Message Transmission Begin Date Partner Commitment: Jan 10 2010

Involve your partners in determining which events should be tracked

You can find full details at *http://sapplanning.org/2009/07/12/collaborative-database-for-event-management-events/*.

When configuring event handlers, you should ask the following questions:

> Which events will be managed?

> What is the relationship between events?

> How will each event be identified?

> What data are needed?

> Who will view and have access to the event information?

> How many events will be tracked?

Only assign event handlers to events important enough to track

However, not every event is going to be part of the implementation and be assigned an event handler. So only those events that are to be tracked will have event handlers. You should only include events that are important enough to track because setting up an event handler requires work during the implementation, as well as maintenance effort after the implementation (Figure 8.6). And, system users will track the expected event list that results from the configuration.

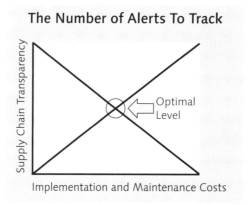

Figure 8.6 SAP EM Complexity Versus SAP EM Payoff

The question of the degree of modeling needed with respect to SAP EM is generally the same as the question of supply chain modeling: the more detail modeled, the higher the accuracy and the better the transparency. On the downside, the more detail modeled, the higher the maintenance and implementation costs.

Event Handler Types

There are different event types for different event handlers. These types are related to the different business processes being tracked, which is an essential organizing structure of SAP EM events. These event types are then prioritized during configuration and grouped into event handler sets, which completes a business process sequence (Figure 8.7).

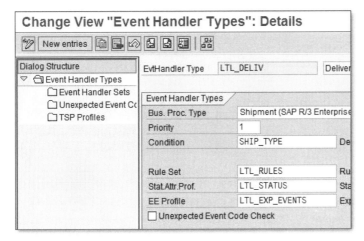

Figure 8.7 Event Handler Type Details

Reacting to Events

SAP EM can trigger, receive, and monitor events, which has the potential to greatly automate the management of not only supply chain execution but also planning because SAP EM can use historical trends to make decisions related to planning. Events can be triggered in the following ways:

> Events can be triggered in three different ways

> SAP EM

> Alert Framework

> SAP Business Workflow

These are all different ways of accomplishing the same task. The SAP EM method is simply using the internal SAP EM functionality.

The Alert Framework is accessed through the SAP NetWeaver Portal providing a second way to initiate reactions. And the third option, SAP Business Workflow, also defines which activities are to be initiated in reaction to incoming events. The difference is that while the normal SAP EM process of event reaction has a flexible sequence response and is integrated into the normal SAP BusinessObjects Supply Chain Performance Management, SAP Business Workflow has a fixed set of tasks as a response and isn't linked to SAP BusinessObjects Supply Chain Performance Management.

 Note

SAP Business Objects Supply Chain Management is an application that allows companies to track important metrics and to perform root-cause diagnostics of your supply chain. This will likely replace the approach on at least some projects where the metrics that are run out to BW.

 Example

Selecting among the various options available for reacting to events really comes down to the extra functionality you want. To go with the standard functionality, you don't need to do anything because it's inherent to SAP EM. However, if you can tolerate less flexibility in event sequences, or it fits with the process to be modeled and you don't need long-term performance tracking, then the flexibility in terms of access offered by SAP Business Workflow can be used.

After the events have occurred, event notifications can be sent.

Event Notifications

Multiple options for communicating event notifications

Event notifications can be communicated using a number of different internal and external channels. Different event codes are used depending on whether the message was internally or externally generated, and whether the partner is using a separate code set. However, you must define the relationship between internal and external codes using the mapping configuration area in SAP EM for setting up the connections between internal and external codes. Every external code must map to an internal code for the external codes to be recognizable by SAP EM. These event notifications can be delivered to the portal interface or to other recipient systems, which include the following:

> Email

> Message services

> Pagers

> Wireless Application Protocol (WAP)

Within the framework of event notification there are discrete event messages.

Event Messages

Event messages provide essential information about the event, and there are a number of data elements related to a message:

> Event code

> Group code

> Generated from

> Priority

> Date rule

> Duration

> Duration sign

> Group number

> Item number

> Date calculation

> Date tolerance

Event messages are used to provide the status of events, and one message can update more than one event

Some of the most important fields relate to tolerance or range. These fields determine when alerts are created for lateness. Reactions can be set up in response to different message statuses, which define what the system does after receiving different event messages.

Service Matching

After an event is received, SAP EM can match a service provider to the location for the subsequent event. These partner functions are defined in the expected event profile.

Action Initiation

The long-term vision is to develop a system that can automate many supply chain tasks

SAP EM can receive event notifications from both SAP systems and non-SAP systems and can initiate actions in SAP systems (Figure 8.8). Examples include the creation of a goods receipt in response to activity. More than one reaction can be configured through the sequence or cascade of reactions called the set rules. This capability is just getting started in SAP EM, and the long-term vision is to create a system that can automate many supply chain tasks. Look for more functionality in this area in future SAP EM releases.

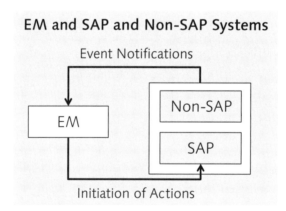

EM and SAP and Non-SAP Systems

Figure 8.8 SAP EM Can Initiate Actions

Analytics: SAP NetWeaver BW and Trend Analysis

Key performance indicators are tracked with SAP NetWeaver BW and updated in SAP EM regularly

SAP EM is designed to be a real-time system. SAP EM builds up notifications, which can be exported to SAP NetWeaver Business Warehouse (SAP NetWeaver BW). You can then use SAP NetWeaver BW to find out who your best and worst performing partners are in their respective areas and adjust your volume allocations accordingly. However, this is just one example of one application for archived SAP EM information. More generally, key performance indicators can be tracked with SAP NetWeaver BW and constantly updated by SAP EM. This isn't automatic, however. The exports as well as the presentation of the reports are part of the implementation effort, and because there is the potential for many different categories of users with an SAP EM implementation, the SAP EM-SAP NetWeaver BW portion of the implementation must determine report design and distribution for a number of different groups.

This concludes our look at the areas and components of SAP EM. Now let's see how you access SAP EM.

Web Interface and Access

The SAP EM portal has an intricate permissions model because not all of the data in the SAP EM interface is to be shared, nor should it be shared with all business partners or the users inside your company. And because different categories of users have different roles and different needs to access specific categories of data, access to SAP EM is provided on the basis of necessity.

A significant amount of the configuration work in SAP EM is simply setting up the web interface and defining events, event messages, document types, and the like. However, less time is spent on traditional SAP SCM configuration work such as optimizer setup, testing, and other advanced planning functionality. What this means is that SAP EM is a different type of project than say implementing SNP. However, the SAP EM team must effectively integrate with the other advanced planning teams to have a successful SAP EM implementation. Integration brings us to the next topic, which is how SAP EM is integrated to the providers of event messages.

SAP EM projects usually need to be staffed differently from advanced planning projects

Integration

SAP EM can accept data from many sources, which is how it provides an integrated view. From a high level, SAP EM is a combination of a monitoring frontend and an integration infrastructure. It can receive data from the following different categories of sources:

> Transportation providers

> GPS

> Scanners (both facility and vehicle based)

> Vehicle computers

> Suppliers

> RF devices

When combined, this provides a comprehensive view of the supply chain. In addition to an integrated view you can also allow the movement of messages between the various systems.

Web Communication Layer

Consider WCL if you're planning to implement SAP EM, so that you can get your business partners involved

The Web Communication Layer (WCL) allows business partners to communicate with SAP EM over the Web, and it's their interface into SAP EM. WCL is actually a separate software package that you need to purchase, but after you do, you can customize the WCL screen layout during configuration. The question of whether to do so has to be weighed against the project budget versus the need to have business partners communicate over the web. Because getting business partners involved is a major contributor to the success of cross-enterprise projects, the WCL should definitely be evaluated if you're planning to implement SAP EM.

That covers the core functionality of SAP EM and hopefully has given you a good overview of the application. It's one of the newer applications so it doesn't have a long release history, but there are some key things to note.

SAP EM Release History

Although SAP EM is one of the more recent additions to SAP SCM, it has only seen a moderate level of new functionality, especially when compared to the similarly new applications of SAP SNC and SPP. Some of the important improvements in SAP SCM 5.1 (also known as 2007) are listed here:

> The ability to track the ocean carrier booking process

> The ability to create hierarchies between event handlers

> The ability to search for event handlers by the message header, the document reference, or the header extension table

> New visibility processes for transportation management, SAP SNC, and Auto-ID infrastructure, which relate to product tracking and authentication visibility processes

> The ability to create tables that store customized parameters for event messages

> The use of the Web Dynpro interface

> New visibility processes for SAP SNC inbound messages, purchase orders, and replenishment orders

SAP SCM 7.0 improvements include the Web Dynpro ABAP interface that now supports almost all of the functions in the original web interface.

Case Study

Company

Although this postal service company has a long history, they recently found new competition from parcel companies. The company wants to integrate a number of new technologies into its business to improve its competitiveness in the market.

Challenge

This company needed a way to create an event monitoring system that could be used to improve its internal operations, as well as position it as a premium service provider to its customers eager for updates on the status of their mail and parcels. And, the solution needed to meet all of the company's needs at a transaction volume that SAP EM had never been implemented with.

Solution

SAP EM was implemented in a way that improved visibility internally to its customers and to its business partners. The key feature of SAP EM that made this possible is that it can have multiple "customers" for the information it produces.

Value Achieved

The company was able to implement SAP EM and provide a significant differentiator for customers, while greatly improving internal visibility. As described in this chapter, the flexibility in SAP EM is key to gaining value from it. Just as the planning modules within SAP SCM are measured by the accuracy of the model compared to reality, SAP EM implementations are measured by the selection of events and the ability of the technical aparatus to provide data to the events that support the overall planning process.

Conclusion

SAP EM provides a view of the status of in-process supply chain activities that range from where transportation units are geo-located to the progress of production planning on contract-manufactured items. The scope of SAP EM in terms of what it can control is broad, and implementations should naturally first focus on the highest areas of potential in terms of monitoring. SAP EM can also be implemented internally only, and perfecting its use internally goes a long way toward bringing supply chain partners onboard to an SAP EM implementation.

As you learned, SAP EM is different from the rest of SAP SCM (except for CIF) in that it's not planning software; it's monitoring software that supports supply chain planning and execution. For those familiar with implementing planning systems, SAP EM is an adjustment. The fact that the success of the SAP EM implementation depends on the ability of the implementing company to get buy-in and effort from business partners means that SAP EM must be planned differently. The fact that both SAP EM and SAP SNC face similar challenges regarding their implementation means that similar methods must be used to increase the likelihood of their success.

Success in supplier collaboration is well documented and covered in Chapter 12, SAP Supply Network Collaboration (SNC). One of the most important lessons from previous supplier collaboration projects is that the two business partners need to have a good relationship and a level of trust before the project begins. Secondly, there must be long-term investment on the part of both parties. We see no reason these lessons don't apply directly to SAP EM projects as well.

Another issue is the capability of transportation companies to provide information to the shippers that implement SAP EM. Although a detailed exposition into the transportation industry is beyond the scope of this book, suffice it to say that the level of technological and IT prowess demonstrated by FedEx and UPS doesn't generalize to other transportation providers because other transportation providers operate on lower profit margins than the parcel companies and their investment in systems isn't the same. While most of them are capable of producing transportation EDI messages, there can be a significant amount of effort to integrate them into an SAP EM implementation. This can have implications for carrier selection in that not

To be effective, SAP EM requires integration of transportation EDI messages every carrier may be able to be brought up on the SAP EM system. And, implementing a system such as SAP EM can change the selection criteria from price to a more IT-capable carrier.

When considering SAP EM, be careful of scope creep

The more you work with SAP EM, the more the opportunities this application offers will become apparent. This is good but also can be problematic because there can be a natural inclination for scope creep on SAP EM projects. And SAP EM is new and still completely dependent on the constant functioning of the underlying messaging system. This means that informed project managers will allocate extra time and resources (as with SAP SNC projects) for infrastructure and integration work. So you should keep all of these things in mind when considering whether to implement SAP EM.

In the next chapter, we're going to talk about the SAP SCM Core Interface (CIF), which connects SAP ERP to SAP SCM and is delivered as an SAP ERP plug-in.

9 Core Interface (CIF)

SAP SCM is basically designed to perform planning and to develop recommendations for executing transactions such as creating purchase orders, stock transport orders, and sales orders; it doesn't actually execute these transactions. So, SAP SCM needs a way to send recommendations to the execution system, most often SAP ERP, and to receive status information and master data from SAP ERP. Although in the newer releases of SAP SCM applications, other integration methods have become more prominent, the main interface system between SAP ERP and SAP SCM is the Core Interface (CIF).

CIF connects SAP ERP to SAP SCM and is delivered as an SAP ERP plug-in. It allows a connection to be made between multiple SAP ERP systems and SAP SCM systems, at least in principle. In practice, however, the most common connection is between one SAP ERP system and one SAP SCM system.

CIF allows SAP SCM to send recommendations to SAP ERP

CIF is within the category of software called middleware, which, if you're not familiar with it, allows two software applications to exchange data regardless of the system on which they are being run. In this way, CIF has more in common with SAP NetWeaver Process

Integration (SAP NetWeaver PI) (formerly known as SAP NetWeaver XI) than with any of the other SAP SCM applications, but we'll discuss CIF in this book because it focuses specifically on SAP ERP to SAP SCM integration.

The Technology Behind CIF

CIF is a combination of remote function calls (RFCs) with a user interface that allows for their setup and configuration. The user interface also allows the setup and running of integration models, which are selections of data to be moved between the systems. CIF also has a number of tools for queue and error management.

 Note

The process of setting up CIF often entails setting up models, running the models, and then checking for errors. This process is repeated until the models run without errors.

CIF isn't easy to set up, but it's part of implementing SAP SCM

While middleware often refers to software that can connect multiple software applications together, CIF is a highly specialized solution that, as we mentioned, focuses on SAP ERP to SAP SCM integration. SAP SCM can be used without SAP ERP, but it's extremely uncommon. One of the main advantages of this for SAP ERP clients is that much of the data required to use SAP SCM is already set up in any live system of SAP that has SD and MM configured. CIF has a structured way to bring this master data and transaction data over to SAP SCM and to bring planning results back to SAP ERP. However, don't think that it's prepackaged because getting CIF to work, or even monitoring it, is a lot of work. But it does offer some important functionality that makes it worth the effort.

Basic Functionality and Concepts of CIF

CIF transfers both master data and transactional data back and forth between SAP ERP and SAP SCM. A few examples of standard data types for master and transaction data are shown in Table 9.1.

Data Type	Examples
Master data	Plant, materials, customer, vendors
Transaction data	Planned orders, stock transfer orders, ATP requests

Table 9.1 Standard Data Types

From just this small sampling, you can probably see that generally speaking, master data tends to flow from SAP ERP to SAP SCM, while transactional data tends to flow from SAP SCM to SAP ERP (Figure 9.1).

SAP SCM has more simplified master data than SAP ERP, which is typical for planning systems versus execution systems

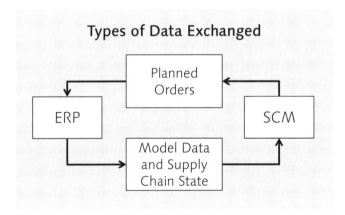

Figure 9.1 Example Model of the Type of Data Exchanged

Other definable characteristics also apply to the data that is exchanged. Comparatively, the data that flows from SAP ERP to SAP SCM is:

> *More numerous* because many more types of data are necessary to populate SAP SCM than data that are sent from SAP SCM to SAP ERP.

> *Less aggregated* because planning systems such as SAP SCM are more aggregated than transactional systems such as SAP ERP.

> *Greater in volume* because much more data in terms of records flows into SAP SCM than back to SAP ERP. This is true of all planning systems versus execution systems.

Because of these factors, in addition to the master data going from SAP ERP to SAP SCM, the complexity tends to be on the SAP ERP to SAP SCM side of the interface. There are CIF configuration transactions in both SAP ERP and SAP SCM, so it's no surprise that the majority of configuration is performed on the SAP ERP side.

Master Data

You can plan the effort required for CIF in part by effectively analyzing what master data is being brought over to SAP SCM

As we mentioned, master data flows from SAP ERP to SAP SCM, while transactional data flows in both directions. In addition to master data, which originates in SAP ERP, there is master data maintained in SAP SCM that has no counterpart in SAP ERP. This data must be set up manually within SAP SCM. This includes but isn't limited to the following:

> Many fields on the product location master

> SAP SCM specific resources

So, the master data in SAP ERP should be viewed as a "starter kit" for SAP SCM. CIFing over all of the master data available from SAP ERP is only the beginning.

As for the master data that does come across to SAP SCM, there are many terminology changes that can be a bit confusing. Table 9.2 shows a few examples of what objects are called in SAP ERP and what they become in SAP SCM.

SAP ERP Object	Same Object in SAP SCM
Plants, customers, vendors	SAP SCM Locations
Routing and BOM	PPM or PDS
Work center	SAP SCM Resources
Material master	SAP SCM Product master

Table 9.2 Object Names in SAP ERP and SAP SCM

Making the two systems work together properly takes a fine level of detail because there are numerous examples of how SAP ERP does things differently than SAP SCM.

Ex Example

Simple things like differences in numbering systems can be confusing; for example, SAP ERP uses 4 digits, and SAP SCM uses those same four digits preceded by a number of zeros. So a vendor master number in SAP ERP that is 2222 is 0000002222 in SAP SCM. Adding leading zeros is standard in CIF for some reason.

Other areas related to your SAP SCM master data are data volumes and data sequence.

Master Data Volume and Sequence

While transaction data volumes stay relatively stable, master data volumes work differently. When you first bring up SAP SCM, there's an initial transfer of master data into SAP SCM to populate the model, and then subsequent transfers are used to modify the existing master data. The reason the changes are often small is because a company doesn't frequently add large numbers of new products or new locations to its supply chain network.

 Tip: Change Pointers

> Setting up the systems for transferring net changes from master data is performed by setting up *change pointers*. Transferring just the net change greatly cuts down on volumes. Change pointers are activated in SAP ERP, and SAP has a documented list of objects that allow change pointers.

Master Data Sequence

It's important to organize your master data based on SAP's recommendation

Master data has an organization and a sequence in which it's loaded because much of the master data depends on other master data being in place first. SAP recommends organizing master data in the order listed here. This list is useful for an implementation; however, it's also useful for simply understanding the different categories of master data:

> ATP Customizing and product allocation customizing

> Plants

> Characteristics and classes

> Material masters, and characteristics and classifications

> MRP area

> Planning product

> Availability check

> Product allocation

> Customers and suppliers

> Work centers

> Production process models (PPMs)

> Scheduling agreement, and contract and purchasing info records

Transactional Data

The following types of transactional data are also commonly transferred between SAP ERP and SAP SCM:

> Purchase orders

> Purchase requisitions

> Sales orders

> Planned orders

> Planned independent requirements

> Reservations

> Stock

Essentially, the state of the supply chain (its on-hand balances, requirements, etc.) is transferred to SAP SCM from SAP ERP. SAP SCM then takes this snapshot and performs processing and communicates *planned orders* back to SAP ERP. But SAP SCM can't actually change the real state of the supply chain; it can only make recommendations for changes. However, SAP ERP may or may not execute depending on many factors. For instance, SAP SCM may place a purchase order that can't be fulfilled by the suppliers. And although SAP SCM is modeling reality, it's still not the actual reality, so there will always be differences between the plan and the actual transactions that result from it. The supply chain state communicated to SAP SCM, followed by recommendations flowing from SAP SCM to SAP ERP, is the natural arrangement between the execution and planning systems.

SAP SCM makes recommendations for changes that flow to SAP ERP

 Tip: Change Pointers

Because variants work differently in CIF than in other areas of SAP, it's recommended that you save different integration models with one variant per model.

Integration Models

Models are a method of selecting different sets of master data and transaction data segmented for export. This is where the data objects that are to be selected for transfer are defined. Integration models are created and then activated. They can be as small as the master data necessary to plan for a single product location, and different integration models can be set up for many different purposes. Integration models are subsets of the overall data available (Figure 9.2).

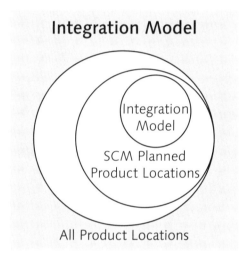

Figure 9.2 Integration Model Subsets

An integration model includes a subsection of the SAP SCM planned product location grouping and, of course, all of the master and transactional data to support it. Not all product-location combinations are planned; however, only critical, long lead time, supply constrained, or expensive products need to be planned (Figure 9.3).

SAP SCM is becomng more execution oriented due to applications such as SAP EWM

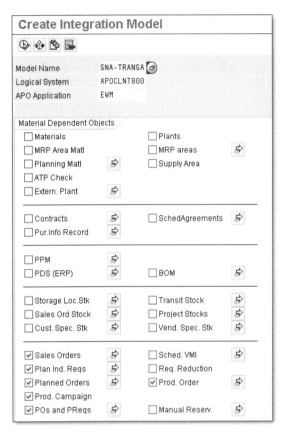

Figure 9.3 Creating Integration Models

The Create Integration Model transaction provides an appreciation for how many different types of data can be brought across with CIF. And as you can see in Figure 9.3, PPMs don't exist in SAP ERP; however, they are included here in CIF because they are created in SAP SCM from the combinations of routing, work centers, and bills of material in SAP ERP. The product locations that are to be included in SAP SCM planning are coded in the MRP Type field on the MRP 1 tab of the material master.

PPMs don't exist in SAP ERP, but they are in CIF

Example: Integration Model Size and Testing

> Very small integration models are beneficial for testing because they can isolate specific data. The best method we know for CIF data testing is to start with small models and then increase them in size (fixing the error messages you receive along the way) until you build up to larger models with more data.

An important feature of integration models is CIF variants, which are instrumental in maintaining integration models.

CIF Variants

Managing CIF effectively is about providing the flexibility to maintain slightly different integration models, especially during testing

In CIF, variants are integration models that are saved and can be reopened and continually rerun. After using CIF for some time, we've concluded that variants should be created and saved for each integration model. The saved variants have to do with the options selected on the integration model selection screen and won't affect the combination of product location or the objects to be brought over. The integration model controls the *data selections*, but the variants control *how this data* will be brought over. A variant can be changed over and over, which provides the necessary flexibility to the integration model as well as being a great time saver.

 Tip

> If variants aren't saved, it can be difficult to bring up integration models after they are created because CIF, at the time of this writing, lacks a transaction for integration model modification. So if you want to change or copy a model (which is typical), you need to create a variant of the model.

Now let's shift gears a bit and talk about models as a generalized concept in SAP SCM, not CIF integration models.

Models in SAP SCM

The generalized models in SAP SCM are particularly important for supply chain planning, although they are also used in execution systems. While SAP ERP represents one reality, SAP SCM is designed to perform scenario testing. The "virtual" nature of planning systems means that they can test and retest different planning strategies. Nothing is executed until the planned orders are exported to SAP ERP. SAP SCM has one "live" or active model and a number of simulation models, which are never exported to SAP ERP. If simulated results are tested and considered beneficial, the configuration changes are migrated to the active model in SAP SCM. This concept isn't unique to SAP SCM because SAP ERP also has versions.

SAP ERP also has a virtual environment within production, but planning systems can take extra advantage of this because they are more aggregated and more suited to simulation

Models and Versions

This design allows SAP SCM to keep many different models in the same instance of SAP SCM. When CIF brings data into SAP SCM, however, it always brings it into the active model, identified as model 000, along with the active version, which is also given the number 000. In addition, multiple versions can be created for a model, although only the combination of model 000 and version 000 are active. The following rules apply for the active version and active model:

Simulation functionality could be better used on projects than it is, if more people understood how planning is different from execution

> The active model can be copied over into other models.

> Simulation models can be created so that different scenarios can be tested. The results can be compared with the active model to see if there are improvements in key performance indicators.

The result of this is that inherent flexibility is built-in to SAP SCM for keeping different versions and models. This serves to enhance planning and provides the ability to perform testing and run scenarios.

CIF Tools

CIF has a variety of queue management and error management capabilities. CIF's queue management is similar in principle to the queue on a printer. As with a printer queue, if earlier jobs or queues don't complete successfully, they tie up the jobs that follow them. So, CIF errors are supposed to lead you to make adjustments to how you're bringing the data over, so that the data fits with the receiving system needs. CIF errors actually say more about the ability of the objects to be used after they get into SAP SCM than about whether CIF intends to bring over the objects. You can really only find out by activating the integration model. When the queue between SAP ERP and SAP SCM is clogged, CIF provides the functionality to remove queues that failed to go through (Figure 9.4).

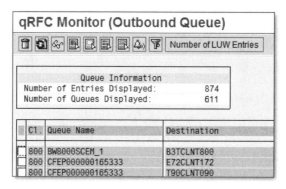

Figure 9.4 qRFC Monitors the Outbound Queue

Planning the configuration and testing of CIF before you begin your project is critical

CIF has both inbound and outbound queue monitoring transactions. The ability to delete queues using this transaction is very important because just as with a printer queue, jobs get stuck and need to be cleared out before other jobs can be processed. This monitoring feature is important during testing because many errors are typically created. These errors often create a lot of effort for those troubleshooting the system. And because CIF isn't particularly intuitive or transparent, time and project resources must be allocated in a serious manner to this work. Configuring and testing CIF shouldn't be an afterthought for your project because the vast majority of errors come during the testing of the system prior to go-live. Additionally, after the testing is complete, the queues must still be monitored to find errors and to ensure that the two systems are sending data to each other properly. SAP has a full list of the areas of CIF to check daily and weekly after SAP SCM is live.

CIF Versus BAPIs and Custom Integration Code

It's important to understand that CIF is an infrastructure component and not a functionality component, so although no user will interact with CIF, they'll quickly notice a problem if CIF is in error. The primary benefit of CIF is that it can kick off pre-built adapters that shuttle data between the two systems. Almost every SAP SCM implementation also implements CIF; however, CIF doesn't necessarily cover every integration requirement between SAP ERP and SAP SCM.

Integration may require some programming, so plan ahead

For some requirements, SAP has developed integration BAPIs (Business Application Programming Interfaces). This is a non-CIF interface that connects the systems for specific data needs. SAP also has BAPIs that connect SAP SCM to non-SAP ERP systems such as SAP NetWeaver BW. To bridge the gap between what is offered by SAP and what is required for the project, you may have to do some custom coding. Project managers shouldn't assume that the combination of CIF and BAPIs will meet all of their implementation needs.

Next we'll discuss how the information flow is managed by CIF, and we'll bring up the topic of the CIF queue.

Queues

With CIF, you have your choice of queue type. You can use either inbound or outbound queues. There are advantages and disadvantages to each. Inbound queues can handle a much larger data volume than outbound queues. With inbound queues, the receiving system controls the data transfer. However, outbound queues are often the preference for lower volume interfaces. The transfer between the two (inbound versus outbound) takes place in the CIF (see Figure 9.5).

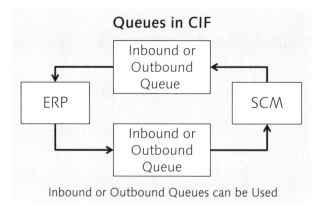

Figure 9.5 General Flow Between the Systems

Error Management

Error management is critical. The first reason is that this is one of the best ways to isolate the errors that invariably come up when breaking in new data transfers. A second reason for breaking up larger sets of data into multiple integration models is to better control the volume flowing between the two systems.

A mammoth number of errors can occur when attempting to integrate systems because a series of master data objects must come across to SAP SCM correctly. If even a few are missing or aren't consistent with the model in SAP SCM, errors will result.

CIF Error Management Components

CIF has the following main error checking components (Table 9.3).

CIF Tool	Description
CIF Cockpit	Shows errors on both the SAP ERP and SAP SCM systems. It is a container for CIF background jobs.
SAP SCM Queue Manager	Oversees the overall CIF process; like the CIF Cockpit, it can see errors on both the SAP ERP and SAP SCM systems.
qRFC monitors	Specifically monitors the RFCs.
Application logs	Shows errors from application data loading issues.

Table 9.3 Error Checking Components

 Note

Not all of these monitoring tools are created equal. It may be a matter of taste, but many users find that the qRFC monitors and application logs (where CIF status can be evaluated) are more effective than the SAP SCM Queue Manager or the CIF Cockpit. In fact, some users don't use these second tools at all, even though they are strongly showcased as important CIF tools in other sources.

Errors in Error

In our own testing, we found that CIF errors aren't as reliable as we had originally thought. That is, data sometimes comes across without actual incident, but a CIF error points to a nonexistent problem. Because we've encountered this issue a number of times, we found it useful to document the examples so they can be identified the next time we encountered these errors. One such error related to storage locations occurred after we received errors from transferring storage locations from SAP ERP to SAP SCM, but we checked to find that the storage locations had been created correctly in SAP ERP. In subsequent interface runs, we gave this particular error much less consideration.

Errors found during testing may not be actual errors, so check them carefully

You should now have a good understanding of how the systems transfer data between one another, so let's move on to discuss the broader integration requirements.

Complete Integration

SAP ERP and CIF must not only be integrated in that they send data between one another, they must also be synchronized so that when the data arrives from the other system, it makes sense. So, it's necessary, for instance to synchronize the calendars used between the systems.

You can see how to synchronize calendars in Figures 9.6 and 9.7 using the Transfer Global Settings options.

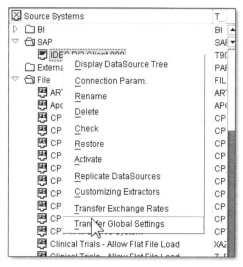

Figure 9.6 The SAP NetWeaver BW
Data Warehouse Workbench

In this transaction, we are transferring the Factory Calendar settings from SAP ERP to SAP SCM. Both systems must plan off of the same calendar. When this calendar is changed for any reason in SAP ERP, this process of transferring global settings must be repeated.

Figure 9.7 Transferring Global Settings from the SAP NetWeaver
BW Data Warehouse Workbench

Real-Time CIF?

While referred to as a "real-time system," this description isn't as useful as it originally appears. This phrasing can make executives or business users think that CIF runs in real time continuously. Although this
sounds good, very few interfaces between the execution and planning
systems must be real time. Also, explaining to business users that in
most cases real-time interfaces are counterproductive is an important
part of many planning projects. In reality, as with most execution
to planning system interfaces, the majority of the transfers occur in
batch. One of the exceptions to this is the availability checks, which
are sent to the GATP application.

Conclusion

CIF is a complicated middleware solution that takes a good amount of effort to master, but any SAP SCM implementation will want to take advantage of its prebuilt adapters to speed the implementation. However, there is still a lot of work involved in getting SAP ERP and SAP SCM to interoperate.

In terms of managing a project with CIF, you can find consultants who mainly specialize on CIF, so it's a good idea to bring in one of these CIF specialists in the initial stages of your implementation. Then you won't necessarily need them after CIF has been brought up and thoroughly tested.

But mastering CIF, with or without a specialist, will really come down to experience and trial and error.

In the next chapter, we'll move on to look at the Service Parts Planning (SPP) packages.

10 SAP Service Parts Planning (SPP)

Many companies struggle to get the right part to the right location at the right time to meet service-level agreements and then end up with excess inventories, poor performance levels and customer satisfaction ratings, and missed up-sell opportunities. There are many causes for these problems, but often it comes down to a few core issues: lack of visibility into service parts inventory levels, inconsistent naming conventions for service parts and suppliers, and insufficient use of automation and analytics, among other things. But to remain competitive and fiscally viable, companies need to fix the issues causing their poor performance problems.

SAP Service Parts Planning (SPP) is designed to address many of these problems. It provides the latest capabilities for parts demand forecasting and for inventory planning and distribution models. It can help you achieve significant improvements in service levels while reducing your inventory costs. The software is designed to meet the unique and demanding needs of the service parts business, and as such supports properly planned inventory across a distribution network based on part volume, velocity, segments, and other practical business rules.

SAP SPP is a subcategory of advanced planning designed for the special needs of the service parts industry. Unfortunately, the vast majority of companies don't use specialized applications for planning service parts, even though there are significant advantages to doing so. This awareness of the difference in finished goods versus service parts planning is very slowly beginning to be understood, and SAP SPP is a major step in the direction of getting specialized service parts solutions generally accepted.

SAP SPP is a step in the right direction for the service parts industry

Basic Functionality and Concept of SAP SPP

SAP SPP can be thought of as if SAP DP and SNP were combined into one application and then customized for service parts. Many people question why a specialized service parts application is necessary, but the fact is that service parts have unique planning requirements that make them difficult to plan well in finished goods planning systems. While service parts represent a sizable percentage of the market for manufactured items (and this greatly varies per industry), the vast majority of supply chain software is designed for the *finished goods* market and not the service parts market. So to date, a small number of niche vendors, and now SAP, have developed software for this specialized form of planning.

Unique Features of Service Parts Planning

The special features of service parts planning make it difficult to effectively plan service parts using finished goods planning systems

Service parts have different planning needs than finished goods. For instance, the demand for a service part at a product location is (unlike the demand for finished goods) not represented by a normal distribution. Instead, a different distribution, which is leftward leaning and called a *Poisson* or *Negative Binomial* distribution, is used (Figure 10.1).

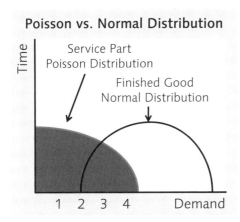

Poisson vs. Normal Distribution

Figure 10.1 Probability Distributions Compared

With service parts, the demand probabilities are bunched up toward the lower end of the demand continuum (Figure 10.1).

These so-called "lumpy" demand patterns are extremely difficult to forecast, so difficult in fact, that a different standard or error must be used. In most cases, the decision the SAP SPP application makes is whether to carry 0, 1, or 2 of an item at a product location. Depending upon the service network in question, this may be the decision for roughly 70% of the product locations.

However, in addition to this well-known feature of SAP SPP, there are several others. Up until SAP SCM 5.1, SAP SPP lacked the rudimentary capabilities to compete in this market because it didn't offer the following capabilities, but today it does:

SAP SPP has added new capabilities that were missing in earlier versions

> Multi-echelon inventory optimization (called inventory balancing in SAP SPP). Inventory balancing is SAP SPP's method of rebalancing inventory across the different levels in the hierarchy. Factors include the following:

 – Move costs

 – Inventory savings

 – Service benefit

 – Warehouse space savings

Surplus and
obsolescence
planning is run as a
service in SAP SPP
and is executed
from the PSM
(discussed in
Chapter 14)

These costs help decide which inventory is to be moved. This is a critical feature because in service parts, if inventory is in the wrong location, there's often not sufficient volume of orders to have it moved out of the system by normal customer demand. So efficient parts planning networks redistribute parts from locations where they aren't needed or repair unserviceable items, prior to scheduling new production or procurement orders. This feature is significantly more important for service parts than finished goods planning, where the repositioning of inventory is less frequent.

The few companies that do invest in SAP SPP applications tend to create long-lived assets and have large service businesses. These companies may receive close to half their business from service parts. However, even in these companies, service parts are subordinated to the finished goods business.

 Note

As of SAP SCM 7.0, inventory balancing was enhanced with the ability to inventory balance unserviceable products as well as perform simulation of the inventory balancing service. The horizon balancing can also be set to consider stock movements outside the shortage horizon. Particularly if the company is using the buy-or-repair functionality, it's important to place the unserviceable item in a location where it can be repaired. Pull deployment can also be used as an alternative to inventory balancing. The concept of fair share deployment is now available within SAP SPP. Already used in SNP, fair share deployment is a method of inventory allocation. Fair share can allocate inventory several different ways, including proportional distribution (based upon previous demand allocation, proportional fulfillment of target stock, and quota arrangements). Deployment is scheduled in the Public Sector Management (PSM), which provides access to services and is for running them in the background. However, a distribution requirements planning (DRP) run is what actually schedules inventory balancing to initiate, and inventory balancing is specifically used to solve the issue of insufficient quantities of products for the repair or buy process at a location.

Supersession *Supersession* is another important difference between finished goods and service parts planning. Supersession is where a planned part replaces another planned part because the second planned part is either made obsolete from the system or simply needs a spot substitution due to a shortage.

Supersession is critical in service parts because, over time, many parts are replaced by new versions of the part (or multiple new parts called *many-to-one supersession* or *one-to-many supersession*), and the old stock out in the field needs to be removed eventually. Due to the low volume of many service parts, frequently the parts sit out in their forward stocking locations for some time with no movement demand. They eventually become obsolete, and normal sales activity doesn't move these obsolete parts out of the system.

 Note

There are a number of forms of supersession. The most common is called *one-way* supersession, which is where one part supersedes another. This is also the simplest form of supersession. However, parts can supersede one another. This is called *two-way* supersession, and it's important because if a part is available at a location that can serve as a substitute for another part, it's beneficial to know this because it strongly affects the resulting fill rate. An enhanced capability to manage this substitution process is both necessary and desirable (Figure 10.2).

Another way SAP SPP differs from finished goods planning is in forecasting. Some, but not all, service organizations are able to take advantage of causal forecasting. SAP calls this *leading indicator forecasting*. Most forecasting is based on applying statistics on historical sales order databases. However, because the underlying factors (e.g., installed base, usage hours, or equipment initiation) can be known, and the part demand (called derived demand) can be calculated from these precursors, forecasting in this way can result in higher forecast accuracy.

Maintaining even one causal value for leading indicator forecasting can be difficult, but SAP SPP is designed to accept causal data, as long as it's accurate

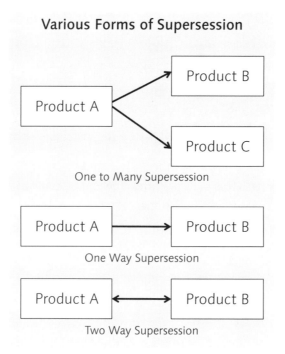

Various Forms of Supersession

One to Many Supersession

One Way Supersession

Two Way Supersession

Figure 10.2 Different Types of Supersession Represented by Replacement Types in SAP SPP

One final way SAP SPP differs from finished goods planning is in the ability to plan repairs. For obvious reasons, repairs don't apply to finished goods at all, so finished goods planning systems don't have functionality that addresses repairs. However, repair planning is very important for service parts. There are several steps to the process. The first is that items must be coded as unserviceable. Second, the repair lead times and costs must be set up as master data. The SAP SPP system then can make decisions regarding repairing, moving, or bringing in new replacement stock to meet planned demand.

Example: Which Causals to Use?

A number of underlying factors, called *causals*, can be used, but by far the most common is the installed base. This is simply the number of serviceable items that are in the field. For instance, if 1000 airplanes are in the field, and a particular part breaks on average once a month per 100 planes, then the resulting installed base forecast is 10 units. This causal forecast can be used alone, or alternatively, can be combined with a historical forecast to arrive at a composite forecast. As a simplified example, we can change the moving average for this same part to 8 units, then combining the historical forecasting with the causal forecast results in a forecast of 9 units. Causal forecasting is particularly helpful for forecasting new items that don't have a demand history.

> If your company has not previously performed causal forecasting, it's likely that you'll need to clean, improve, and test the accuracy of your causal data

You should now have a good understanding of how SAP SPP differs from finished goods planning, so let's look at some key functionality within SAP SPP.

Important Functionality of SAP SPP

The following sections cover some of the most important conceptual areas of functionality that you need to know to understand SAP SPP.

The Bill of Distribution (BOD)

SAP SPP works differently from SAP SCM's other network management software application, SNP, in that it overlays the concept of a *bill of distribution* (BOD) over the planning network. A bill of distribution is simply a play on the term "bill of material," and is just a subnetwork of the larger network (think of the larger network as every product location in the system), which declares which locations are applicable locations for planning. Just as a BOM states which *materials* go together, a BOD states which *locations* go together, or at least those that are active during a planning run.

> Bill of distribution is a play on the term "bill of material"

Example

> While the BOD appears to be a dominant feature in SAP SPP, it's not active for all parts of the SAP SPP planning process. For example, when inventory balancing is used, the BOD is dispensed with. This essentially opens the system and allows demand to drive the relocation of product without the restrictions of the BOD. The issue with inventory rebalancing generally is that in the initial stage, the software often recommends more repositioning than the company has a budget for.

Service Level Planning

Planning in SAP SPP goes well beyond the service parts industry

Service level planning is a functionality that should eventually migrate out of SAP SPP and into SNP. With service level planning, a service level is set at a product location. Planning then works backwards from the service level to determine the ordering and production quantity and timing. This functionality is at the cresting point in the industry, and its interest goes far beyond SAP SPP and into finished goods planning generally. Unfortunately, companies won't take advantage of it because the functionality resides in SAP SPP, which many consider only applicable to service parts.

Surplus and Obsolescence Planning

Surplus and obsolescence planning is how material that isn't sold to customers is managed in the planning system. Surplus and obsolescence is very important with service parts because they tend to have much higher percentages of their inventory that eventually become obsolete, and SAP SPP must manage surplus parts more frequently than finished goods. With SAP SCM 7.0, more detail was added. For example, if a product's mandatory retention period has elapsed, the product is no longer produced, and the demand for the product is below a certain limit value, it's described as obsolete stock. SAP SPP goes through the entire BOD and either scraps the material or provides a scrapping indicator, which is set at the product location. SAP SPP removes locations with the smallest inventory first. Whether products can be set as obsolete is also a controllable parameter.

Differential Planning

With 7.0, SAP SPP picked up the ability to plan inventory of different products for certain customers or dealers. So, their locations can simply be part of the planning network, and material can be moved to the location through a stock transport (an internal movement) rather than a purchase order (an external document). This can be done for either customers or dealers. To do this, the sales, inventory and external locations from the customer or dealer need to be incorporated into SAP SCM. The dealer or customer can log in, see the projected stock movements, and approve and disapprove specific movements before they happen. This functionality is under OEM-Managed Inventory in SAP SPP.

SAP SPP gives dealers and customers a view of projected stock movements so they can approve or disapprove them before they happen

Kit to Stock

Kit to stock is critical functionality, and kitting is an important feature of SAP SPP. In cases where a number of service parts are related and are considered a standard maintenance pack or kit, it's important to consider this kit in the planning process. Release 7.0 allows the kits to be performed either internally or by a subcontractor.

The Logic Creation of the BOD

At this point, you may be wondering why a BOD is necessary for SAP SPP but not for finished goods planning. A BOD is desirable, although not absolutely necessary, to prevent the system from looking at too many possible location movement decisions. The BOD essentially

Why is a BOD necessary for SAP SPP but not for finished goods?

limits what shipping relationships can be realized in normal deployment (Figure 10.3).

This need to reduce the "problem space" is the primary reason that the BOD was developed. By limiting the number of location flow combinations, computational effort and time is drastically reduced. And this is more necessary for SAP SPP than finished goods planning because SAP SPP has far more repositioning decisions to make on any given planning run.

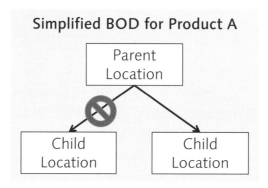

Figure 10.3 The Bill of Distribution

A BOD essentially removes locations from the planning process for a specific product. Locations not in the BOD aren't considered for planning for that particular product. But every product in SAP SPP has at least one BOD assigned to it.

The replenishment indicator sets the stocking location for products

More model simplification can be provided by explicitly declaring at any given product-location combination a stocking location for a product. This is explicitly set in the product location master of SAP SCM and is called the *replenishment indicator*. There can be a number of operational reasons not to stock a part at a location, and the replenishment indicator can be set on the basis of this factor. In addition, SAP SPP comes with a service that provides a stocking or de-stocking recommendation based on SAP SPP's analysis of the product location history.

Note

As a product flow controller, the BOD sets some locations as sources for other locations. And although a product can only apply for one BOD at a time, multiple BODs can be configured for different groups of products that have different validity periods.

BOD in the Interface

The BOD not only controls the location combinations during planning runs, but it also serves as a structural element in the interface. As of SAP SCM 7.0, the BOD can be displayed for every combination of user and various planner screens (e.g., EOQ/Safety Stock, DRP Matrix, etc.). Related to this capability, SAP SPP has many *worklists*, which are sequences of activities or things to check. Customers also have worklists, but they are different and far fewer in number than planner worklists. The planner worklists allow planners to go into the system to do the things that are specifically designed for them such as stocking agreements and stock transfer order approval.

Worklists are sequences of activities or things to check

Planning for External Locations

As we'll discuss in Chapter 13, SAP Forecasting and Replenishment (F&R), SAP SCM has become increasingly focused on collaborative planning. Consistent with this, the BOD has been designed to include both internal and contract locations. Interesting questions arise as to how the external entities or partners decide to accept these recommendations, but we touched on this in most of the other application-specific chapters, particularly in Chapter 6, Global Available to Promise (GATP).

VCL and the IBA

The BOD is a dominant feature of SAP SPP, but it's not the only overlay on the service parts network employed by SAP SPP. SAP also provides the following structures for controlling the service parts network. Unfortunately, a full explanation of these structures is beyond the scope of this book, so we'll just list them here.

> Virtual Consolidation Locations (VCL)
> Inventory Balancing Areas (IBA)

This concludes our look at the important functionality of SAP SPP. But to help put this in perspective, let's review the release history of this application.

SAP SPP Release History

SAP SPP is one of the more recent SAP SCM applications and has seen some of the most enhancements in the past few releases, so we wanted to go into more detail about SAP SPP's developments in the recent releases.

SAP SPP First Releases in SAP SCM 5.0

SAP SPP has been enhanced significantly to address critical service parts planning issues

SAP SPP was first introduced as a product. Developed at CAT logistics along with SAP EWM (SAP Extended Warehouse Management), SAP SPP was SAP's first attempt to break into the service parts planning market. The BOD was established early as one of the key features of SAP SPP, which doesn't exist in the rest of SAP SCM. What follows is some of the most important features of the first release.

> Product grouping, which was an enhancement for SAP SCM across the board, had particular benefit for SAP SPP where grouping is used as part of service parts planning processes.
> Shortage analysis allows both internal planners and suppliers to observe critical situations. (through ICH at the time and now through SAP SNC).
> Service fill monitor displays the service level.

Note

In its first release, SAP SPP lacked several features that were critical to service parts planning, thus 5.0 can be seen as somewhat of a beta. This, among other reasons, caused companies to hold off on implementing SAP SPP. The chief purpose of SAP SPP in SAP SCM is primarily symbolic, as it communicates to the market that SAP is serious about service parts planning.

Recognizing the limitations in SAP SPP, SAP searched for a partner to approve as an xApp and selected the tiny but well respected MCA Solutions as its partner in service parts planning. The new xApp is named Service Inventory Optimization (SIO). This xApp employs MCA's Service Parts Optimization (SPO) for higher-level target setting (called strategic analysis), and then employs SAP SPP for its DRP functionality (i.e., calculating and aggregating demand to locations, backward scheduling, and generating the recommended STOs and POs). SAP pursues and promotes a "single" approved solution for the integration between SAP and MCA.

SAP SPP as of 5.1 (also called SAP SCM 2007)

In SAP SCM 2007, the following were added to SAP SPP:

> Leading indicator forecasting.

> The ability to generate the demand history for service parts planning from a stock transfer from SAP ERP. This is an enhancement to the standard method of create demand history from SAP CRM.

> The ability to copy forecast profiles from one product location to another product location. This is important because the forecast profile contains the forecast strategy and operates off of historical data.

> An additional forecast error model selection.

> Enhanced safety stock and economic order quantity.

> Repair or buy functionality with DRP.

> Shortage analysis, which enhances the monitoring capability of SAP SPP to provide new alert types (such as critical product, DRP repair or buy) that communicate probable areas of shortage to the planner.

> Service fill analysis, which uses the supplier delivery performance rating to calculate the goods issue date and the issue quantity. This enhances the reliability of the lead-time estimates.

SAP SPP as of SAP SCM 7.0

Changes to SAP SPP in SAP SCM 7.0 include the following:

> Because of the ability to include customers and dealers in the planning process, the user administration area of SAP SPP has been enhanced. This is based in the SAP NetWeaver Identity Management (SAP NetWeaver ID Management), and requires release 7.1 installed and connected to SAP SPP.

> Simulation (also known as "what-if analysis") allows planners to see how different plans compare to one another. Simulations can be applied to planning services as diverse as the forecast service or the DRP service. These simulations are performed in different versions, so they don't interfere with the actual planning results. Numerous simulations can be performed in one planning box.

> SAP SPP now allows you to override stocking and de-stocking indicators manually. This is overriding the stocking portion of the BOD.

> SAP SPP is now able to take the lead time from the supplier to the entry location into account when planning a supplier shutdown. This is defined in the product location master.

> SAP SPP can now set a TSL or time-related supply unit.

> The monitoring capability has been enhanced for overdue items, including POs, subcontract orders, refurbishment orders, product orders, stock transport orders, and so on. This monitoring can be switched on or off for these different items. There are also a wide variety of alert types that have been enhanced.

Conclusion

SAP SPP has several concepts that are not found in the rest of SAP SCM: the BOD, leading indicator forecasting, and repair planning. Service parts are different from finished good in terms of their planning needs, and they are greatly sub-optimized by using finished goods planning software. If your company is using a finished goods planning system to manage your service parts, SAP SPP could radically improve the management of your parts. And despite the fact that SAP SPP is a product with far more development effort than market acceptance at the time of this writing, SAP SPP has a lot to offer and is one of the most capable products in the SAP SCM suite.

In the next chapter, we'll talk about the SAP Extended Warehouse Management application.

11

SAP Extended Warehouse Management (EWM)

Warehouse management is the process of executing your warehouse activities — everything from shipping to receiving. Warehouse management is primarily thought of as a transaction-oriented process, but there's a planning component as well, which is why SAP developed Extended Warehouse Management to perform both planning and execution activities.

Extended warehouse management isn't a common term in the supply chain, but you can basically think of an extended warehouse as a contract or overflow warehouse that manages material for other warehouses. Currently, this term is most strongly associated with SAP EWM within SAP SCM, and is used by SAP to differentiate the two warehouse management solutions offered: SAP EWM and the older, more established warehouse management within SAP ERP. Warehouse management was formally called SAP WM, but this is no longer considered a full application, just *functionality* available in SAP ERP.

Choose between SAP EWM and the warehouse management functionality in SAP ERP

So if you're just getting started with SAP and haven't chosen your warehouse management tool yet, you can choose between these two options.

 TechTalk

SAP EWM was developed to provide more enhanced capabilities than those available in existing warehouse management functionality, including enhanced performance capability and improved process flexibility. While SAP ERP has some of the functionality of SAP EWM, including slotting and cross docking, SAP EWM has more advanced functionality. SAP EWM is also considered by some, including Catalyst, a consulting company that specializes in warehouse management, as the more appropriate option for warehouse environments that have high SKU line item volumes, fast moving products, complex cross-docking requirements, detailed packaging and shipping processes, and 3PL on inbound, outbound, or both.

To help you really understand these two options, before we delve into the details of SAP EWM, let's look at the core differences between them.

Differences Between SAP EWM and Warehouse Management in SAP ERP

SAP EWM is the choice for warehouses with high SKU line item volumes

The official SAP position is that the warehouse management functionality in SAP ERP is stabilized, which means that presently and in the future, the more advanced warehouse management development efforts and functionalities will go into SAP EWM and SAP ERP. SAP EWM is interesting for another reason — it's the most transaction-oriented of all of the software in SAP SCM. This isn't to say that there aren't any planning capabilities within SAP EWM, but in our estimation, SAP EWM has the highest percentage of its functionality devoted to execution management versus the other SAP SCM applications and components.

The following is a brief look at the other core differences.

> **Warehouse management in SAP ERP includes the following functions:**

  - Picking waves

  - Quality management

  - Handling unit management

  - Storage units

> **SAP EWM can do everything that SAP ERP can do, but also includes the following capabilities:**

  - Slotting

  - Rearrangement

  - Routing

  - Labor management

  - Batch management

  - Order creation

  - Resource management

  - Task interleaving

  - Expected goods receipt

As you can see from this quick comparison, SAP EWM offers much more functionality and will likely be the warehouse management solution companies who use SAP will choose. So let's look into what SAP EWM has to offer you and investigate how it's structured within SAP.

SAP EWM offers more functionality than warehouse management in SAP ERP

Warehouse Organization

SAP EWM uses many of the same organizational units as the warehouse management functionality in SAP ERP — it just calls them by different names. If you're already familiar with SAP ERP, you'll need to translate these organizational structures, as detailed in Table 11.1.

Organization Unit	Description
Supply Chain Unit	This represents a location — plant, DC, customer, or supplier.
Warehouse Number	These represent the warehouses and are assigned to the supply chain unit.
Storage Type	These define the physical storage areas — assigned per warehouse number. Examples include a work center, where activities such as picking, counting, or deconsolidation occur. They also determine the maximum number of bins that can be assigned to a type. Putaway control is also configured for each storage type. Examples include the following: - High Rack - Fixed Bin - Bulk Storage Type
Storage Section	This is a subdivision of a storage type.
Activity Areas	This is a section of the warehouse where storage bins are defined. Picking or physical inventory might be allocated to an activity area.
Storage Bin	This is defined after the storage type. This is the lowest level of organization within SAP EWM. Storage sections are divided into storage bins. Storage bins are the smallest space unit in SAP EWM and represents the exact location of an item in the warehouse in SAP EWM (see Figure 11.1). For instance, bin 02-05-07 refers to - Storage Bin Aisle 02 - Stack 05 - Level 07
Party Entitled to Dispose	This important term is the business partner at a location that holds the title to the goods. This is a required field in the product master. Every product must have an "owner" assigned.

Table 11.1 SAP EWM Organizational Structures

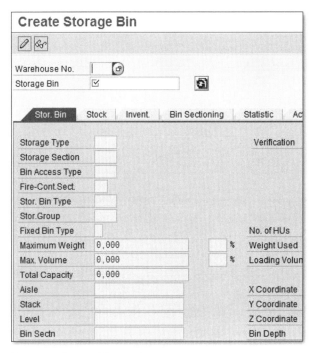

Figure 11.1 Storage bin creation

These are the key organizational units you'll use in SAP EWM, so let's move on to the supported processes.

Supported Processes

SAP EWM can be used to support a number of your processes that are necessary for sophisticated warehouse management:

› Slotting
› Rearrangement
› Value added services
› Waves
› Handling units

> Quality inspection engine

> RFID

> Serialization

> Stock replenishment

> Yard management

> Cross docking

> Labor management

We'll look at each of these briefly to help you understand what they are used for and show you how they can be customized for your own requirements.

Slotting

Slotting finds the best locations in the warehouse for storing received items, so that they are located in the most efficient location for removal from the warehouse. Slotting uses the following information to make its decisions.

1. Product data

2. Storage requirements data

3. Packaging data

4. Demand forecasts

For your operations, for example, you may have one or two items with a high turnover rate. Slotting ensures that you're storing these items in the right locations, typically toward the center of the warehouse, so that you can minimize pick movement, reducing the effort needed to retrieve the item on the outbound side. There are some constraints on doing this. For example, some materials need to be placed in certain locations because of special storage requirements, such as their size. Slotting in SAP EWM takes these many considerations into account in the material location decision.

Rearrangement

Rearrangement is sort of like re-slotting after the material has been put away. New information may have come to light after the initial slotting; for example, items in your warehouse that were previously moving out at a high rate may begin moving out at a lower rate, so re-arrangement would increase warehouse efficiency. Rearrangement can also be considered a warehouse housekeeping function, meaning that it's necessary to keep the warehouse running smoothly. Rearrangement is performed during down periods when lower volume is scheduled to move through the warehouse to keep it from interfering with normal picking and balance the work level across labor and equipment.

Housekeeping activities such as rearrangement can improve warehouse efficiency

 Example

Warehouses have a limited ability to manage the work performed within them because, on the outbound side, they typically receive orders that need to be shipped out as soon as possible, and on the inbound side, vendors send materials when it suits their schedules, not necessarily when it suits the receiving warehouse. So there can be periods of heavy activity followed by periods of very light activity. End-of-quarter buys, seasonality, promotions, and a host of other factors can cause changes in warehouse throughput. So it's during the slower times that "housekeeping" activities such s rearrangement can be performed.

VAS

Value added services (VASs) aren't the traditional tasks of warehousing. They involve performing extra services or light manufacturing, such as kitting or light assembly. When warehouses pick up increasing amounts of VASs, it adds more value to the warehousing process and increases the complexity of warehouse operations. VASs are for performing light assembly, packaging, and configuration in the warehouse. VASs are associated with the concept of *forward stocking locations* and *product postponement*. Product postponement allows your company to meet more demand, with less overall inventory, but specifically with less inventory obsolescence and waste. Postponement is

A forward stocking location is a concept where inventory is held close to the final destination, allowing for a short lead time from order placement to delivery

a broad classification of techniques for deferring final assembly and is addressed with several functionalities within SAP SCM, of which VAS is just one. VASs in SAP EWM include the following:

> Kitting

> Packing

> Labeling

> Light assembly

Let's look at kitting specifically because it can provide a significant advantage for your warehouses.

Kitting

Two types of kits— *kit to stock* or *kit to order*

Kitting is the process of combining items so that they result in a *kit*. Examples of kits include an automotive repair kit that is sold with cars or a service kit that is sent out with machinery or aircraft. The items in these kits are necessary for performing essential maintenance on the support item; however, kitting is a far broader category than service items. For instance, in the medical device industry, kits are created for everything from operations (e.g., a specialized kit that includes everything needed for a particular type of surgery) to general hospital admission kits. In SAP EWM, kitting can be performed two different ways, as described in Table 11.2.

Kitting Types	Description
Kit to Stock	Kits are created and put away as stock for future consumption.
Kit to Order	Kits are created in response to a specific order. This requires SAP Customer Relationship Management (SAP CRM) 5.0 or higher. In this scenario, a requirement for a kit initiates the ATP check in GATP. If a stocked kit isn't available, then assembly of a kit is attempted based on present or future on-hand items.

Table 11.2 SAP EWM Kitting Types

One thing to note here though is that kitting requires the importation of kitting information from SAP ERP in the form of an outbound delivery. This means that the kitting arrangement and combination must be maintained in the transaction, which is the outbound delivery document. This is because SAP EWM doesn't maintain the information internally but instead relies on SAP ERP to send the information over for each kit. You can initiate kitting within SAP ERP or within SAP EWM; however, reverse kitting, which is the breaking down of material that has already been added into kits, must be initiated in SAP EWM. Reverse kitting is valuable for lowering the overall inventory by providing for more interchangeability on inventory items.

Reverse kitting allows for interchangeability on inventory items

 Example

Kits don't always simply go from the vendor to the buyer. In some specialty kits, especially when the kits are expensive, the kits come back after use. One example is back surgery kits. In this case, a kit contains a number of instruments for back surgery. The kits cover all of the bones necessary for any number of individuals and for operations on different vertebrae. This type of kit is comprehensive, and the surgeon only uses a small portion of what is contained in the kit. After use, the kit is returned to the vendor, which then sterilizes the kit, charges the hospital for only the items used, and then re-sells the kit. This is a perfect use for reverse kitting in SAP EWM

Waves

This is a grouping of warehouse request items that are processed at roughly the same time. Waves or "picking waves" refers to a premeditated method of maximizing the efficiency of picking efforts used in all warehousing. SAP EWM allows these waves to be planned for high degrees of efficiency. Waves are controlled with a wave template, which means that many different configurations of waves can be set up. In SAP EWM, waves can be paused and even merged with other waves.

One type of wave is picking by zone

Example

> As suggested in the white paper by Ciber and Red Prairie, *Achieving Best Practice Performance In Automotive Parts Distribution*, to be effective at order management, you should use best practice methods that have you segregate orders by type, either by consolidating same customer orders or picking and processing by type. An example of this is an emergency order that is usually small and can be picked by zone with the parcel documents already applied.

Handling Units

Handling units are not just for packages; the term broadly applies to the management of the yard as well as other transportation functions. Handling units are simply the units being moved and managed by SAP EWM. For instance, the handling units that refer to transportation are called *transportation units*. Handling units are quite flexible in SAP EWM. For example, a truck could be a handling unit for yard management, and within the warehouse, handling units can be placed within other handling units. In their final stage, warehouse handling units are inserted into transportation units. Creating a handling unit is called *packing,* and bins must have a storage type configured for handling units.

Quality Inspection Engine (QIE)

Good quality management ensures discrepancies can be quickly resolved

This functionality allows you to manage the quality inspection engine (QIE) during the inbound process. QIE offers many different dimensions of quality checking, of which counting is the most basic, but they're all focused on ensuring that the information about the material matches the reality of the material in the warehouse. In general, quality inspections are critical to inventory management because the sooner you find discrepancies, the more quickly replacement material can be ordered.

Storage Control

Storage control gives you a more sophisticated way of managing the *putaway process*. It offers both layout-oriented control and process-oriented control as detailed in Table 11.3.

Two types of storage control are process-oriented and layout-oriented

Control Method	Description
Process-oriented storage control	Based on handling units and used for complex stock movements. Process-oriented storage control is performed by default. However, the items are checked by SAP EWM to see if they would conform to a layout-oriented storage control. This analysis can change the steps in the process, adding or removing steps.
Layout-oriented storage control	Based on handling units but requires more configuration. Layout-oriented storage control also has a connection to VASs because it's the storage control used if items are not directly put away but are moved to intermediate storage first.

Table 11.3 Storage Control Methods

SAP EWM and RFID

SAP EWM is especially integrated with Radio Frequency Identification (RFID), which as of this writing, is a popular topic of discussion in warehousing. While more slowly adopted than the industry anticipated, RFID is positioned to one day provide comprehensive serial-level identification in warehouses and throughout the supply chain.

RFID is forecasted to make an impact on retail

RFID allows entire pallets to be scanned during goods receipt, and RFID tagged goods can actually be scanned without stopping. So a forklift could drive through a specially designed scanning area and wouldn't even need to slow down to read all of the contents of the pallet, including the pallet itself (equipment is also tagged for asset tracking), into inventory. Also, unlike bar codes, some RFID tags actually store information on the tag. So instead of being simply read, they are *read-write*. This brings up interesting applications for modifying information on the tag as it passes through the supply chain. On the other hand, passive RFID tags, those with small batteries that can be read over short distances, are extremely inexpensive, allowing them to be placed in individual item boxes.

RFID is really a different way of managing a warehouse but also in managing the flow of items through the supply chain. While currently expensive, RFID will decline in cost, and as more RFID implementations occur, the capability to perform future RFID implementations will increase as well.

RFID relates to the advanced shipment notification (ASN); ASN is the information from the sender of the goods, while the RFID provides the verification. RFID also impacts serialization by making it more attainable for more product categories.

RFID and ASN

As items are received into the warehouse, the advanced shipment notification (ASN) can be compared against the RFID items and quantities to check the integrity of the shipments. This is part of the quality inspection engine we described earlier.

RFID and Serialization

Read-write tags act more like miniature hard drives or flash memory devices in that they can both store and have the information on them continually updated

Serialization is an important functionality because it allows SAP EWM to track serial numbers in the warehouse. This means you can track at the item level, which provides you with the highest level of detail in supply chain tracking. This is also consistent with RFID technology, which also tracks at the individual item level. At the time of this writing, serialization isn't that common in warehousing. This is evidenced by the dominant tracking technology, which continues to be the bar code. Identical bar codes are applied to each individual stock keeping unit (SKU), but there's no serialization because one identical bar code is used for every SKU. In fact, until RFID became popular as an industry concept, serialization was considered necessary only for specialized items such as pharmaceuticals or expensive repairable items where maintenance of service histories was necessary. In SAP EWM, the serial numbers are copied into the inbound delivery notification as well as the outbound delivery request. As RFID grows, it will allow increased serialization of different item categories that weren't previously serialized.

Stock Replenishment

Stock replenishment is the functionality that controls how bins are replenished. You have several options for replenishment that are related to whether the replenishment quantity should be the minimum replenishment or minimum quantity and the planned replenishment or the replenishment quantity. In addition, the minimum quantity can be set as a percentage of the maximum quantity. The controls for this essentially set whether the replenishment should be more based on future expected inbound quantities or current quantities (Figure 11.2).

Stock replenishment can be controlled based on expected inbound or current quantities

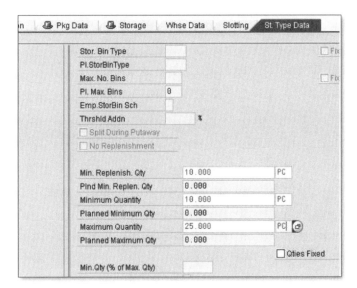

Figure 11.2 The St. Type Data Tab on the Product Location Master

In addition to quantities, SAP EWM replenishment has two possible strategies:

1. Planned replenishment
2. Order-related replenishment

This tells SAP EWM if it should be concerned with present orders only or present and future planned orders (Figure 11.3).

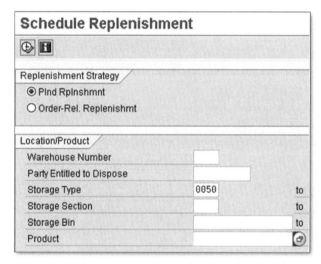

Figure 11.3 Replenishment Strategy Selected in the Schedule Replenishment Transaction

Yard Management

Poor yard management causes frequent delays

Yards are the vehicle parking areas that are connected to warehouses. This is where your company's vehicles are staged and queued in preparation for the loading and unloading of material. Unfortunately, according to recent research, many yards are not run as effectively as they could be, and a lot of delays are caused by not having the right equipment lined up in advance. But you can remedy this with better planning and the right tools.

Yard management is far more important than most users recognize, so if you're attempting to improve your transportation, you'll need to look at yard management as well. Yard management is made up of three components (Table 11.4).

Collaborating Method	Description
Yard location management	In this component, the physical locations (parking lots, doors) are mapped to the objects (trucks) and to system entities (storage bins and transport units).
Yard movements	This component represents the physical movement by the trucks by moving transport units and vehicles within the yard locations.
Yard stock	This component reports the transport units content to support and control the loading and unloading activities.

Table 11.4 Yard Management Components

Although a yard is a distinct physical area from the warehouse, it's still represented as a storage type in SAP EWM, as are other storage items in the application. SAP EWM simply uses the same approach to managing a warehouse that it applies to managing a yard. In yard management, bins are created. These bins can represent three things in the yard:

> Doors

> Parking spaces

> Checkpoints

A good way of thinking about this is that there are three places, or three bins, a truck can be at in a yard. The handling unit within the yard is called the transportation unit (TU). Trucks, or TUs, are moved with warehouse tasks. As you can see in Figure 11.4, SAP EWM manages the yard in the same way that it manages the warehouse. Parking spaces and checkpoints are set up as bins in the system, so the park-

SAP EWM manages the yard the same way it manages the warehouse

ing spaces are set up as bins, just as with a warehouse bin. But the key difference is that the bins in this case use the Yard Storage Type.

You can choose between YM in SAP ERP or SAP SCM

Fortunately, companies don't need to learn two different methods to expand their implementation from warehouse management to yard management because they essentially work the same way. This is important because trucking delays from mismanaged containers in the yard are responsible for more delays than direct transportation delays. If warehouse management is an underinvested area of the business with regards to IT, then the yard is even more so.

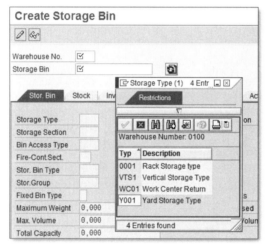

Figure 11.4 Yard Storage Type

 TechTalk

Please note that SAP also offers Yard Management (YM) with the warehouse management functionality in SAP ERP. So, YM is SAP's yard management solution for customers using SAP ERP. But for companies interested in using SAP EWM for yard management, you'll need to perform a solution comparison between the two alternate solutions. The question of which solution to use most likely has to do with how sophisticated a solution you need. The official position of SAP is that the more advanced planning functionality has gone into and will continue to migrate to SAP SCM and therefore, SAP EWM. So if you have a sophisticated operation, YM in SAP EWM is probably the better choice.

Cross Docking

Cross docking is complementary to yard management and labor management because it requires knowledge of inbound and outbound transportation and labor to actually perform the cross docking. *Cross docking* is the movement of material in and out of a warehouse without ever having the stock put away. This allows the material to be broken down and reconfigured and for VASs to be applied to this material. When possible, this is clearly desirable, and having a system such as SAP EWM that can effectively compare inbound to outbound material is critical for this process.

Cross docking is a great concept, but the systems must be in place to allow it to happen

 TechTalk

Warehousing is becoming increasingly sophisticated, and cross docking is an example of this. Cross docking requires, or is at least enabled, with warehouse planning systems. This can let the warehouse managers know what material should be assigned to cross-docking locations based on future outbound documents. This along with VASs allows warehouses to take on more and more value-added activities. And functionalities such as slotting and rearrangement are partially what support the more advanced warehouse capabilities.

Labor Management

Labor management allows for planning, directing, and controlling labor in the warehouse. This allows the times required to process work to be tracked, so that unproductive time spent in the warehouse by the workforce can be identified. Specifically this includes the following:

> Ensuring that workers are in the right place

> Tracking work performed by each worker

> Providing alerts when worker productivity declines

When rearrangement is configured with management, labor can be allocated as needed

Labor management is one of the more advanced functionalities within SAP EWM and is a significant differentiator from the warehouse management functionality in SAP ERP. The strength of labor management in SAP EWM is its integration to the rest of the SAP EWM functionality, meaning that labor management is co-planned with the other SAP EWM functionalities. For example, labor management can directly respond to the variations in the warehouse schedule by scheduling labor in terms of working hours and in terms of what work is performed. To borrow from a previous example, the act of rearrangement is integrated with labor management (when configured), which can allocate labor to rearrangement during low periods.

This concludes our look at the core processes supported by SAP EWM functionality. Now let's look at the process types.

Process Types

Warehouse process types

You plan and schedule work in SAP EWM through warehouse process types. A warehouse process type determines what's available as a process within SAP EWM, and it controls the movements within the warehouse. These process types are then assigned to warehouse documents so that work can be performed. For example, a task is created in response to an inbound delivery document that includes the following information:

> What should be moved

> The quantity to be moved

> From what storage bin should the product be moved

Warehouse tasks are then assigned to warehouse orders. And the final link in the chain is the work packages, which are created in response to warehouse orders. Below the warehouse process type, configuration sets up what the warehouse process type can do, and this is just a partial list of its settings (see Figure 11.5). By creating different warehouse process types, a fine degree of control is allowed for the processes in the warehouse.

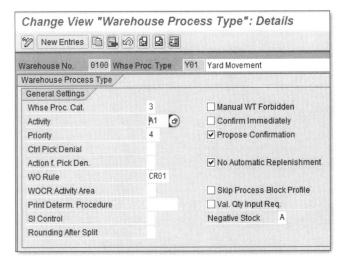

Figure 11.5 Many Controls for Process Types Can Be Used to Change Their Behavior

Integration to SAP Event Management (EM)

As we mentioned in a previous chapter, SAP EM can accept data from many sources, which is how it provides an integrated view of activity in the supply chain. SAP EM is a combination of monitoring frontend and backend integration components. It can receive data from the following categories of sources, which when combined, provide a comprehensive view of the supply chain:

SAP EM accepts data from various sources

> Transportation providers

> GPS

> Scanners (both facility-based and vehicle-based)

> Vehicle computers

> Suppliers

> RF devices

As you can see, the majority of the listed areas are related to either warehousing or transportation, so in a 100% SAP solution, this would include integration with SAP EWM and SAP TM. SAP EWM is especially important if your warehouses are run by a third-party logistics provider because you'll then need to update regularly with the supply chain information.

Let's move on to wrap up this chapter with a brief look at the release history of SAP EWM.

SAP EWM Release History

SAP EWM is a newer application within SAP SCM, so it has seen significant improvement over the past few releases. SAP EWM received many major improvements with SAP SCM 5.1, and some key enhancements in Release 7.0, which are listed here:

> Allows for the integration of production supply from SAP ERP. This enables SAP EWM with SAP ERP to move and stage products to a production staging area (PSA).

> Enhanced cross-docking capability allows for unplanned cross docking. Prior to Release 7.0, only planned cross docking was possible within SAP EWM.

SAP EWM Server Setup

It's recommended that SAP EWM runs on its own server and not be combined with a planning server that is performing planning. Secondly, due to its transactional nature, SAP EWM is less memory intensive and more database intensive than the other SAP SCM applications or components, and this is another reason that it makes sense for SAP EWM to sit on a server designed for its more transactional needs.

Conclusion

SAP EWM has a broad set of functionality that addresses some of the most sophisticated needs in high-volume warehousing. This includes higher end warehousing capabilities such as cross docking and VAS. In addition, it provides advanced warehouse functionality within SAP SCM that is integrated with the other tools and applications. The past few years marks the first time that SAP has addressed warehousing within the SAP SCM application.

One of the more frequent questions people ask after they learn the differences between SAP EWM and the warehouse management functionality in SAP ERP, is what type of customers are good candidates for implementing SAP EWM. These candidates include clients who have very high warehouse management needs such as third-party logistics providers. The larger the warehouses managed, the more SAP EWM can provide benefits. Not surprisingly, SAP EWM was developed with Caterpillar Logistics, a third-party logistics provider that specializes in service parts. SAP EWM was also developed in conjunction with SAP Service Parts Planning (SPP). So, a company implementing this combined solution would certainly benefit from the previous work SAP has performed in integrating these applications.

SAP EWM is best suited for larger warehouses such as third-party logistics providers

In the next chapter, we'll cover SAP Supplier Network Collaboration (SAP SNC).

SAP Supplier Network Collaboration (SNC)

Supplier collaboration is a frequently desired but elusive capability. The concept is to provide more notice on tracked objects such as scheduling agreements, work orders, and purchase orders, and to provide forecasting information that can improve the forecast of the implementing company by enlarging the number of business partners who can provide input. Overall, the design of the software is to improve the cross-enterprise integration.

SAP Event Management, covered in Chapter 8, also addresses cross-organizational needs

SAP Supplier Network Collaboration?

SAP Supplier Network Collaboration (SNC) is on the vanguard of a strong trend within SAP SCM development to make the application suite cross-organizational. That is, SAP SCM is transitioning from being mainly focused on internal planning to more aggressively incorporating data from outside the organization into planning decisions.

One of the reasons for this change in SAP SCM is that there's increasing agreement that even more opportunities for supply chain improvement lie between organizations rather than within them. SAP's vision is for its customers to use SAP systems to communicate with many suppliers and customers to such a degree that the information from these partners is completely integrated with supply chain planning and execution.

SAP has a forward-thinking approach to the development of SAP SNC

While we can appreciate SAP's strategy, we also note that the supply chain management field is presently not close to this state. In addition, SAP has been pressing forward with SAP SNC and EM development (also a cross-organizational application) for some time, essentially pushing the software functionality out in advance of industry need. SAP's vision is clear, however, in its development emphasis for these newer products in SAP SCM in general, but particularly in the development of SAP SNC (Figure 12.1).

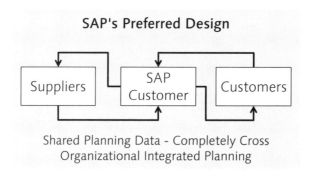

Figure 12.1 SAP's Preferred Design Concept

Although not yet as common in practice as SAP would like, there's significant evidence to support SAP's vision of shared information for multiple aspects of the supply chain. According *Successful Strategies in Supply Management* (IGI Global, 2005), researchers have shown that under the scenario of a vendor supplying a product to a single buyer, a coordinated inventory replenishment policy is more desirable from a total system perspective than each party operating its individual optimal policy.

The research in the area, as well as SAP's experience with leading planning companies has clearly convinced them where the future is headed.

Setting the Stage for Effective Collaboration

If companies are generally not where they could be in regard to collaboration, you may ask "why not?" Well, technology limitations are one of the reasons why many companies have difficulty with their collaboration projects. But before we jump to the technology of SAP SNC, let's discuss the nontechnical factors necessary for collaboration:

> Reducing the overriding focus on internal optimization and focusing on one's partners

> Bringing suppliers, customers, and supply chain partners closer, and sharing information that was not shared in the past

> Changing the supplier relationship culture to work collaboratively with their supply chain partners rather than merely competitively (a euphemism for this is "coopetition")

> Making collaborative efforts a priority

Extensive research into how many Japanese companies enable supply chain supplier collaboration point to sharing and trust as significant reasons for their frequent success

Ex **Example**

On average, suppliers provide 70% of the value of a car. This means supplier management is of paramount importance in this industry. GM, a company with poor supplier relations and poor supplier collaboration, eventually ran into financial trouble. Toyota, on the other hand, with its renowned supplier relationships has continued to thrive. However, for some reason, media and academic attention has tended to focus on the inventory management or production process differences between GM and Toyota rather than the differences in how they manage their suppliers.

Suppliers and customers share more than inventory or demand information

SAP SNC is on the leading edge of allowing shared inventory management and procurement. However, optimally, the supplier and customer end up sharing more than just inventory or demand information. This cultural change, along with the actual software implementation, is another big challenge to moving toward a cross-enterprise design (Figure 12.2).

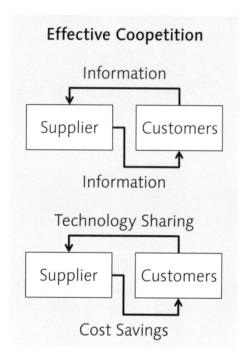

Figure 12.2 Supplier to Customer "Coopetition"

Exchanging information is ideally just the beginning of the collaborative relationship. The Japanese manufacturers have been successful partially by enabling their suppliers to both share information and to improve. This has been demonstrated to lead to richer relationships in other ways. According to *The Power of Two* (Palgrave Macmillan, 2008), too many companies are stuck in the price reduction rut. While this has been the standard way of dealing with suppliers, it's not functional for collaborative relationships.

Now that we have covered the important nontechnical preconditions for effective collaboration, let's move on to the details of SAP SNC.

Basic Functionality and Concepts of SAP SNC

Users are often surprised at how many different types of collaboration partners SAP SNC supports. SAP SNC Implementations tend to have the following entities involved:

> Suppliers

> Customers

> Outsource manufacturing partners

> Third-party logistics providers

However, SAP SNC can collaborate with almost anyone because its web interface can be accessed by anyone. With this flexibility, there are many other collaborations possible with SAP SNC that go beyond those we'll describe in this chapter because while SAP SNC is mainly positioned and known in the marketplace for supplier collaboration, it actually supports many other collaborative processes. One of the challenges of understanding SAP SNC is learning all of the different collaborative choices that are available to you. Let's begin by looking at the different collaboration types.

SAP SNC supports many collaborative processes beyond supplier

SAP SNC Collaboration Types

The different forms of supplier collaboration supported by SAP SNC are varied, so it's important to have a working familiary of each of the broad collaboration types before we move into more detail. Table

12.1 provides a detailed description of each type and should give you the insight you need for the rest of the chapter.

Collaborating Method	Description
Demand	The supplier receives forecasts from the customer. This collaboration method is driven by the customer. If performed correctly, it replaces the need for sending replenishment orders; instead, they're created by service level agreements versus inventory levels. This form of collaboration is very advantageous for promotions planning.
Inventory	Inventory collaboration combines demand collaboration with replenishment orders no longer sent to the supplier. Instead, the agreed-upon service level initiates replenishment. This form of collaboration is driven by the supplier and provides a higher level of integration than demand collaboration.
Procurement	Identical to inventory collaboration, but procurement is driven by the customer.
Capacity	This method of collaboration is perfect for outsourced manufacturing because it communicates the capacity of factories to the customer and translates the different sequences of production to phases as well as the status of these phases. This collaboration method's main object is a work order.
Transportation	This is collaboration with third-party providers on transportation services.

Table 12.1 SAP SNC Collaboration Types

You can also see other collaboration types as they are offered in the SAP SNC menu in Figure 12.3.

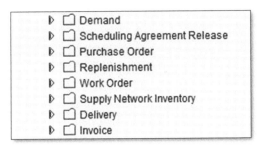

Figure 12.3 The SAP SNC Menu Shows the Different Collaboration Types Available

Different Collaboration Methods and Objects

To collaborate between supply chain partners, a number of different types of collaboration are supported. The end result is that a different object is transferred between the business partner system and another application of SAP SCM. Therefore, SAP SNC is somewhat misnamed. It performs supplier collaboration, demand collaboration, and other forms of collaboration, so a better name for the product might be simply Network Collaboration. Within SAP SNC, however, different types of collaboration result in different objects being transferred between the supply chain partners. Each collaboration method is organized around a specific object as shown in Table 12.2.

SAP SNC is basically a delivery mechanism; ultimately the collaboration object will be interfaced with one of the other SAP SCM applications

Collaborating Method	Transferred Object(s)
Demand collaboration	Forecasts
Replenishment collaboration	Replenishment orders
Release collaboration	Scheduling agreements
Purchase order collaboration	Purchase orders, ASNs
Work order collaboration	Phases (which are based on resources assigned to PPMs and PDSs) work orders, ASNs

Table 12.2 Collaboration Methods and Transfer Objects

Collaborating Method	Transferred Object(s)
Supplier network inventory collaboration	Current stock, subcontract reservations, receipts, requirements
Delivery collaboration	ASNs
Invoice collaboration	Invoices

Table 12.2 Collaboration Methods and Transfer Objects (Cont.)

Let's have a look at each of these methods so you can understand which ones would work best for your business.

Demand Collaboration

Demand collaboration is used by Wal-Mart

One of the most common forms of demand collaboration is Collaborative Planning, Forecasting, and Replenishment (CPFR). This is where the retailer shares forecasts with the OEM suppliers. When done correctly, it supports a high level of in-stock inventory positions. In addition to being widely understood in the retail industry, it has also been a main driver for collaboration in other areas. The SAP Forecasting and Replenishment application (which we'll cover in the next chapter) is designed to support retail replenishment and can interoperate with SAP SNC. However, a client doesn't have to have an SAP system to engage in collaboration with SAP SNC demand collaboration. In fact, this applies to all of the SAP SNC collaboration types listed here.

Replenishment Collaboration

SAP SNC provides the ability to essentially collaborate on different types of purchase orders

The replenishment collaboration functionality determines the quantities of products or projected stock that must be delivered in every period to cover requirements. SAP SNC uses replenishment orders, which only exist within SAP SNC, and if confirmed, they are then converted into purchase orders. These purchase orders can be collaborated on as well. Finally, the supplier can perform replenishment planning with the planning service manager (PSM). Replenishment orders aren't "real orders" in the SAP ERP sense in that they only exist within SAP SNC. It may seem strange to collaborate on an object that doesn't exist in either business partners systems, but replenishment orders are simply transitional objects. They have a lifecycle where both the supplier and customer perform different actions on the order that move it toward completion or rejection. The replenishment orders are also used to provide transparency, and, if confirmed, are eventually converted into purchase orders.

Release Collaboration

This method allows partners to track scheduling agreements, which can be thought of as longer-term purchase orders. Scheduling agreements are used in situations where orders are placed frequently between the customer and supplier. When SAP SCM manages scheduling agreements, it allows the application to perform delivery scheduling as well. So, release collaboration is really a way of collaborating on schedule agreement releases.

Collaborate on schedule agreements

Purchase Order Collaboration

With this method, also known as procurement collaboration, your partners can track purchase orders. The tracking of purchase orders helps you and your partners know whether you need to make adjustments or possibly expedite other sources of material if certain purchase orders are late.

Work Order Collaboration

This form of collaboration is designed to monitor the production progress at your contract manufacturers by tracking phases in the production process. The work orders that are passed between the contract manufacturer and customer contain the following items:

> Delivery dates

> Delivery times

> Quantities

> Components used

Work order collaboration tracks the status and completion of manufacturing operations

The "customer" in this SAP SNC collaboration creates the work order. Multiple contract manufacturers can bid on work orders, with the winning contract manufacturer getting to build the work order. After the optional bidding and the winner is chosen, the work order moves through its lifecycle of tracking the work performed. This is called the *execution phase*. The SAP SNC Web UI provides visibility both to the contract manufacturer and the customer, but primarily to the customer as the work order is fulfilled.

Work orders often have a number of complex design documents, called *attachments*, which provide instructions to the contract manufacturer regarding the item to be built.

Attachments

SAP SNC SAP SNC allows the following types of attachments to be easily organized and associated with the work order:

> Work instructions

> Design drawings

> Specifications

> Test programs

> Packing instructions

All work orders can be associated with a purchase order (which, as we previously discussed, can also be used for collaboration).

Supply Network Inventory

This form of collaboration provides visibility to demands, receipts, and inventories. Projected stock is calculated as with replenishment collaboration. It compares the projected stock against a "target stocking level" range, which is the agreed-upon level of stocking between the supplier and customer. SAP SNC then makes inventory decisions based on the difference between the projected stock level and the target stock level.

SAP SNC adds visibility to demands, receipts, and inventories

 Note

A target stocking level is actually a concept that is rarely applied within SAP SCM. The target stocking level is "the quantity available to meet demand within lead time and thus becomes the basis for computing service levels" – MCA Glossary. It's an important concept because it encapsulates the decision making around stocking level into a single number. The difference between the actual stocking level and the target stocking level is what drives procurement, production, or the relocation of inventory. We expect to see the term target stocking level or TSL to become far more frequently used in the future.

Delivery Collaboration

In this method, the main object transferred is the advanced shipment notification (ASN). Delivery collaboration can be the only type of collaboration used, but more often than not, it's used in conjunction with other forms of collaboration. So, the ASN communicated by delivery collaboration is related to a purchase order, replenishment order, or scheduling agreement. What this demonstrates is that collaboration is possible on multiple levels, all of which are supported by SAP SNC.

ASNs are central to delivery collaboration in SAP SNC, and are used in SAP EWM for warehouse planning (Chapter 11)

Invoice Collaboration

Like delivery collaboration, invoice collaboration creates a collaboration for an object that may have already been the subject of collaboration, including purchase orders, replenishment orders, ASNs, and schedule agreements. Creating an invoice for each of these objects is subject to different rules; however, in all cases, it gives both the supplier and customer a better idea of when funds will depart from and arrive to the company.

From a very narrow type of collaboration, invoice collaboration, we move to a very broad type of collaboration called supplier managed inventory.

Supplier Managed Inventory (SMI)

Supplier managed inventory (SMI) is a broad definition of collaboration used by SAP SNC to describe a number of different collaboration types:

> Forecast delivery release process

> Purchase order process

> Subcontracting

> Supply network inventory

> Work order collaboration

> Kanban

> Dynamic replenishment

> ASN processing

> Invoice collaboration

Replenishment decisions are driven by pre-defined service level agreements

This is the type of collaboration where the supplier is managing and essentially holding the inventory for its customer. If this sounds familiar, it should, but the industry term for this is *vendor managed inventory (VMI)*. This concept connects with the concept of service level planning in that rather than an order triggering a movement between the supplier and the customer in an SMI/VMI arrangement, "replenishment decisions" are driven by predefined service level agreements between the supplier and customer. Inventory collaboration is a service that is usually required by the customer.

This concludes our review of the different collaboration types available within SAP SNC, so now we can move on to one of the important ways that the collaboration objects are tracked: confirmations.

Confirmations

All of the transferred objects for each collaboration type can be confirmed or rejected during the multi-stage collaboration process. The process begins when data is sent, and the loop is closed when the confirmation is received. This is the basic cycle of collaboration. Collaboration is important for telling your partner which requests you can fulfill which ones you can't. As with the rest of SAP SCM and planning in general, collaboration should be managed on an exception basis, which means responding to alerts. Just as with alerts that are set up to inform the planner of inventory overages in normal supply planning, the relationship between business partners is managed with a series of alerts that can be displayed in the SAP SNC web browser (this is explained in the SAP SNC Web Browser section coming up), in the event manager, in email, or in all three. Table 12.3 shows several of the SAP SNC alert types categorized by collaboration type.

Collaboration should be managed on an exception basis

Alert Types — Demand Collaboration	Description
Cumulative received quantity is smaller	The cumulative quantity is less than the received quantity from the predecessor forecast delivery schedule.
Unloading point has changed	The current forecast delivery schedule differs from the unloading point in the predecessor forecast.
Forecast delivery schedule overdue	The forecast delivery schedule contains schedule lines with a due date time in the past.

Table 12.3 SAP SNC Alert Types

Alert Types — Procurement/ Subcontracting Collaboration	Description
Purchase order rejected	Supplier has rejected the purchase order item manually.
Purchase order overdue	The purchase order contains due schedule lines in the past.
Over-delivery tolerance not reached	The quantity of the purchase order item confirmed by the supplier is greater than the total requested quantity of the purchase order item plus the over-delivery tolerance.

Alert Types — Capacity Collaboration	Description
Publish changes	Changes in the work order have not been published.
Respond to proposal	A response to the proposals of the other business partner is required.
Projected data out of tolerance	Quantity or date/time deviations between planning data and projected delivery data are outside the permitted tolerance.

Alert Types — SMI (Unmatched)	Description
Demand	The gross demand is given in a time bucket.
Planned receipts	The total quantity that the supplier intends to deliver to the customer in a time bucket.
Days' supply	A key figure that specifies how long the projected stock of a time bucket will last to cover the demands of subsequent buckets.

Table 12.3 SAP SNC Alert Types (Cont.)

Alert Types — SNI	Description
Below min – projected stock	The projected stock is below the minimum stock level.
Above max – projected stock	The projected stock exceeds the maximum stock level.
Stockout – stock on hand	The actual stock on hand is zero.

Table 12.3 SAP SNC Alert Types (Cont.)

Alerts aren't necessarily binary; they can also have shades of gray. For instance, a tolerance level can be set so that a transfer object that is above or below a certain quantity, or a number of days early or late, can be confirmed. This functionality is configurable and needs to be to fit the company and business environment. The review process can be made more automatic or be made to require more manual intervention depending on the need of the business.

We already talked about how broadly SAP SNC supports different collaboration types; however, one assumption regarding collaboration needs to be challenged, and that is that the collaboration is always between the supplier of the materials and the customer of the materials. This isn't always the case, which brings up the topic of third-party logistics providers.

Third-Party Logistics Providers

Supplier collaboration is generally considered to be between a supplier and a customer; however, the types of organizations that can fill the partnership role are quite flexible. For example, if your company is a third-party logistics (3PL) provider that provides logistics services and increasingly manages inventory and warehousing for clients, you can be either the supplier or the customer in the collaboration relationship. So as the 3PL provider, you can take the supplier role in SAP SNC and communicate inventory positions to a customer for whom

Third-party logistics providers can be the supplier or customer in SAP SNC collaborative relationships you provide warehousing and transportation services. You can also fill the role of the customer in a collaboration and have information communicated to you that will help you perform your 3PL tasks. There are many opportunities for innovative approaches to collaboration with 3PLs as well as 4PLs.

One of the most important components to an SAP SNC project is the integration. Rather than spending significant project time on planning methods, SAP SNC projects spend more of their time attempting to get various data feeds properly integrated. This brings us to the topic of SAP SNC integration.

SAP NetWeaver PI Integration Scenarios

SAP NetWeaver PI is used to integrate both SAP systems and non-SAP systems with SAP

SAP SNC is supported by SAP NetWeaver Process Integration (PI) (formerly called SAP NetWeaver XI). The SAP NetWeaver PI scenarios support each of the collaboration objects listed in the previous paragraphs. This includes direct mappings between SAP SNC and SAP ERP. SAP SNC projects have a heavy integration load to manage, particularly because there's a messaging infrastructure that supports every SAP SNC implementation. If you're implementing SAP SNC, you need to be aware of this and be sure to have experienced SAP SNC consultants and staff, sufficient integration technologists, and functional SAP SNC resources. SAP SNC projects involve a lot of change management issues and technical integration requirements, which makes them resource-heavy projects to undertake.

In addition, projects that require the involvement of external business partners are always more resource consuming than internal projects. For this reason, it's important to staff your SAP SNC projects with sufficient resources. Some of the resource requests we've personally fielded seem to indicate that many companies mistake SAP SNC projects for other SAP SCM application implementations, which is definitely not a correct interpretation.

Part of obtaining business partner buy-in is providing them with the SAP SNC user interface so they can interact with the system. This brings us to our next few topics.

Visibility Profile

In SNP there is a view called the Product View, which shows planned inbound and outbound stock. This is a very frequently used transaction by planners. SAP SNC has something similar called the *receipt and requirements list*, which provides visibility to the various SAP SNC objects.

Receipt and
requirements list

SAP SNC Web Browser

To work effectively, SAP SNC needs to allow multiple people who aren't internal to the company to actually log in to the SNC system. The natural way to accomplish this goal is through the use of a web browser. Due to its cross-enterprise nature, SAP SNC is the most browser enabled of all of the SAP SCM applications.

You can see a sample SAP SNC web interface in Figure 12.4.

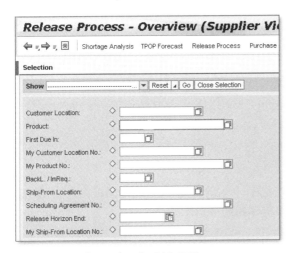

Figure 12.4 Web Interface for SAP SNC

Because SAP SNC must receive input from so many users, and many outside of the organization, it has been designed so that users interact with it SAP SNC through its browser. This makes it an easy-to-access application both internally and externally.

For more details on SAP SNC see the book, *Supplier Collaboration with SAP SNC* by Hamady and Leitz, SAP Press, 2008

There is certainly more that we could talk about in SAP SNC, but this overview should give you a good understanding of what it has to offer. And as with many of the other SAP SCM applications, SAP SNC continues to improve with each new release. So we'll wrap up the chapter with a look at the release history and a brief case study.

SAP SNC Release History

SAP SNC is an important focus for SAP

SAP SNC is a clear focus of attention for SAP development as evidenced by the fact that of all of the SAP SCM applications, SAP SNC received the most improvements in 7.0.

There were many improvements 7.0, including the following key improvements:

> The quick view can be used as the entry screen to the SAP SNC web applications, and it can be personalized to display the building blocks for different users and various scenarios.

> The ability to create users SAP SNC using SAP NetWeaver Identity Management (SAP NetWeaver ID Management) means the users don't need to be created in SAP SNC. Also, existing users can be migrated from SAP SNC to SAP NetWeaver ID Management.

> XML messages are used for delivery confirmation as well as for purchase orders.

> Alerts are created for things such as a partially confirmed purchase order, and new notes are used for purchase orders.

> A customer can request a specific manufacturer part number in a purchase order to procure a particular part. If the supplier procures a product from different manufacturers, the customer can specify

the preferred manufacturer and manufacturer part number in a purchase order.

> A supplier that differs from the requested price in the purchase order item can confirm prices. The customer can also specify tolerances that constrain the confirmed price.

> The web interface for views such as the purchase order and replenishment order has had significant enhancements.

> Work orders can be sent automatically to the customer backend system and to the supplier backend system. SAP ERP can receive production progress notifications.

> Net requirements calculation allows the product allocation check from GATP. You can use the replenishment quantities for a product provided by a particular ship-from location that don't exceed product allocations.

> Min and max lot size can be incorporated into the replenishment service and the TLB service for a customer location product.

Case Study

Company

This consumer and professional audio equipment products company does significant sourcing overseas (as most electronics companies do), making collaboration one of the most important areas of its supply chain.

Challenge

With international lead times and a global supply base, this company needed to collaborate with suppliers in a very detailed way, including giving them a very high degree of transparency into the company's overseas suppliers.

Solution

SAP SNC was selected for multiple types of collaboration, including delivery schedules, release schedules, forecasts, ASNs, proof of delivery confirmations, and SMI.

Value Achieved

The result was one of the more advanced collaboration systems to be fully integrated into a planning system. This case study is an interesting one due to the degree of collaboration involved in the implementation. The company was forward thinking in its willingness to share information, unlike many companies that treat some of the most basic information as proprietary, because they don't realize that sharing is necessary for improved supply chain integration. However, increasing numbers of companies have outsourced their manufacturing, so the type of collaboration implemented by this company will become more common in the future.

Conclusion

As you learned throughout this chapter, SAP SNC is a highly flexible application that supports many collaborative processes. Supplier collaboration is just one modality of collaboration it can support. We've highlighted the others, but you need to spend time working with the system to fully appreciate them. Progressive companies should ask what forms of collaboration are most important to them before settling on one collaboration type. After one form of collaboration has been successfully implemented, it becomes significantly easier to implement others.

Industry developments clearly favor SAP SNC, and SAP has planned ahead of the curve by investing in the development of SAP SNC prior to collaboration becoming the trend that it has. Many predict that the trend is really just getting started and will broaden out into a standard way of doing business in the coming decade. Collaboration may become simply standard, the same way that no one uses the term "e-business" anymore as it eventually became the rule rather than the exception.

While the opportunity is great, SAP SNC projects are challenging because they combine factors related to technical integration between collaborating partners, along with extra-organizational implementation issues that don't arise on internal IT projects. In terms of staffing, SAP SNC is understaffed because it has both a heavy functional and integration component that can't reasonably be filled by one person. No less than two dedicated SAP SNC resources (one integration and one functional) are recommended to complete an SAP SNC implementation, and this doesn't count junior resources, project managers, or other non-hands-on and experienced resources.

The complexity of the many collaborative processes offered, as well as significant cultural changes for most of the companies that will implement SAP SNC, means a more challenging road than more traditional SAP SCM implementations. However, the research is in; those companies that work cooperatively and collaboratively with their partners do better than those that don't. They benefit from lower total supply chain costs and receive higher priority from their suppliers and customers. The evidence from research in this area is that collaborations where partners are genuinely interested in investing in other partners, rather than simply exchanging information, result in the most successful partnerships.

In the next chapter, we'll discuss SAP Forecasting and Replenishment (F&R).

SAP Forecasting and Replenishment (F&R)

SAP Forecasting and Replenishment (SAP F&R) is a specialized application within SAP SCM for the retail sector that allows for rapid replenishment and a high degree of collaboration between the warehouse and retail store. It's the only SAP SCM application to be directed toward one specific industry.

SAP F&R is a specialized solution for the retail industry

For customers using SAP ERP, there's a sister application called SAP for Retail, and SAP Retail IS (industry solution). SAP F&R integrates with SAP for Retail, and the high-level interaction between them allows SAP for Retail to transfer purchase orders to SAP F&R and SAP F&R to transfer order proposals to SAP for Retail (Figure 13.1).

 Note

Industry solutions are areas of functionality that have been enhanced allowing SAP ERP to address specific industry needs but aren't themselves different applications. And because SAP IS Retail is its own topic, and won't be covered in this book. If you're interested, however, there is an SAP PRESS book that covers it in detail called *SAP for Retail* by Heike Rawe.

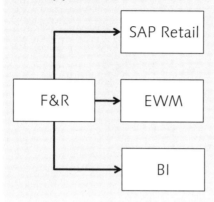

F&R Application Interactions

Figure 13.1 SAP F&R Application Interactions

SAP F&R connects
to SAP for Retail,
SAP NetWeaver BW,
and SAP EWM In addition to SAP for Retail, SAP F&R connects to SAP NetWeaver BW for analytical needs, and its most natural coupling in SAP SCM is with SAP EWM because this is the retail store to warehouse connection. However, because SAP EWM is specialized for high volume and third-party logistics (3PL) warehouses, there may end up being few SAP F&R to SAP EWM implementations in practice.

SAP for Retail has been around for several years, so it has many implementations. SAP F&R, on the other hand, as of this writing is just beginning to be implemented. There haven't been many functionality updates since release 5.1, but it has a lot to offer in the current 7.0, so let's take a look at the basic functionality.

Basic Functionality and Concepts of SAP F&R

The first thing you'll notice if you're familiar with SAP SCM is the new terminology associated with SAP F&R, and there are a couple of common retail industry terms that don't apply to the rest of SAP SCM:

> Order proposals

> Assortments

Of all of the planning areas of the supply chain, retail replenishment is the most divergent from the other planning types modeled in SAP SCM. SAP F&R is different in other ways as well. It has an interface that allows store managers to participate in the ordering and planning process, which makes it close to a collaborative planning tool in that it is decentralizing decision making to the most numerous location type (the retail store) in the supply chain. This is a collaborative model, although it may not meet the strict definition of collaboration because the data is being exchanged within one organization, and the store managers work for the same company.

Collaborative approach

This decentralizes decision making to the stores, which are the closest to the factors that influence ordering. This is just one example of an overall trend in SAP SCM to decentralize decision making in the application, which should be familiar for those of you with SAP SNC exposure or those who've read Chapter 12.

This collaborative approach is patterned upon a technique called *Collaborative Planning, Forecasting, and Replenishment (CPFR)*, which we'll discuss shortly. But first we need to talk about the SAP F&R processor.

SAP F&R Processor

SAP F&R has a processor that performs automatic replenishment. It's the result of a combination of the forecast calculation and the requirements calculation. This combined value is then adjusted by any relevant requirement quantity optimization. The SAP F&R processor produces the forecast and performs multilevel requirements calculations that can be performed in substitution for the Demand Influencing Factors (DIF) forecast, which we'll discuss later.

It also performs order balancing, which effectively optimizes the replenishment orders by performing calculations such as rounding. The main takeaway from all of this is that the SAP F&R processor is a critical component within SAP F&R that does a number of things to support automatic replenishment, which leads us to the topics of collaborative planning, forecasting, and replenishment.

Collaborative Planning, Forecasting, and Replenishment (CPFR)

The SAP F&R solution has a folder item in the IMG called Collaborative Planning, Forecasting, and Replenishment (CPFR). Understanding CPFR will help you understand SAP F&R because it's essentially based on this workflow.

The SAP F&R processor performs automatic replenishments

CPFR developed into a new way of performing retail replenishment based on a study run from 1995 to 1996 between Wal-Mart and Warner Lambert. In this test, rather than the store or the centralized planners controlling the replenishment function, CPFR provided the technology, authority, and visibility to allow both of these groups to collaborate on the final released replenishment orders. This experiment resulted in the following for Warner Lamberts' Listerine product, which was the test product in the study:

> An increase in service levels from 87% to 98%

> A decrease in lead times from 21 to 11 days

> An increase in sales of $8.5 million over the test period

Wal-Mart capitalized on this success by expanding CPFR into a broader program, which is frequently cited as a contributing factor to Wal-Mart's ability to maintain such high in-stock positions. CPFR uses the planning data time series as does the SAP F&R processor. The use of planning data time series is initiated when the CPFR material staging date's usage time is exceeded. Many companies can benefit from this in the same way that Wal-Mart does; however, again it comes down to compliance. Wal-Mart can dictate that suppliers get onboard with its CPFR system because it has the volume, but for smaller companies without the clout of Wal-Mart, incentives and relationship building are necessary to ensure compliance.

SAP DP is used to drive the supply and production plans, while SAP F&R is used for the retail and replenishment areas of the supply chain

Forecasting

As we discussed in Chapter 2, SAP SCM has a very detailed and widely used forecasting product called SAP Demand Planning (DP). However, SAP F&R also has a large area of functionality dedicated to forecasting. So you might be wondering why a separate forecasting solution is necessary for SAP F&R. This is a good question, and the best way to answer it is to look at the fact that DP is designed to create the overall demand plan. This demand plan is used to drive the supply plan and the production plan. SAP DP simply has no focus on the retail or replenishment part of the supply chain.

Important distinctions between SAP DP and SAP F&R also arise in the area of forecast time horizon. SAP DP has one of the longest forecast time horizons, while F&R has one of the shortest and is only concerned with replenishment from the warehouse to the retail store. In addition, SAP DP often looks out over a year, while SAP F&R often only looks out six weeks. So as you can see from looking at their time horizons, SAP DP and SAP F&R are also performed at opposite ends of the supply chain planning process. SAP DP is considered the starting point of the supply chain planning process, and SAP F&R is its end. Overall, this is actually a different process, so SAP has created a different application to manage it. SAP F&R creates forecasts for stores and warehouses based upon the individual store forecasts. This is a bottom-up approach to forecasting as opposed to a top-down method, which is more popular in centralized forecasting systems such as SAP DP. A synopsis of these differences between SAP DP and SAP F&R forecasting is outlined for you in Table 13.1.

Application	Characteristics of Forecasting
SAP DP	Long term, not specific to supply chain area, early stage of the supply chain planning process
SAP F&R	Short term, specific to retail, late stage supply chain planning process

Table 13.1 Forecasting Characteristics of SAP DP and SAP F&R

SAP F&R Forecast and Time Series

SAP F&R time series is actually a storage component

SAP F&R has a particular name for its forecasting, called *time series*. This is frequently referred to in the documentation and can take some getting used to because time series, of course, is a forecasting method. However, SAP uses the term time series as a proper noun within SAP F&R describing its forecasting results; for example, the results of the SAP F&R forecast are stored in the time series. The SAP F&R time series is actually a storage component. It's a logical database that is created at runtime and can be displayed in the following interfaces:

> Replenishment Workbench

> Product Workbench

> Cause Determination

> DIF Workbench

You can see where the time series is calculated in Figure 13.2.

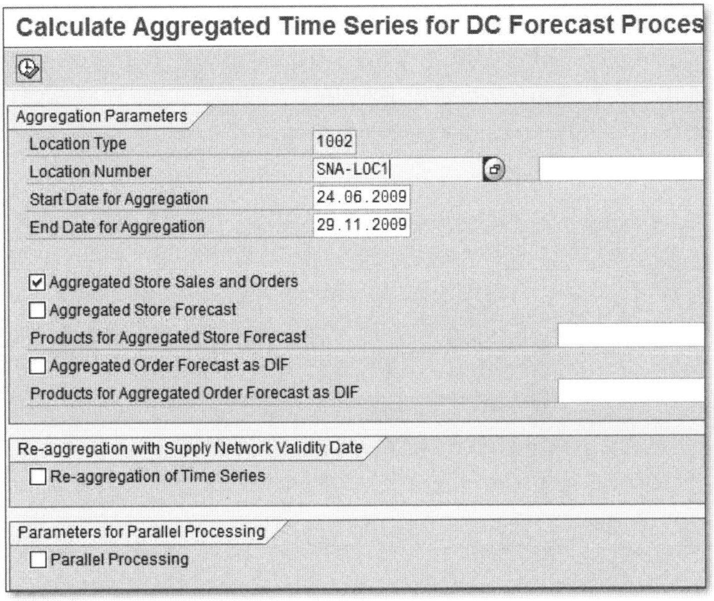

Figure 13.2 Time Series Can be Calculated Per Product Location

To see where the time series is changed in aggregation, look at Figure 13.3.

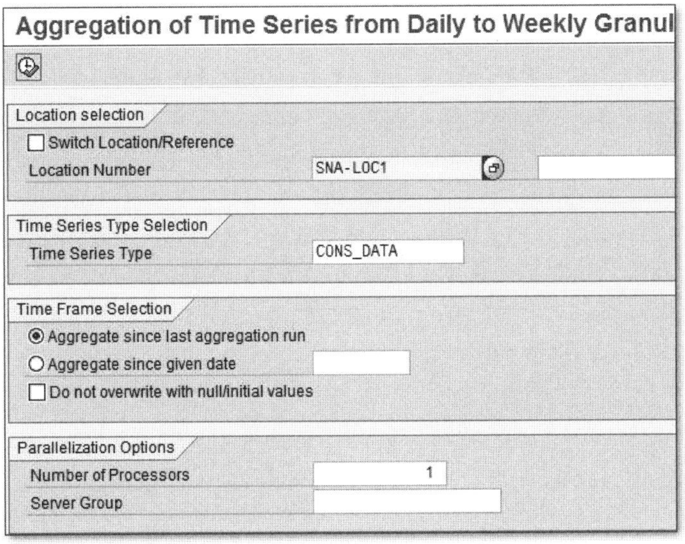

Figure 13.3 Time Series Changed in Aggregation

Demand Influencing Factors

One thing that you may find interesting is how forecasting is performed differently in the other SAP SCM forecasting applications — SAP SPP and SAP DP — versus how it's performed in SAP F&R. SAP F&R uses a concept called *the Demand Influencing Factors (DIF)* to adjust and create its forecasts. DIFs can be anything that adjusts the forecast, and they are managed from the DIF application (not to be confused with an actual SAP SCM application) within SAP F&R. The DIF application provides input data for the automatic replenishment process and allows the adjustment of DIFs. It also helps you manage any unusual events such as promotions, holidays, price changes, and so on, and can be defined for any factor.

 Example

> In a retail store environment, one factor is the aggregated store sales or even store traffic. DIFs work by creating occurrences that then influence the forecast after the factor is created and applied to the demand history. For instance, a common retail environment factor that must be modeled is promotions. A DIF can be applied for a promotion that can help improve the accuracy of the forecast.

Like SAP SPP, SAP F&R allows for the use of causal forecasting. However, unlike SAP SPP, it doesn't use the term *leading indicator*, but instead applies the industry standard term *causal*. And as with forecasting in SAP DP, SAP F&R has best-fit functionality. For example, it can perform auto-selection between more than 100 forecast models, which allows for DIFs such as calendars, promotions, and price changes. And, reports can be generated from the DIFs, including the Detection of First Time Occurrences report, which reports on DIFs that have recently been put into service and aren't yet affecting the forecast.

In addition to the flexibility provided by DIFs, forecast frequency is also flexible in SAP F&R, which is important because short-term tactical forecasts can vary widely in the frequency requirements. Forecast frequency can be controlled by a process control profile that allows for different frequencies based on characteristics of the product. So, this allows an automatic adjusting of the frequency by product need. Some examples of product characteristics that can cause the frequency to adjust include the following:

> The ABC classification of the location product

> The selling class of the location product

Ex Example

> Auto-adjustment of frequency is one of the very important functionality introductions in SAP F&R. Auto-fit functionality, where the forecasting methodology is matched per product demand history is a near universal capability within forecasting systems now. However, auto-adjust forecast frequency based on product characteristics is a more recent development. This cuts down the configuration time of SAP F&R as well as some of the project decision points. Also, once set, it doesn't have to be revisited as the product's characteristics change.

Auto-adjustment of frequency functionality

Order Proposals

The main integration object to SAP for Retail is the order proposal. After a manual overview of the order proposals, your order items can be released. However, in addition to releasing orders, old order proposals can be copied over to create new ones. This saves time and improves planning efficiency by reusing old order proposals. Also, the existing orders can be grouped or split based on criteria such as the vendor, receiving location, or planning date. Because the store managers use this interface, it is web based. Within this display is a product list view that allows the rounding of quantities on proposed items, which can help ensure that the orders are of efficient order quantities.

Order proposals are the main integration point between SAP for Retail and SAP F&R

> The following functions apply:

> Order proposals

> Store exceptions

> User administration

> Responsibility management

All of these capabilities provide store managers with the order management information they need to effectively manage the ordering for the store. As stated earlier, the intent is to move the tactical order decision making to the store to take advantage of the local knowledge possessed by those closest to the process.

Now let's get into the detail of SAP F&R's order management capability, beginning with order release.

Order Proposal Release Management

Profiles are used throughout SAP SCM to save parameters and time, and improve management of the system

SAP F&R delivers exception-based capabilities for order release. Most releases are automatic and are subject to checks. For instance, an order proposal may be held up if it doesn't meet quantity requirements. In this case, the order is cancelled, and an exception is issued. These restrictions can be set in the restriction profiles. SAP F&R can also perform economic order quantity order creation in a way that incorporates supplier discounts. Profiles can be set up to optimize the requirements quantity. These are set up in the maintain requirements quantity optimization profile.

> **Ex** **Example**
>
> It's important to consider that often in-store personnel don't have a great deal of time to apply to order management. So SAP F&R has significantly automated the ordering process, which is apparent in the order proposal release management in that most of the orders will go out as scheduled, but some orders can be automatically held back for further review. This is customizable in the profiles and can be assigned to a single store, but it's more likely to be assigned to groups of stores.

SAP F&R also allows the application of a filter on some of the orders so you can manually evaluate them. These are then placed in the Replenishment Workbench where orders can be adjusted. Again, as with release management, profiles can be created that determine the release criteria. This workbench supports the central replenishment of stores. Orders can also be balanced, which is the SAP F&R term for leveling, so that you can control how many orders are being released at a time, particularly during heavy times.

Balancing orders can greatly improve stocking and logistics efficiency. This is similar to the capacity leveling performed in SNP and PP/DS, when both applications run heuristics without constraints. Although it's important to note that SAP F&R has far less flexibility in pushing out or postponing requirements than SNP and PP/DS when routinely performing leveling because the timeline it's evaluating is much shorter.

Substitution

Substitution is important for SAP F&R because of the short time horizon. So, in many cases, the options are between using a substitute product or a lost sale. This is one of the reasons that SAP F&R has a strong substitution capability that allows products that have demand history to be substituted for other products. Another reason is to use the demand history of one product for what could be a new product or a product that is new to the geography. There can be any number of reasons for this. For example, a new product might lack demand history, or a demand history might be "borrowed" from a similar product with a history at a particular location, if the company wants to graft that history onto a product that is new to that location. So, SAP F&R's substitution capability can be leveraged for either short-term tactical decisions that can help reduce lost sales or long-term decisions that can leverage demand history of an applicable product. Figure 13.4 shows where substitutions are configured.

Substitutions can prevent lost sales

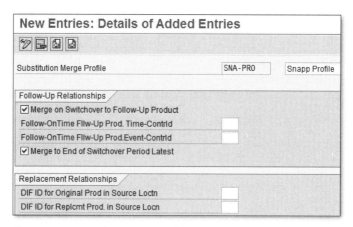

Figure 13.4 Demand Histories Can be Switched in Product Substitution

The next topic is critical to understanding SAP F&R but also has implications for supply chain planning in general. Service-level planning is a concept that originates in SAP SPP but is beginning to migrate to finished goods planning. It's actually a very elegant concept that can tie together the desires of the customer with the operations of the seller and can help sort out the appropriate level of inventory to be held and the frequency of delivery, among a host of other supply chain decisions.

Service-Level Planning

Service-level planning can tie the customer's desires to the operations of the seller

Service level planning is an important capability that is gathering wider application in supply chain planning. Service-level planning essentially allows the service to be set, and then the system attempts to meet the service level by making the necessary ordering and inventory holding decisions. Service-level planning is available within SAP F&R through the amount that SAP F&R increases the forecast, which responds to the level the service level is set to. The service level can be set a number of different ways. The service level can be set based on the inventory turnover or the importance of the product within the classification (also known as ABC analysis). Service levels can even be changed depending on the season.

Service-level planning in SAP F&R is set up with the service-level profile. It contains parameters that impact the service level and can be assigned at a location product. The service level can be set on the ABC indicator and the selling class (Figure 13.5).

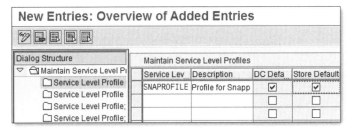

Figure 13.5 The Service Profile Is Under The SAP F&R Processor

SAP F&R Reporting

Reports are an important part of SAP F&R which can be connected to SAP NetWeaver BW to monitor investments in merchandise inventory, not just at the retail location, but all of the way through the supply chain. Table 13.2 describes the types of reports provided.

Generate a wide variety of reports

SAP F&R Reports	Description
Lost Sales	Due to stock outs
Over Stock	Too much stock for demand
Under Stock	Too little stock for demand
Forecast Quality	Actual consumption compared against the forecast
Service Level Development	Estimate of the actual service level

Table 13.2 SAP F&R Reports

SAP F&R Reports	Description
History of Manually Changed Order Proposals	How manual changes have affected the performance of the different items in terms of fulfillment
Development of Range Coverage	The actual range of coverage and a range of coverage factor, which is created for each hierarchy of the product
Stock History	The stock history of a location product
Gross Margin Return on Investment	The development of the stock value for the location product for things such as gross margin percentage
Replenishment Exceptions	Statistics on the exceptions reported by both replenishment and forecasting
Dead Stock	Stock that is above zero but for which there is no more demand (a.k.a. obsolete stock)
Variances Dynamic Versus Minimum Stock	All cases where the static and dynamic minimum stock or a location diverge from one another
Automatic Order Proposal Processing	Information about the number of order proposals created per day and the percentage that could be released automatically

Table 13.2 SAP F&R Reports (Cont.)

As we discussed previously, SAP F&R can manage ordering in a way that develops economical orders for the store. This is called *order optimization*.

Order Optimization

SAP F&R supports optimizing the order quantity as described in Table 13.3.

Order Optimization Methods	Description
Logistical rounding	Rounds quantities based on the order proposal quantity and the unit of measure. This function also updates the dependent data.
Vendor restrictions	Restrictions are used when there is too much stock for demand.

Table 13.3 Optimization Methods

This concludes our look at the functionality of SAP F&R. These details should clarify the unique focus and nature of SAP F&R as compared to the other SAP SCM applications. It's still a newer application, so there aren't many real-world case studies to discuss, but we'll review the release history to help you understand where SAP F&R has come from.

SAP F&R Release History

Unlike most of the other newer applications, SAP F&R didn't receive improvements in SAP SCM 7.0. However, a number of important changes were made in 5.1:

> The ability to define DIF-related sales dependencies between products such as cannibalization and simultaneous purchases. This can also be imported from SAP NetWeaver BW or a third-party system.

> Pre-allocation to move deliveries earlier than originally planned. This is a form of capacity leveling.

> The ability to import product substitution data. Data from the original product can be merged with data from the new product to perform forecasting. Can be integrated with DIF functionality.

> CPFR order forecasting enhanced to allow a tactical order forecast on a weekly basis for the CPFR exchange. Also the CPFR output stimulation includes detailed tactical order forecast information.

> A number of added time series management methods.

> Addition of the SAP F&R processor.

> DIF enhancements in the ability to distribute forecasts across multiple weeks.

> Improved analytics that allow detailed tracking on items such as cross-selling effects.

> Addition of the Replenishment Workbench's ability to use planning data to substitute forecast data.

> Addition of the Product Workbench, which allows a concentration on the location products, not just the order proposals (which is the focus of the Replenishment Workbench).

As you can see, there were a number of important enhancements made to F&R and it will continue to develop through enhancement packs.

Conclusion

As you learned throughout this chapter, SAP F&R is a young application in terms of the number of implementations. It's intended to be used with SAP for Retail, so its potential customer base is smaller than the other applications due to its industry-specific usage. SAP F&R is, however, a third forecasting option in SAP SCM, and it approaches forecasting somewhat differently from either SAP DP or SAP SPP. Additionally, SAP F&R is a highly collaborative solution that includes input of store managers as an essential component of its workflow. SAP F&R is strongly based on the CPFR method of retail replenishment, which has shown success at several of the large retailers where it has been implemented.

Next, we'll take a step back and look at the technical beginnings of SAP SCM so you can really understand how and why it's designed as it is.

14

SAP SCM's Direction as of Release 7.0

How SAP SCM has developed over the past few releases is both an interesting story and a topic of strong interest to the potential and current customers. In this chapter, we'll provide an overview of what the individual changes mean for the overall suite.

SAP SCM has seen some very significant enhancements in the past few years. Many of these changes started in release 5.0, and they have continued until the present release, which at the time of this writing is 7.0. Numerous enhancements have been made in the past few releases, so we were only able to list some of the most important ones in each of the application chapters. In this chapter, however, we'll cover a select few of these in greater detail, with the goal of providing insight into the high-level direction of the suite.

High-Level Direction

From a high-level perspective, the changes in SAP SCM are easy to chart, primarily because SAP SCM has added new applications with categories of functionality that cover entirely new areas of the supply chain, or that do something SAP SCM didn't do in the past (e.g., service parts planning, or at least providing specific planning solutions for service parts, and various forms of collaboration). The list of new areas includes the following:

> Collaboration with suppliers

> Sophisticated warehouse management

> Cross-enterprise supply chain monitoring

> Service parts planning

> Retail replenishment

So at a high level, without yet getting into any detail, we can see a significant change in the focus of SAP SCM.

New Approaches and Tools

SAP SCM has a major new interface as of release 7.0

SAP SCM has so much functionality that it's a full-time job just keeping up with the entire suite and all of the new developments that come out with each release or enhancement pack. Often the improvements are incremental; however, occasionally new capabilities are released that mean a different way of doing things in SAP SCM. In the next few sections, we'll outline areas of functionality that are examples of very significant improvements to SAP SCM. Among the many additions, the following changes represent significant new directions in SAP SCM.

A Major New User Interface

The user interface to SAP SCM has been consistent since its inception.

The major interface tools included the following:

> The product view
> The planning books

Many interfaces have been added, but none have been such permanent fixtures as the product view and the planning books. Each has been enhanced through the various releases, but the basic concept and design of each has remained relatively stable. Both have their advantages:

> The planning book allows you to view different intersections of characteristics.
> The product view shows receipts and issues at a location.

The interface is one of the most underappreciated factors that drive system adoption. This is because the people that make the decision to buy corporate software (executives) aren't usually the people who actually work with the system on a daily basis.

The DRP Matrix interface is only available in SAP SPP. It's been quite a while since SAP SCM offered a major new interface for users, except for the DRP Matrix. The DRP Matrix is one of the most interesting and effective new capabilities in SAP SCM, and the highest degree of analysis is provided by the DRP Matrix. Using the DRP Matrix provides you with those "ah-ha" moments that were often missing from the planning book and the product view. However, currently the DRP Matrix is only available within SAP SPP. So let's evaluate what is currently available in the planning book and product views, and then look at what the DRP Matrix offers.

> DRP Matrix available in SPP only

 Note

The DRP Matrix is much like a job running screen. It provides the services to be run (and more services can be configured), and these services can control functionality in different areas of SAP SCM.

The planning book allows flexible selections of characteristic value combinations (CVCs). However, it lacks the integrated analysis features of the DRP Matrix (Figures 14.1 and 14.2).

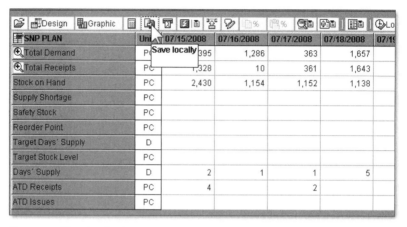

Figure 14.1 Planning Book

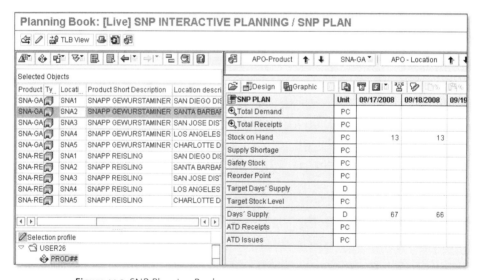

Figure 14.2 SNP Planning Book

The planning book interface provides a simple spreadsheet view that allows for the flexible addition of rows, which are based on data, and for dynamic or calculated rows that are calculated by macros. This provides effective views on aggregation, but it lacks an immediate analytical impact.

The screenshot of the DRP matrix demonstrates that it provides a level of transparency and intuitive understanding that the planning book lacks. Figure 14.3 illustrates how intuitively more usable the DRP Matrix interface is as compared to the planning book in Figure 14.2.

Macros allow all types of calculations and can even be used to perform inventory management calculations that SAP SCM doesn't have

> **Note: Product View**
>
> The product view shows the planned inbound and outbound material at a location and is a frequently used view by planners. For instance, when material is planned to be transferred between locations, the movement shows on both the *from* and the *to* locations. This allows the planner to see the changes to the system recorded.

☐ TPOP								
Forecast	Change	Save	Save Profile		Fine-Tuning		Model Selection	
Key Figures			M 06.2008	M 07.2008	M 08.2008	M 09.2008	M 10.2008	
Demand: Final History			200,000	155,217	150,000	133,636		
Demand: Outlier Correction								
Demand: Std Dev. Outlier Correction								
Demand: Forecast						144,200	147,306	
Demand: Expost Forecast								
Demand: Disaggregated Forecast						143,804	146,809	
Demand: Manual Forecast								
Demand: Manual Disag. Forecast								
Demand: Final Forecast						143,804	146,809	
Demand: Std Dev. Forecast						36,050	36,826	
Demand: Std Dev. Disag. Forecast						0,000	0,000	
Demand: Std Dev. Final Forecast						0,000	0,000	
Demand: MAD						28,840	29,461	

Figure 14.3 The DRP Matrix

The DRP Matrix provides a maximum degree of transparency. Instead of a group of products, the DRP Matrix applies for a single product forecast. Also, a row interacts with a graph below it, which provides very fast feedback (Figure 14.4).

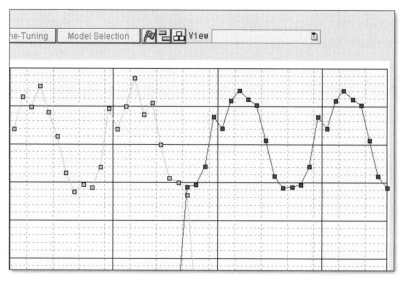

Figure 14.4 DRP Matrix Graphics

By selecting a line item, a graph will be drawn below the spreadsheet to illustrate the data (Figure 14.5), which in this case is a historical forecast, and it will also provide the future forecast.

Additionally, farther down (on the same screen) a number of forecast parameters or controls are available. This provides a high level of transparency to the forecast and ensures that the basic factors adjusting the forecast don't stay hidden from the planners.

Linear vs. Discrete Optimization

Figure 14.5 DRP Matrix Parameters

Another important new area is The Planning Service Manager.

Planning Service Manager

It's always interesting to find a truly new part of SAP SCM. Planning profiles and the Planning Service Manager (PSM) certainly meet this description. While originating in SAP SPP, PSM can be used to access services in many SAP SCM applications. Up until PSM was introduced, all of the SAP SCM applications were primarily self-contained, addressing only their own functionality. The design has been to perform the application-specific processing and then pass data from one application to the next for the subsequent steps. This modular approach reinforced a sequence between the different applications, which while structured, limited the workflows that were practically possible for SAP SCM implementations. For instance, in the most traditional sense, SAP DP sends the demand plan to SNP, which then processes it and sends it to PP/DS. There are a few exceptions to this generality though. For example, SNP can execute heuristics that actually reside in PP/DS. For most of SAP SCM's history, however, the functionality has been modularized, in that you went to that specific application to run its functionality. PSM changes this by providing the ability to access functionality across the applications through the use of *process profiles* (Figure 14.6).

Process profiles are used to set up the functionality to be accessed as services to be run from the PSM

283

Figure 14.6 PSM Can Access Functionality in SAP SCM Applications

PSM allows you to access functionality across applications

Planning Service Manager Profiles

One reason that PSM isn't yet highly adopted is its strong association with SPP, which as of this writing is just gaining visibility with clients

There are many process profiles, and, of course, an unlimited number can be created from scratch by customizing the processes that come standard with SAP SCM. Now, PSM allows multiple types of functionality that reside in different applications to be accessed from a single location (Figure 14.7). This greatly simplifies the approach to accessing SAP SCM functionality. For instance, if you wanted to run a forecast, you could create a process profile and schedule it in PSM. We believe most companies who have implemented SAP SCM are still using SAP SCM in a very modular approach and not taking advantage of PSM to more flexibly unlock SAP SCM functionality. This should change as users begin to better understand the capability.

This is just a small sampling of the services available. The number of services goes on for pages, and any of these can be initiated and scheduled from PSM.

Now let's discuss service-level planning. We discussed it in passing in Chapter 13, SAP Forecasting and Replenishment (SAP F&R), but here we want to discuss it more broadly in SAP SCM.

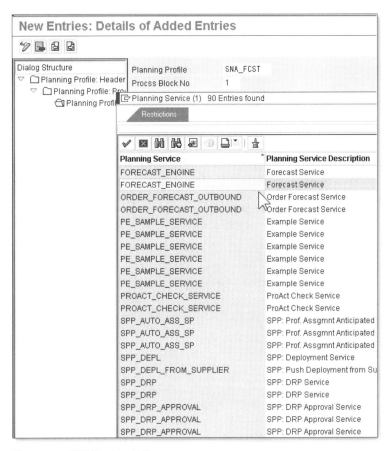

Figure 14.7 PSM Services Listing

Service-Level Planning

As discussed previously, service-level planning is a very important method of planning that SAP has included in recent SAP SCM releases. Service-level planning allows the system to set service levels and determine the appropriate inventory, safety stock, and production activity based on a specific service level. Service-level planning is called different things in different industries (e.g., aerospace and defense calls it performance-based logistics [PBL]), but for all companies, it's where they agree to service-level contracts with their customers.

Service-level planning has different names within different industries

285

There are often financial implications to not meeting the service-level contract.

Service-level planning is new to SAP SCM 7.0

However, service-level planning can be far less formalized than this. A company can simply keep internal service-level values assigned per product location. However, service level increases impose costs on the supply chain. So as the service level climbs, the cost of maintaining the service level increases drastically after a certain level. This is why service levels are never stated in terms of "100% fill rates" because it's simply too expensive. The profitability of different areas of the business can help a company determine what the appropriate fill rate should be, and more specifically different customers (and different industries) have different abilities to pay and different preferences to pay for service levels (Figure 14.8).

Figure 14.8 Service-Level Planning Trade Off

Concepts of Service-Level Planning and Finished Goods

Service-level planning functionality has been predominantly introduced by specialized service parts vendors. However, this is only because service contracts are often sold on the basis of an explicit service rate. But the concept is beneficial for both service parts and finished goods. In the area of finished goods planning, different factors can be used to determine the appropriate fill rate. For instance, the profitability of an item is a major factor. Profitable items, which are often more differentiated in the market, have a higher lost sales value than lower profit items. So it pays to hold more inventory to prevent the company from being out of stock on that item.

There are multiple levels of the product geography hierarchy where the service level can be set. For example, one of the most important areas of functionality in several service parts planning applications is the ability to perform "global" service-level planning. Global service-level planning allows the planner to set the same or different service levels for the locations in the network that result in an overall service or availability level for the supply chain network. However, finished goods service-level planning tends to set the target service level on either product or product location. But the service contract planning requires customer product location level planning. SAP SCM has some ability to manage finished goods with service levels (which we discuss next), but we also expect this functionality to grow and the concept to gain even more momentum.

So how does SAP SCM handle service-level planning and goods services?

Service-Level Planning in SAP

There are some older and some newer areas of SAP SCM and even SAP ERP where service-level planning exists, although it may be called something else. But regardless of what it's been in the past, the service-level planning capability of SAP is growing, and it exists in the following areas of SAP.

The material master in SAP ERP is much like the product location master in SAP SCM — both store master data information about the product and parameter data that controls the model

Service-Level Planning in SAP ERP

> SAP ERP: service-level planning at the part level exists on the material master where safety stock can be calculated dynamically. This is a part-specific level of availability that doesn't extend to a broader view (it's local, not global) of the overall part database service level. However, SAP SCM has many more areas where service-level plan-

ning is incorporated (although we're confident that future versions will have even more). So if your company is interested in service-level planning, the place to look is SAP SCM. These areas of service-level functionality (both implicit and explicit) are listed in the next section.

Service-Level Planning in SAP SCM

It's important to note that service-level planning functionality, or at least service-level concepts, aren't in just one application but are distributed through different application as detailed in the following list.

> Capable to Match (CTM) can prioritize requests so that some customers get inventory allocated versus lower priority customers.

> In Production Planning and Detailed Scheduling (PP/DS), reservations can be defined on the capacity of resources, and they can be made on the basis of profitability and service-level agreements.

> In SAP Supplier Network Collaboration (SAP SNC), a service fill analysis component is now part of the supplier delivery performance rating.

> In SAP F&R the forecast and estimated safety amounts are based on both the forecast error and the safety stock.

> SAP F&R periods with expected similar patterns can be combined, and separate service levels can be assigned to each ABC classification.

> In SAP F&R Demand Influencing Factors (DIFs), which are the primary mechanism of forecasting in the application, service-level profiles can be set up for the DIFs.

> In Service Parts Planning (SPP), target service levels can be set at the location or product location level. As of Release 7.0, targets can be set depending on whether the location is an entry, intermediate parent, or child location.

> Safety stock (which is in SNP) can be set by using the enhanced method. This is where the safety stock responds flexibly to the service level in the product location master.

Safety stock is covered in Chapter 15

Figure 14.9 shows what the Service Level Field screen looks like in SAP SCM.

Stock Data			
Safety Stock		Safety Stock Method	
Reorder Point		Service Level (%)	
Max.Stock Level		Demand Fcast Err.(%)	
Stock	0	RLT Fcast Error (%)	

Figure 14.9 The Service Level Field in the Lot Size Tab of the Product Location Master

The extended safety stock functionality in SAP SCM requires a service level and a forecast error.

 Note: Forecast Error

The forecast error is used to change the safety stock value. A higher error results in a higher safety stock value. This results in higher inventory, which is one reason why improve forecasts are perennially desired by companies. There are many process approaches to improving the forecast that are typically greatly underused such as reducing the number of promotions, reducing the model changes, and new product introductions, but typically most companies try to employ a complex product and promotional scheme, and ask for the planning system to fix any issue.

Service-Level Planning as an Evolved Approach

There's a good reason why several service parts planning applications are built around service-level planning. The concept is that with service parts, you're providing a service level to a customer and signing a contract to this effect. So, with service parts planning, service-level based planning is explicitly necessary to meet the contract terms.

However, shouldn't it be just as important for the company to plan its inventory level based upon service levels? For example, knowing what's a profitable versus unprofitable in-stock position allows your company to know how many financial resources to allocate to inventory and at what level to stop holding inventory by using the rough average profit margin of your company's products. This concept is fundamentally different, however, depending on whether you're planning service parts or finished goods.

Finally, the recent developments in SAP SCM in the area of service-level planning are a likely indicator that more service-level capabilities will be added in future releases.

Now let's look at some of the cross-enterprise capabilities offered in SAP SCM.

Cross-Enterprise Capabilities

Manage your supply chain across enterprises

One of the major directional changes with SAP SCM is the ability to manage the supply chain across enterprises. There are a couple of reasons why this cross-enterprise focus matches the actual supply chain environment:

> Large-scale supply chain outsourcing means that most companies have some or most of their supply chain in the hands of other companies. However, outsourcing brings up and increases integration issues.

> The large amount of contract overseas manufacturing and international suppliers means that companies increasingly don't have control over the origination of their products.

Cross-Enterprise Monitoring

SAP EM can report on the entire cross-enterprise supply chain

Several applications within SAP SCM improve cross-enterprise integration. As we discussed in Chapter 8, SAP Event Management (SAP EM), SAP EM is a supply chain nerve center that spans enterprises.

SAP EM is based on the Alert Manager, which provides advanced warning of problems with the plan related to material, capacity, transportation, and storage constraints. It was originally designed to bring up an issue that needed to be addressed. SAP EM, on the other hand, not only lists open issues for planners and operational personnel but also provides notifications when important things happen in the supply chain. Although not deliberately marketed this way, the Alert Monitor is actually an excellent reporting tool on the state of the supply chain. We think that SAP EM will be used in a similar manner by progressive companies to report on the entire cross-enterprise supply chain.

The Alert Manager looks inside of SAP SCM, while SAP EM looks both inside and outside of SAP SCM. This highlights the increasingly cross-enterprise nature of SAP SCM. While SAP EM is often viewed as providing benefits to the implementing company, in truth, the other supply chain partners also benefit. This is because all of the partners can log in to check the process as proposed by SAP.

The Alert Monitor provides alert capabilities and reporting functionality

Ex Example

The role-based approach of SAP EM is a great feature because it allows a variety of people in your company to view the same business process from various points of view.

We're really in the early stages of building cross-enterprise supply chain monitoring systems. The current design is that companies integrate with another company's alert system, such as SAP EM. Currently, this cross-enterprise integration is primarily being handled by sending EDI transactions. It isn't clear that this is the best approach because the model is inherently limited. A better solution is a publish-and-subscribe model where companies publish status and notifications to a company that can be read by preselected business partners, and vice versa. This way, a single feed can update multiple business partners, and work effort and repetition can be seriously reduced. Currently, SAP EM, and little else in the marketplace is set up to work this way. Until that happens, SAP EM can still provide comprehensive status information to multiple supply chain partners through one-off integration.

Collaboration

We covered collaboration in Chapter 12, SAP Supplier Network Collaboration (SNC). However, we wanted to emphasize the increasing number of objects that can be collaborated on within SAP SCM and that key figures have been added for the following:

> Purchase orders

> Advanced shipping notifications (ASNs)

> Invoices

> Scheduling agreement releases

> Work orders

So in addition to the growth in the breadth of collaboration, the depth is growing as well. Early versions of SAP SNC provided higher-level collaborations, but the more recent versions are increasing the detail capability of collaboration, or increasing the transparency of the collaboration for you. Specific improvements in this area include the following:

> Customers can now request a specific manufacturer part number. This is a higher level of detail that provides transparency into the manufacturer, which is useful to the customer when multiple manufacturers are sourced for a product.

> Batch numbers can be used for the product produced by the work order (for production collaboration). This allows the customer you are collaborating with to more readily identify the product being produced by the work order.

Responsive replenishment is a type of collaboration used between warehouses and retail stores, which is supported by SAP F&R

> New user interfaces such as the Responsive Replenishment Monitor allow receipts and requirements to be accessed. Additionally, SAP EM now provides visibility processes for purchase orders, inbound messages, and replenishment orders.

> SAP SNC is now more reflective of ordering realities with the introduction of the ability to integrate lot sizes from the product location master and with the new ability to round order volumes through the creation of rounding profiles.

> SAP SNC is increasingly better integrated to other SAP SCM applications. For example, SAP SNC can use the product allocation check that resides in Global Available to Promise (GATP).

> Up until SAP SCM 5.1, SAP SNC was focused on collaboration on objects related to products. However, with the addition of invoice collaboration, SAP SNC now spans the entire collaborative workflow from work order to payment.

> Collaboration is being opened up to more business partners, which is indicated by the number of user role types that have been added to SAP SNC. This allows several business partners to agree on quantities, dates, and prices. Consensus collaboration is built-in to the following areas of SAP SNC.

  – Collaborative Sales and Forecasting

  – The Order Forecast Monitor

  – Work Order Processing

  – Purchase Order Processing

  – Replenishment Order Processing

Simple collaboration can be considered a more limited form of collaboration that just connects a few big suppliers to a customer. Consensus collaboration enlarges the concept and involves more parties (Figure 14.10).

Simple collaboration and consensus collaboration

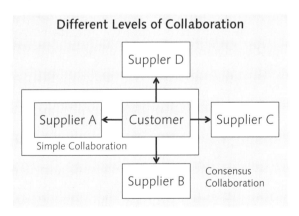

Figure 14.10 Limited Versus Consensus Collaboration

The consensus collaboration functionality effectively demonstrates that there are different degrees of collaboration. It's important to remember that cross-enterprise systems aren't easy to install because of they are involved in the integration of company systems that have until recently only been loosely coupled through things such as EDI messages or phone calls.

Although there are plenty of barriers for the cross-enterprise aspects of SAP SCM, SAP SCM has one thing that EDI didn't have, and that was the ability to collaborate with supply chain partners over the web. The web is a fantastic resource for collaboration. In terms of motivation, if your company is evaluating whether to invest in cross-enterprise systems, you need look no further than Amazon.com. Much is discussed about Amazon in terms of the customer experience and top-flight web site that is a feature in many people's lives. Less discussed, however, is the cross-enterprise systems that support Amazon and that make what it does possible. This is borne out by Amazon's IT investments, and many of these investments have nothing to do with the frontend website.

As we pointed out in Chapter 6, SAP SCM Global Available to Promise (GATP), Amazon shows an integrated (although simplified) Available to Promise to Customers model that allows them to select from a number of sellers. Amazon performs inventory collaboration with these sellers to have this information to provide to consumers. It fulfills the orders for some of its partners under the Fulfillment by Amazon (FBA) program, and it has built a supply chain monitoring exchange. Amazon also links to its suppliers in a way that auto orders and in a number of cases eliminates human interaction. Because of this, Amazon can collaborate with its suppliers at an extremely high level.

Ex **Example: Follow Amazon's Technology Lead**

It's definitely misleading when business books point to a single company, or even several companies, to try to demonstrate a trend. So this isn't what we're proposing here. We propose that Amazon is an outlier: Its web and supply chain capabilities are far superior to those of almost any other company. In many ways, Amazon is similar to Apple (which dropped the word computer from their name, so they are now just Apple). Apple is like no other company in the computer industry. While PC proponents dismiss Apple, what's often unrealized is that Apple actually does the majority of hardware and software innovation in the industry. (Here we aren't speaking of component innovation because we're aware that Seagate and Intel continue to bring out more advanced hard drives and improved microprocessors.) But the other technology from Apple, such as the iPhone has now been thoroughly copied, as has the iMac (by HP and ASUS), and there's even a Sony keyboard that appears to have been backward engineered from Apple's lower profile keyboard. So neither Amazon nor Apple are typical companies — they are both heavy innovators. They are also great companies to analyze to get an understanding of what is possible. In terms of learning how to best integrate supply chain management with systems, there really isn't a company farther out on the technology edge than Amazon. And, Amazon can easily be followed because it puts so much of its capability on its website to lure merchants into selling. You can learn a lot about how Amazon is designed by simply reading the information it makes publicly available (Figure 14.11).

Another important area that has been added to SAP SCM in terms of planning is the warehouse and retail store. This highlights how SAP SCM is broadening its scope, in addition to becoming deeper in the areas that it already covers with each subsequent release.

Figure 14.11 Check Out Amazon's Processes Online

Addition of the Warehouse and Retail Store

With the introduction of SAP Extended Warehouse Management (SAP EWM) and SAP F&R, SAP SCM now covers areas of the supply chain previously not covered. This means that SAP SCM can now be used by users in your company who haven't been previously exposed to SAP SCM.

Calculate projected
or future order
proposal line items
with SAP F&R
and CPFR

In addition to normal retail replenishment SAP F&R offers support for CPFR order forecasting. This is a tactical forecast that works on a weekly basis and calculates projected or future order proposal line items based on forecast consumption, current stock on hand, open receipts, goods issues, and scheduling. This process hasn't been supported in SAP SCM before. The addition of SAP EWM allows for very advanced forms of warehouse management that many companies may not have fully evaluated in terms of how SAP EWM compares to warehouse management or other existing warehouse solutions.

And, both of these systems support RFID. SAP has bet heavily that RFID will be the tracking method of the future. In a 100% SAP solution, RFID records the item leaving the warehouse as well as the item being received into the retail store with SAP F&R.

SAP SCM's focus in terms of development has changed over time. Downstream processes such as warehousing and retail planning and replenishment have been added to the footprint (Figure 14.12).

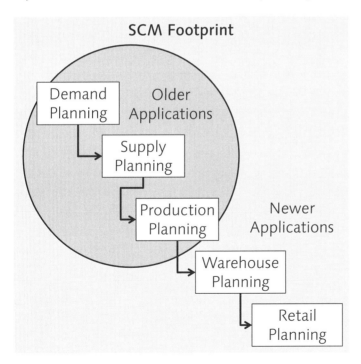

Figure 14.12 Growth of the SAP SCM Footprint Over Time

Note

> As the preceding examples demonstrate, there's a host of new functionality in SAP SCM that companies need to analyze to see what fits with their requirements. Some things that SAP SCM couldn't do just a few years ago, it can do now, and some areas of the business that couldn't be planned by SAP SCM, can now be planned. This means that companies looking to get the most from their SAP SCM licenses should analyze these areas by either looking for functionality not yet implemented within previously implemented applications or by looking to the new ones for more business value.

Conclusion

SAP SCM has developed since its introduction as SAP APO more than 10 years ago. The applications that make up SAP SCM have become much more feature rich and broader in scope. It has added an important new user interface in the DRP Matrix and has developed an ultra-powerful services scheduler, the Planning Service Manager, which can reach out and call functionality in different unrelated areas in SAP SCM. SAP SCM is beginning to use the concept of service-level planning in different applications, a positive trend that we predict will continue and grow. SAP SCM has picked up new areas of the supply chain, namely the warehouse and the retail store. While it previously could only plan service parts with a finished goods solution, SAP SCM now offers a specialized Service Parts Planning application, which for the first time now has the necessary functionality to tackle service parts.

In the next chapter, we'll look at how to get more from SAP SCM.

15 Getting More from SAP SCM

In an ever-changing economic environment, it's becoming more important to get the most from your SAP SCM investment. And because SAP SCM has more applications and functionality within each release than ever before, figuring out the appropriate area of functionality to leverage can make the difference in your SAP SCM projects. This chapter focuses on how to improve the utility of your SAP SCM implementation.

Now that you've read about the core offerings with SAP SCM, you should have a good idea of the basic functionality it provides. But there's obviously a lot more that can be done with the applications to really make it work well for your business. So, throughout this chapter, we'll look at some ways you can use the functionality to enhance your SAP SCM implementation. So whether you're just considering it or you're already up and running with SAP SCM, you'll find valuable insights about how to get the most out of the applications.

Where to Look for Improvement

The question of where to look in terms of improving, expanding, or enhancing an existing implementation is easier in some ways than the question of which application to initially install and how to implement it. The major reason is that your company is already familiar with SAP SCM, and you have the experience to know how long SAP SCM implementations take, their level of complexity, resource commitments, and so on. However, there are still a number of unknowns because your company may not be familiar with other applications you want to evaluate, or there may be new functionality within new releases of applications you're already using.

Depending on your situation, you'll either need to take an offensive or defensive approach to getting the most out of your SAP SCM implementation

When evaluating how to improve your SAP SCM implementation, you can take an offensive or defensive approach. So if you need to try to salvage an SAP SCM implementation that fell short of expectations, you'll need to look at it defensively. But if you want to improve on a current implementation that has been successful, or you just want to add another application to continue the momentum and bring advanced planning into other parts of a company's supply chain, you'll be taking an offensive approach.

Let's begin by looking at ways to salvage an unsuccessful implementation.

Why do SAP SCM implementations fail, and how can you fix them?

Recovering Failed SAP SCM Implementations

This is the most difficult position for any company to be in: After a number of promises, the implementation didn't have its intended effect, and the software has lost credibility with the user base and the executives. In this situation, the implementation recovery must both fix the problem and improve the reputation of the software. So the first thing to do is make sure that everyone understands that not every attempt to implement a complex system succeeds the first time, but that your company is dedicated to getting it right. But before we look at how to recover, let's step back and look at the possible reasons why the implementation might have failed. There are a number of reasons for SAP SCM implementations to fail. This list is by no means complete but comes from real-world situations:

> The solution is not designed correctly during prototyping. The most common problems are

  – Development of an overly complex solution.

  – Believing the representatives from within the company who declared, "If the system can't do XYZ, the entire implementation is useless."

  – Not incorporating maintenance into the design decision.

> Picking an implementation partner more focused on monetizing the account than in getting the software implemented correctly

> Not properly understanding the importance of user acceptance

> Not understanding how the new system is supposed to be used and interface with existing systems (both technically and functionally)

There are not that many unique reasons for failure

The first step in recovering an SAP SCM implementation is properly diagnosing what went wrong. Often this process is short-circuited entirely because instead of a logical process of forensics being applied, the weakest departments are singled out for blame. Companies that take the politically convenient route and engage in finding scapegoats have a significantly lower chance of being successful the second time around because if the problem is misdiagnosed, the likelihood of fixing the implementation is low. This is where outside assistance can be helpful.

The Recovery Analysis Team

The most effective recovery team will be small and unaffiliated with any of the players from the original implementation or planned implementations, so that there will be no conflicts of interest. This team needs access to everything, every document, and every person and group involved in the original implementation. It's also important that the team not be comprised of generalists, and at least one of the team members should have content experience in the application in question. It's unlikely that the most senior member of this team will have this experience, but that isn't a problem as long as one of the junior members does. When the team is in place, they'll work to determine the root causes of the failed implementation and provide guidance on how to get it back on track. One key to getting back on track, however, is being sure that those accountable for the initial problems that led to failure are held accountable, and systems are put in place to avoid the mistakes they made.

Accountability of Partners

Application knowledge is necessary in order to evaluate what is possible. Furthermore, applications specialists must be actively engaged

It's surprising how infrequently implementation partners are held accountable for below par implementations. If a partner unsuccessfully manages an implementation, then your company shouldn't feel uncomfortable about switching out the partner. Also the degree to which many firms are specialized isn't well understood. Some partners can implement SAP NetWeaver BW or SAP ERP very well, but that doesn't mean the same partner can implement SAP SCM. Meeting the team that will be actually on your account is important to improve the likelihood of project success. The consulting partner may control its pool of consultants, and subcontractors and other firms may be involved, but ultimately, the money is all coming from the client. It's important that the client actually oversee the consulting partner and not simply outsource the project to the partner.

While it's simple, convenient, and less of a political headache to depend completely on the consulting partner, this won't necessarily lead to the best outcomes. Small, focused SAP SCM consulting firms or even a team of contractors can work alongside a major implementation partner effectively. But the focus of the team, regardless of their size, should be on the implementation and not gaining future contracts.

Implementation Partners

An implementation partner is doubly at fault if an unsuccessful implementation goes live. They are most likely culpable for mismanaging the implementation, but also, no implementation should go live and then fail in adoption without the implementation partner knowing. It's the partner's responsibility to inform the client of the problem beforehand. If the partner doesn't perceive the problem, then that partner lacks the proper experience or instincts and shouldn't have been selected for the implementation in the first place. If the partner does perceive the problem but doesn't bring up the issue to the client, the partner is abrogating its responsibility as an advisory team. If things aren't going as expected, it's best to postpone the implementation rather than go-live with a system that has little chance of being adopted. If either the client or the consulting company lacks confidence as the go-live date approaches, there's likely a good reason for the feeling, and the project needs to be analyzed for postponement. Postponement is appropriate because it's easier to fix an implementation that isn't yet live, than to go back and recover a failed implementation.

To help you identify when you might be having consulting partner issues, we've compiled the list in Table 15.1 of "warning signs."

Method-heavy consulting partners have a tendency to be bureaucratic, and bureaucracy is the enemy of successful projects

Warning Signs	Description
The consulting partner never pushes back on requirements.	It's extremely rare that all business requirements can be accommodated by SAP SCM. Some reasons can be performance related, some relate to doing things in the system that may be customizations, or uses of standard functionality in ways that are possible, but not advisable. Every severely problematic implementation of SAP SCM that we've heard of has combined both unrealistic expectations on the part of the client and an unwillingness of the consulting partner to push back for fear of losing business.

Table 15.1 Consulting Partner Warning Signs

Warning Signs	Description
Resources "show up" on the account without proper evaluation.	Every new resource added to the project needs to be discussed at length. Questions such as: › Why this resource? › What have they recently done that makes them a great fit? › How do they tend to work on projects? › What are their strengths and weaknesses? While every consultant may be part of the consulting company, each is a unique individual, and their addition to the team needs to be justified.
The consulting partner can't differentiate between functionality directions and explain pros and cons.	Although there are many pathways in SAP SCM, not all are equally advisable. A big part of having a successful implementation is matching the right pathway with the client need. Some areas of SAP SCM may be perfect for some clients, but disastrous for others simply because of different performance needs. A skilled partner can explain the different pathways and make recommendations that result in a sustainable system.
The consulting partner is overly wedded to its implementation method.	The use of a specific methods is one of the main ways consulting companies try to differentiate themselves from one another. The problem is that the method doesn't substitute for product knowledge, openness, or the ability of consultants to work together and resolve differences in ways that push the project forward. Companies that overly emphasize their "method" are in a way attempting to dazzle the client but in an area that won't make a significant difference in the project. This usually takes away from where the emphasis should be, which should be on the skills they bring, the experience they have, the functionality with which their consultants interact with each other, and the client, among other factors.

Table 15.1 Consulting Partner Warning Signs (Cont.)

Warning Signs	Description
The consulting partner is director focused or partner focused.	Make no mistake, the people who will be designing the solution, testing, and doing the actual work will be managers and below. The role of the higher-ranked members of the consulting partner team is to put the actual people doing the work in the position to succeed, not to make the project about themselves. Consulting partners with rigid hierarchies where the lower-ranked consultants are overly deferential and too afraid to contradict those higher ranked, who are further away from the actual system, will result in a less effective solution for the client.

It is important to understand who is doing the work versus directing resources

Table 15.1 Consulting Partner Warning Signs (Cont.)

The best implementation partners are sometimes hard to find, but doing the research and finding the right partner is worth it in the long run. This leads to successful implementations in which you can take the offense to improve on it as your company succeeds with the existing system.

So let's move on to look at a variety of ways that you can enhance and improve a successful SAP SCM implementation to truly get the most out of this powerful application.

Improving or Enhancing Successful SAP SCM Implementations

Expanding or enhancing a currently successful SAP SCM implementation is a nice position to be in. This isn't to say that adjustments in terms of implementation approach shouldn't be made for the next phase, but the company now has momentum to build on what's working well. After the application has proven its capability, your company and team will have confidence in the system and be open to enhancing it.

Expanding an existing planning solution that is successful is easier than beginning a multimodule implementation without this experience

It's important not to get overconfident though because the new application or new functionality won't be the same as the last application, and you may have new team members who aren't as familiar with the process. But after you decide to enhance the system, it's just a matter of applying what worked to a new area of the supply chain or simply enhancing the current supply chain area with extra functionality. Areas to look at for enhancing a successful SAP SCM implementation include the following:

> Areas of functionality that were desired but not included in the previous implementation due to budgetary or complexity reasons.

> New functionality that wasn't available during the previous implementation.

> New processes implemented in your company that require new tools.

As SCM is constantly evolving, new modules or new releases should be evaluated to see what new functionality can be leveraged

So let's look at some of the areas that you can work with to address these issues.

Areas of Functionality Worthy of Analysis

What follows is an analysis of some of the promising areas of SAP SCM that you should evaluate and analyze if your company is attempting to get more from SAP SCM. Some of these areas of functionality are new as of this writing, so you may not be completely familiar with them. However, whether old or new, all of these areas are particularly effective functionalities that have a high potential for providing a strong return on your investment.

Subcontracting in SAP SCM

Subcontracting can be a difficult concept because often it's confused with simple outsourced manufacturing. However, there's more to it than that, and SAP has provided a definition that we'll base this discussion around.

> *Subcontracting is a form of procurement in which the manufacturer orders a product from a subcontractor (vendor) and provides the vendor with certain components needed to make the ordered product.*

The optimizer is appropriate for when multiple procurement decisions can be made, and where the company is indifferent, and the main differentiator either is price or can be represented with costs.

Subcontracting has many financial benefits, however, it does make the planning more challenging

When subcontracting is enabled in SAP SCM, it allows your company to better meet demand because the subcontract manufacturer is essentially competing against the in-house manufacturing to fulfill the sales order. This is especially useful if costs are set correctly in the SNP optimizer (assuming the optimizer is used) because then the company can allocate demand to capacity most efficiently. As you'll recall from earlier in the book, when the optimizer is used in either Supply Network Planning (SNP) or Production Planning and Detailed Scheduling (PP/DS), the system chooses the lowest cost production process model (PPM) or production data structure (PDS) that can meet the time and quantity requirements of the order.

So if your company is under capacity at the time of the sales order subtracted from the production lead time, it makes sense to manufacture the order internally. If, however, your company is over capacity at the date of the sales order subtracted from the production lead time, giving it to a subcontractor can be a better alternative over either having to postpone the customer request or having the customer go to a different source.

A subcontract purchase requisition is connected to the subcontract purchase order through the material that the company is receiving as well as the material that the company is providing to its subcontractor. The planned order shows all of the requirements for the subcontract components. In SAP, subcontractor agreements are brought into

Scheduling
agreements can be
sent from SAP ERP
or from SAP SNC
SAP SCM through the CIF, SAP ERP, or SAP SNC (Figure 15.1), where they are put to use in both SNP, which allocates batched requirements to them, and Global Available to Promise (GATP), which allocates real-time requirements to them.

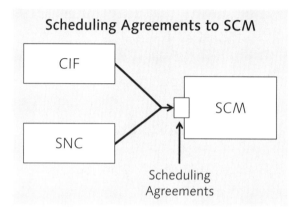

Figure 15.1 How Scheduling Agreements Arrive to SAP SCM

To use subcontracting to the fullest extent, you have a few options. For instance, PPMs can be created. As we stated in Chapter 5, Production Planning and Detailed Scheduling (PP/DS), subcontract modeling in SAP SCM can be performed in either SNP or PP/DS, depending on the level of modeling detail desired.

 Example: Subcontracting Service Parts Repair

Outsourced service parts repair is also a form of subcontracting. This meets the definition because a material is provided from the company that needs the work done to the subcontractor (in this case, not a component, but the whole part). In this situation, the part is kept at the owning company's location and is then sent to the outsourced repair partner before it's sent back to the owning company. Here the subcontracting interacts with Service Parts Planning (SPP). This is the buy versus repair functionality that was described in Chapter 10, SAP Service Parts Planning (SPP), and will be described further in this chapter.

The next area of enhancement to consider is in collaborative forecasting.

> All of the planning methods have advantages and disadvantages.

> Although the SNP optimizer is still not the best solution for high prioritization levels, it can now do limited prioritization.

Prioritizing Demand for the SNP Optimizer

If you've implemented the SNP optimizer and had to give up the concept of prioritizing customers, it's now possible to use optimization with prioritization. As of SAP SCM 5.1, priorities can be set per customer by assigning customer-dependent penalty costs. The higher the penalty cost, the higher the priority of the customer. This is defined in the Business Add-In (BAdI) (/SAPAPO/SDP_RELDATA) and is used to assign penalty cost groups to forecasts and sales orders. With a relatively small amount of data creation and configuration, this allows the provision of a priority to customers that didn't exist before. Companies that benefit from this are those that need to use the optimizer for procurement or make or buy decisions but want to have some limited prioritization. Until release 5.1, the only real way to allocate according to the priority of customers was to use CTM. However, the prioritization capabilities of SAP SCM have now expanded; optimization and prioritization can be used together so that those customers that choose the optimizer aren't totally left out of prioritization functionality.

Prioritization in the SNP optimizer is just one example of how the functionality is constantly evolving

In addition to enhancing older applications such as SNP, SAP SCM has seen rapid development and functionality enhancement of the new applications such as SPP.

Repair Functionality in Service Parts Planning (SPP)

SPP added repair planning functionality as of release 5.1 and was discussed in Chapter 10. This is one of the functionalities that made SPP competitive in the market for service parts planning. With repair planning, SPP can compare the cost and lead time of bringing new parts versus repairing unserviceable parts at any location. This is a powerful functionality that can be used by service organizations and isn't duplicated in any other area of SAP SCM. Repair or buy functionality is well suited to high-value service parts that are cheaper to repair than procure. Almost every company that manufactures or supplies this type of service part has a repair planning program (in various states of effectiveness); this functionality systematizes the repair planning function. This functionality can be used for both service parts sold to customers as well as parts that are used to maintain equipment in the supply chain. In the second case, the parts may be inducted into repair by SAP Plant Maintenance (PM). This functionality requires the maintenance of several types of data:

> Repair or buy functionality is capable of looking into the future and inducting into repair in anticipation of future demand

> Unserviceable (i.e., to be repaired) inventory per product location

> Repair lead times per product location

> Repair costs per item

Buy versus repair functionality allows the company to keep the item at the location it's needed in an unserviceable state, without incurring repair costs, until either a forecasted need increases to a certain level of probability, or until an actual order comes through for the item. Because companies haven't had the ability to do this before in SAP SCM, it requires considerable effort on your part to implement and employ this functionality. But again, this is chiefly a master data exercise in developing repair lead times and costs per product location, so this is quite a bit of work. An important step is developing a method for properly identifying unserviceable items and coding them appropriately in the location product master (which we demonstrate later). However, the benefit is that once complete, the company can let SAP SCM make the buy or repair decisions. Based on the forecast, SAP SCM can induct parts into repair so they can be brought into a serviceable state in time to meet demand.

The functionality works in the following way. When this functionality is activated, the system checks whether enough unserviceable products to be repaired are available and how the costs compare with procuring new products. Alternatively, the system can be configured to skip this analysis and instead always schedule a repair (which is processed as a repair order or refurbishment order by the execution system). A product location can have two statuses with respect to repair or buy functionality. They are listed in Table 15.2.

Coding Options for Repairable Parts	Description
Serviceable	A location product has the serviceable status if the part is either new or has been repaired.
Unserviceable	A location product has the unserviceable status if it hasn't yet been repaired but is scheduled for repair (or is ready to be scheduled for repair).

Table 15.2 Coding Options for Repairable Parts

To get to where the serviceable field is set, you need to first configure the SPP product location tabs to appear.

As we discussed, there's a lot of master data work to get to the point where buy versus repair can be used, but once it's active, it can make decisions much easier.

The Storage and Packaging Data tabs, including new tabs, are shared with SAP Extended Warehouse Management (SAP EWM)

Backward Consumption Enhancement for GATP

For those clients that have already implemented Global Available to Promise (GATP), there's an added ability to specify the period consumption strategy that companies may want to evaluate. SAP's definition of backwards consumption is:

> *This defines the sequence in which periods are consumed by product allocations during backward consumption.*

Backward
consumption should
be evaluated by
companies that have
implemented GATP

This means GATP looks for the planned independent requirement quantity that lies directly before the sales order. Backward consumption means that the company can provide available to promise quantities prior to customer need dates, which may be acceptable to the customer. If the customer accepts the new date, this is a more efficient use of capacity. Backward consumption allows the system to look back even a short period of time prior to the current date, scheduling resources that are unscheduled or under capacity. The company can literally gain business at a very low cost because the production takes place on resources that would have otherwise sat idle.

As Figure 15.2 shows, product availability can be evaluated for products whose lead time end date is prior to the current time of the check, or for products whose lead time spans prior and post the current time.

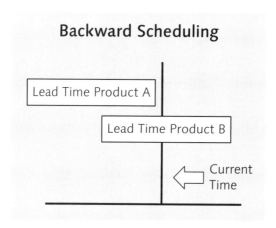

Figure 15.2 Backward Scheduling

The nice thing about this functionality is that there's little that needs to be done to execute it. The functionality is simply opening up to allow GATP to consume more flexibly.

Another area that should be leveraged by companies and that is always a topic of interest is the more advanced methods of safety stock management.

Improving Safety Stock Management

Safety stock is the quantity of redundant inventory that is held to mitigate variability in the supply chain. Its existence is necessary to manage the lead-time variability from supplier to customers. The formula for safety stock is:

Safety Stock = {Z*SQRT(Avg. Lead Time*Standard Deviation of Demand^2 + Avg. Demand^2*Standard Deviation of Lead Time^2}

An old concept and elementary to implement in its more simple forms, safety stock is still significantly and surprisingly mismanaged in the industry. So, implementations of SAP SNP should pay considerable attention to safety stock settings.

 Tip

To stabilize safety stock, there's a rule regarding safety stock that really shouldn't be broken but often is. Safety stock needs to be either kept stable, or depending on the method used, the parameters shouldn't be changed. This means it's not a quantity that is to be altered to meet short-term objectives, and reductions in safety stock values shouldn't be decreed from on high to meet short-term financial objectives. When safety stock is manipulated this way, it's always very damaging for the company.

We recommend using dynamic methods for safety stock, which means that safety stock can and will flex depending on the variability of supplier lead time or the forecast error. For some reason, safety stock isn't well understood in corporate America at least. If lower inventory levels are desired (which they almost always are), then either forecast accuracy must be improved, or supplier lead times or variability must be reduced. There are ways to work on improving both the forecast and supplier reliability through any number of methods. If these inputs are improved, the safety stock (under dynamic methods) will naturally improve with no interference whatsoever. So the rule with safety stock is don't put the cart before the horse. Safety stock is the cart, not the horse.

Safety Stock Functionality Offered by Supply Network Planning (SNP)

SNP provides a high degree of flexibility in terms of safety stock management. The functionality is complete, and unusually straightforward to configure for SAP SCM. The biggest challenge is to understand what it's doing to supply chain inventory and having the discipline to implement it properly. There are two high-level ways in SAP SCM to implement safety stock and then several derivations of each. The two high-level methods are listed in Table 15.3.

Safety Stock Method	Description
Standard	Includes static and dynamic methods
Enhanced	Based on service level

Table 15.3 Safety Stock Methods

The most common method of setting safety stock is referred to as static safety stock, in which the value is hard-coded into the product location master. This value may or may not be an externally calculated value (it may be calculated in Excel or in a third-party inventory management software package), or it may simply be entered based on the planner's experience with the product.

The more advanced safety stock methods in SNP are categorized as enhanced, and this uses some of the same inputs as in standard dynamic forecasting. It allows for the incorporation of service levels in the setting of safety stock levels. As with many areas related to safety stock; the settings for this are on the product location master. However, safety stock can also be set using a safety stock profile (Figure 15.3).

Example: Flexing Safety Stock

The problem with simply hard-coding safety stock is that if it lacks a transparent and consistent method, safety stock has a very strong tendency to become altered in an inconsistent fashion to meet short-term financial or inventory objectives (as just discussed). A second problem is that static safety stock settings don't allow for flexing in the supply chain, which is the primary point of safety stock. If lead times, forecasts, or other input factors change, the safety stocks can rapidly become out of date, causing the company to store either too much or too little inventory. For these reasons, we recommend using the dynamic method or better yet the enhanced method (based on service level) of determining safety stock. The dynamic method provided within standard safety stock functionality does allow for the safety stock to flex along with the supply chain as input factors change over time.

Figure 15.3 The Safety Stock Planning

There are many options to set for the safety stock profile, and this is just a small sample, but we can't cover them all here.

The basic things you need to do when implementing safety stock planning include the following:

As discussed several times, service level planning is a powerful capability

> Determine if you can work from service levels. If you can, and they can be assigned per product location, SAP can drive the safety stock from the service level.

> Find out if you can provide SAP the inputs it needs to perform dynamic safety stock calculation as it enables the system to auto-flex to the changing environment.

> If static methods must be used, make sure that the external system, and the external method, is very robust, and that the policy for setting safety stock is well documented and not subject to manual overrides or to constant changes based on management trends or short-term financial objectives. Companies that are involved in frequently manually changing their safety stock, or changing their safety stock policies, lose many of the benefits of stability that a planning system can provide.

Production Planning/Detailed Scheduling (PP/DS) Implementation Tips

Because master data can always be improved, this topic should be one of the first places to investigate when a planning project begins. PP/DS projects are driven by the need to improve the production process. PP/DS is one of the most detailed of the applications in SAP SCM because PP/DS provides the capability to plan for the many work centers (known as resources in SAP SCM) in the factory. Another reason for PP/DS's detail is due to the fact that the time intervals being planned are short and numerous. The rule of modeling is the higher degree of details modeled, the faster the model can become out of synch with reality, and the more maintenance the model requires to stay in synch.

Production process models (PPMs) and production data structures (PDSs) (the SAP SCM containers for the resources) require accurate and constantly updated constraint information. This shouldn't be considered part of the SAP SCM implementation, but instead needs to be understood as a different project altogether or at least a separate endeavor. That is, one is a planning project, and the other is part of master data maintenance. The planning project sets up a model of the supply chain, while the master data maintenance project declares what the network looks like, what the lead times are between locations, what the constraints of the model are, and so on. The most expertly configured planning system can't substitute for accurate master data maintenance, and the less accurate the master data, the less effect the SAP SCM has in improving the condition of the implementing company. Also, the emphasis on master data should increase when a planning system such as SAP SCM is installed. Only on very rare occasions is the pre-existing level of master data maintenance acceptable prior to a planning system installation.

Constraint information should be developed *before* the SAP SCM project begins and needs to be constantly monitored and updated after the SAP SCM system is live. If a company has not implemented constraint-based production planning in the past, it probably won't have this data and will have to engage in a parallel project to build this master data. SAP SCM can't provide your company with a feasible production plan without quality constraint data.

The way to check the validity of the production plan produced by PP/DS is simple. The first question to ask is whether the factory managers are following the plan, or simply using it as a "guideline."

Master data is one of the most overlooked areas of advanced planning implementation

Example

We worked with one client where the factory plan generated production batch sizes that were so small that they would have seriously compromised the productivity of the plant. These batch sizes were set by the inventory management group that resided at headquarters and who participated and gave input to the implementation. But the production managers, who were out in the factories, were not able to give input. So, the plan became the expression of the will of the inventory management group. But what was forgotten was that the plan doesn't control how the plan is actually executed. So, using perfectly rational logic, the plan managers simply aggregated the individual batch sizes into larger production runs. And unfortunately, it's not uncommon during implementations for the team to forget that if one group is given extra influence on the system configuration, they might use this power to steamroll the other departments. This happens with such frequency that it's pretty safe to say it will continue to happen. So it's important to consider that plans that are seen as unreasonable by the people that execute the plan will probably not be followed.

Real Constraints for Real Planning

We say "real constraints" because it's possible for PPMs and PDSs to exist and be configured in the system, but to not be constrained. This was actually an issue with a company we worked with. Because they had "implemented PP/DS," they thought they were performing constraint-based planning. More on this case study is covered in Chapter 5. PP/DS can be configured without constraints so that it can schedule an infinite number of unconstrained PPMs and PDSs. In fact, this is how the system is run if heuristics are used. However, if there are no constraints, that capacity must be leveled. This client neither constrained the resources, nor ran capacity leveling, and thus ended up with an infeasible plan. To increase the likelihood of getting accurate PPM and PDS information, you can follow these approaches.

> Address the master data maintenance issue early. Begin asking questions as to work center, routing, and BOM accuracy. There will

be areas of improvement. These need to be addressed as soon as possible and need to continue to be addressed. Business groups will always have the content knowledge to update their business information, but they need the assistance of a data-oriented team, a master data maintenance team, to help them systematically manage their master data. This team can ensure consistent processes between business groups, provide tools for master data entry, perform archiving of the master data, and keep the business out of some of the technical details that are not their forte. If you don't have a master data maintenance group that interfaces between IT and the business, consider very strongly creating one.

> Many times factories are distributed internationally, or in areas of the country far from where the planners and those that maintain the SAP SCM system work. In many cases, factories believe that corporate headquarters doesn't take enough input from them. Don't let this happen to your PP/DS project. Stay in constant communication with factories in terms of their constraints, and for SAP SCM, the planned constraints, and update the model to match what the factories are saying. There are a number of methods for implementing this, but they don't need to be complex to be effective.

The issue of by-in extends to every part of the project

Don't Rely Too Heavily on the Planning Book for SAP SCM Success

The planning book does some things well, however it has a learning curve so, planners shouldn't be blamed for not readily and enthusiastically adopting it. If the planning book is holding up user adoption, work around it. There are all types of customized reports that can be developed to support the planners. This will mean more work on future upgrades, but planner acceptance is critical to all of the hard work and expense that was put into the configuration being accepted. One way of doing this is allocating enough money for this activity during the project planning stage. During the implementation, there's often an option between selecting a simple and straightforward solution versus a more complex but fully featured solution. If the more complex and fully featured solution doesn't leave sufficient post-implementation money for system adjustment and employee education, the company is almost always better off selecting the simple solution. This is dramatically the case at not just a few, but at every company we've consulted for.

Provide Ample Non-consulting SMEs or Super Users

Those expected to become experts in the system and evangelists, cannot be expected to keep the same operational responsibility level

While consultants can provide specific expertise, there's a difference in approach and style between a consultant and planner. Consulting firms tend to hire two types of people to help users: those with SAP SCM configuration experience, and those with change management experience. Neither is generally best suited (although there are exceptions) for providing long-term support to planners and users. Secondly, it's quite expensive to continually use consultants to support the company users. SAP SCM reduces the amount of work to be done. So we recommend that one to two of the "line" planners be converted to SAP SCM SMEs (a.k.a super users) to serve as a training and support resource for the other planners. This SME continues in the role after the planners become comfortable with SAP SCM in training new hires, serving as a liaison to first-level and second-level support, and in producing cross-planner or cross-material research on a continual basis.

Ex Example: SAP SCM SMEs

While the concept of a super user isn't at all new, transforming them into SAP SCM SMEs and removing their line responsibilities have a number of advantages. Freed up from day-to-day planning responsibilities, they can really focus on making the other planners better. They also can become valuable conduits for information to support managers. However, if their day-to-day planning responsibilities aren't removed, and their compensation isn't changed, there is little reason to expect them to take their SME "responsibilities" seriously.

Individuals need to be courageous and vocal enough to be viewed as advocates for planners. And, if it's one person, that person must represent all of the planners (if there are two or more people in this role, then each must represent a portion of the planners). This individual must keep good relations with all of the planners and not simply represent the interests of the materials that they used to plan. This is a bigger and more complicated job with political implications, and thus their pay should be increased accordingly. The reason we're being so particular in defining this role is that one of the most common reasons for a lack of planner acceptance is a combination of insufficient support and planners thinking no one is addressing their issues and concerns to either support or to management. In our experience, companies most often expect planners to simply pick up a complex new system with very little tutoring and with little appreciation for the effort they have to put in to learn the system.

 Note: The Myth of Instant Use

The previous discussion leads to a discussion of one of the great myths of product adoption. New technologies, particularly significant technologies, take time to be effectively adopted. For instance, the seatbelt was actually invented in the 1920s (on the race track). It wasn't introduced into passenger cars until the mid-1960s. However, its use was extremely low until the mid-1980s. The same holds true of the printing press. It takes a while for any new technology to go from curiosity to being generally accepted. Full acceptance and adoption comes when the item or concept is no longer seen as an innovation. One example is the arch. At one time, the arch was considered very innovative. Now, it's just part of the backdrop of architecture.

History shows that new technologies are often overestimated in terms of their impact in the short term, but underestimated in the long term

After the Implementation

Implementing companies and outside observers place a great deal of focus on the countdown to go-live. After the go-live and the system is rolled out, there's a tendency to underestimate what happens. A frequent question for SAP consultants interviewing for new projects is how many full lifecycle implementations they've been involved in. This question assumes that the really important work happens during the implementation.

The idea that the interesting work and learning opportunities are primarily in the design stage is a popular myth

However, what is often missed is that much of the diagnostic work efforts occur after the project has gone live. This allows a consultant to get into a lot of the issues that were passed over or even incorrectly designed during the actual implementation. Consumer software is the best example of how inaccurate this general understanding is

For example, after consumers install Excel or Word on their computer, do you think that the most interesting part of the process is over and that the users simply begin using the software at the optimal level? Clearly no one would propose this. Having the software available is just the beginning.

There's a learning curve with all software and because SAP is far more complex than Excel or Word, the learning curve is much steeper. And the learning curve isn't limited to the users of the system because gradually as the system is put into use, information about its capabilities and limitations are communicated up to the executive level, so they begin to think about what other functionality they want to get out of the system in the future.

Improving Usage Efficiency with Model Maintenance Methods

One of the biggest challenges for maintaining an SAP SCM system is to simply understand the master data. When a user or consultant approaches the SAP system, he must be cognizant of the location and product combinations, at a minimum, to progress through the transactions. Too often, this information isn't well documented or easy to find, and employees and consultants end up wasting valuable time hunting and pecking through the system trying to find the right combinations. As anyone who has used SAP can attest, without the right combination, it's impossible to progress through transactions. Finding master data such as the product names in the model, the location names, and so on is very important, and the master data for the SAP SCM application can be found using the methods in Table 15.4.

Methods	Description
SAP tables	The more technical resources can find the master data relationships though looking at tables.
Supply chain engineer	This shows the model master data setup in a graphical form.

Table 15.4 Methods for Finding SAP SCM Master Data

However, neither solution is optimal. Using tables takes significant SAP experience and isn't efficient even for technical experts or the supply chain engineer, because it has a difficult-to-use interface and is rarely used on projects. It also doesn't appear to have received any development in years. Far more preferable to either approach is the creation of a simple website on the company intranet that presents the model setup both in text and graphical form. This way, the model design can be accessed with or without SAP access, which means it can be used by non-SAP resources as well to understand what has been modeled. It's surprising how infrequently we've seen this at companies, and yet how comparatively easy a site like this is to set up. We're also not aware of any consulting companies that offer the creation of a web-based model as a service. While some may consider using SAP Solution Manager for this, Solution Manager is a document management solution, which primarily focuses on storing project documents. It's not a replacement for what we're discussing here. It's something a company would have to either build itself or contract with a non-SAP consulting company to build.

Tip

Using the right tool for the job is critical to the success of any SAP implementation.

In addition to working as an SAP consultant, we also write and maintain the largest non-SAP affiliated SAP SCM blog on the Internet (which you can find at *http://sapplanning.wordpress.com*). Doing this for a number of years, we've become very familiar with the WordPress blog platform. In our view, WordPress is one of the best information management software applications currently available. Either WordPress or other similar software (such as Typepad, which is also quite good) should be the first choice when it comes to selecting a platform to manage information about SAP SCM configuration or master data about the implementation. Blogging software is typically free (although there are some minor costs for upgrading to extra functionality) and constantly improving. It's amazing to us that Microsoft SharePoint has taken over the corporate information/document market. Unfortunately, this is completely counter-effective for information management. However, because Microsoft's relationship with companies is so strong, it's likely to take more than a decade for companies to realize they are migrating their documents to an inefficient platform. We have a hard time convincing either consulting companies or clients that you can't have an efficient and cost-effective implementation with inferior document and information management tools. This is a massive blind spot for the vast majority of companies engaging in IT implementations. However, this blind spot doesn't exist outside of companies as few take information management seriously. There is no such confusion on the web. Many millions of people have started their own blogs, and we often find that blogs started by individuals have better content and more reliable (less promotional) material than nonblog websites. Google seems to think so as well because they rank blogs high in search results. To see for yourself how effective WordPress, or blog-based software is for this type of work, head over to *http://sapplanning.org*.

Modern document and knowledge management concepts and methods have passed many companies by, however, this capability is critical to managing IT projects

Conclusion

The SAP SCM applications can be connected in a number of different ways to address client needs. As SAP SCM has grown, it has meant more applications addressing more areas of functionality. Having a high-level understanding of the overall architecture of SAP SCM is important to making good decisions about which are the best applications, as well as the best areas of the application to configure for a particular company.

Companies often don't realize how much time consultants and users spend simply trying to find combinations of master data that allow the individual to proceed. So every company implementing SAP SCM (and SAP ERP for that matter) should invest in an intranet website that provides detailed information on the basic master data of the configuration (locations, products, planning areas, planning objects, etc.).

From all of the information we've covered in this chapter, it should be clear to you that SAP SCM implementations are not finished when they go live. Significant knowledge is gained after an implementation, if your company is open to understanding how the solution is behaving. Finally, after a system goes live, companies should not cut off the opportunities to learn as use of the system progresses.

16 SAP SCM and ROI

When evaluating the decision to implement a new application in SAP SCM, the most compelling argument for executives is the financial benefit of the implementation. Determining this isn't as simple as it may appear at first glance because as with most analysis, everything rests on the assumptions. Many of the variables to the analysis are unknown and can only be estimated. But the act of going through and evaluating these assumptions can be very educational and beneficial for your company if it's done correctly. However, if biases are involved, the process can easily be degraded.

The mathematics of this type of financial analysis is simple, and it can — and should — be calculated in a small spreadsheet. However, the challenge is digging into a level of detail on the SAP SCM products. For instance, if a particular application can reduce inventory costs by a certain percentage, what is the likelihood that the company will attain this level of improvement? What specific functionality within the SAP SCM application will bring about this improvement? Have other companies obtained a similar improvement? And if so, how was this improvement quantified?

To start your ROI evaluation you have to ask the right questions

By asking and answering these types of questions, a detailed financial analysis of the implementation of different SAP SCM applications can be a truly beneficial exercise.

Return on Investment (ROI)

Not all companies evaluate software and IT investments based on ROI

ROI has become a very popular driver in estimating the potential and actual financial impact of major system implementations. ROI is a standard practice in mergers and acquisitions, as well as in decisions to purchase major pieces of equipment for manufacturing and distribution companies. But its use to justify software acquisition is significantly less understood and less straightforward. In fact, operational and financial practitioners often don't readily accept the use of ROI as a budget justification in software acquisition; even though it's considered standard practice for the purchase of other capital expenditures.

For those companies that do seek to evaluate their ROI, there are two main parts:

> Projected benefits

> Projected costs

Benefits

While costs are relatively easy to estimate, the real issue is the estimation of the benefits. For instance, in the case of a new assembly line, knowing the throughput from technical specifications presents a clear-cut way to calculate the positive potential impact. This isn't the case with software, however. In the software sales process, the industry relies heavily on benchmarking data. For example, you may have heard the following statement:

> *An increase in customer service level by 1% will translate into a 5-10% increase in your revenue.*

This statement may sound reasonable, but the problem is that it's based on the following:

> It depends on the market share and competitive position of the company in question. A direct relationship can't be assumed but rather depends on a number of factors such as the current size of the company's market share, the preferences of the customer base, and so on.

> Service level is directly related to a company's sales only when the company is operating in a more competitive market and lacks significant monopoly power.

> The number itself (5-10% in our example) is very difficult to verify. While this may sound "right," these numbers may have been obtained based on a sample that doesn't represent the company in question or your particular market situation (e.g., company size, level of product line maturity, degree of demand elasticity,... the list goes on and on).

Improvements in Sales

When a company has a higher availability of finished goods or service parts, it loses fewer sales, and as it improves its reputation, it tends to take sales from other firms. Overall, SAP SCM is designed to improve the availability of the company's product. For instance, Demand Planning (DP) can improve the forecast, putting the company in a better position to meet future demand. SAP Forecasting and Replenishment (F&R) can improve the in-stock position at the retail store, resulting in fewer lost sales. And Global Available to Promise (GATP) specifically communicates the future availability of goods to customers. Companies that can make reliable commitments into the future regarding their product availability also gain more business, generally speaking, than those that don't. This type of benefit is difficult to quantify because it depends on some of the following factors:

> The current in stock and commitment capability of the company.

> The competition in the industry.

> The buying relationships between the company and its customers.

Software-based ROI is not always sustainable

Another key component of software-based ROI is an assumption that whatever improvement has been achieved is sustainable, but this isn't necessarily always the case. You also need to understand that it's not automatic, so that you have an appropriate appreciation for the complexities involved with system adoption and system lifecycle management. The following are some of the reasons why software improvements are not always sustainable:

> Systems, as we pointed out previously, don't go live and immediately reach the top level of usage by users, just people don't become experts in Excel or PowerPoint the day they buy and install the software on their computers. Rather, the system goes through a period of trial and error and learning. Some systems, and consumer software applications, are eventually adopted and become relied on applications, but others don't. Success is never assured.

> Business and market situations never stay the same; they evolve multidirectionally. This brings an additional component into the benefit estimate: the quality of the SAP ERP implementation and how well it addresses not only the current but also the future situation.

> The quality of implementations varies significantly. Stories of disastrous experiences of companies going through multimillion dollar initiatives aren't uncommon.

> Some implementations begin well, but ill-advised changes are made to the configuration, or the system "drifts" from its original design,

330

causing the value of the system to decline. On the other side, some implementations are mis-designed from the beginning, but through diagnosis and adjustments, they are eventually made effective, improving the value of the implementation to the company.

Finally, the part of the ROI benefit calculation most open to a challenge is the link between operational improvements, especially the financial results of forecast accuracy increase and increase in inventory visibility across the enterprise. As noted earlier, the use of benchmarking is most commonly employed in benefit calculations. However, the applicability of a given benchmark is a very serious question (due to the sample on which the benchmark was based) as are the specifics of the current market segment (in which the company operates).

This doesn't mean that the ROI calculation for a large software implementation is a futile exercise. However, ROI estimation requires a significant amount of thought and analysis specific to the company's particular business situation and how this situation will evolve in the future to be truly effective.

Costs

The cost side of ROI is far simpler, although it also has its caveats. While there are some very straightforward cost components, such as license and maintenance fees, SAP ERP implementations contain many costs that are either "hidden" or don't have a constant nature.

First, the costs of implementing a new system must be separated from upgrading an existing one. Typically, labor dominates both of these initiatives; according to Forrester Research, labor constitutes only 65% of total cost for implementation versus 76% for upgrades.

ROI evaluation needs to include all costs —constant and variable

Second, there is a difference between what a company intended to implement and what a company actually ends up implementing. This is due to an almost inevitable product footprint extension, which is a well-documented issue in system implementations generally.

Don't underestimate
internal support
costs

Third, companies frequently underestimate their internal support costs. With a new system, a need for a new set of skills becomes mandatory. A major SAP ERP implementation almost always leads to a headcount increase in both operations (due to a rising need for people who know how to effectively use new technology, so-called "super users") as well as information technology support. Strangely enough, this relatively simple fact is almost always underestimated.

The following is a list of the areas that may be positively affected due to an SAP SCM implementation:

> Inventory management

> Reduction in transportation expense

> Reduction in labor cost

> Reduction in direct material cost

> Reduction in indirect material cost

> Reduction in selling expense

> Reduction in procurement expense

> Increase in R&D efficiency

> Increase in use of fixed assets

> Improvement in gross margin

> Increase in incremental revenue from increases in values

> Key financial ratios

These value areas may be impacted as the result of operational improvement in multiple functional areas. Depending on the situation and surrounding circumstances, all, some, or only one of these value areas may be influencing the ROI estimation. Therefore, a comprehensive, forward-looking analysis must be done to determine the true financial impact on ROI and its sources. Let's describe some areas (as they pertain to benefit generation) in more detail. We'll address several of these improvement areas that can be tracked to specific applications next.

Inventory Management

You can achieve inventory improvements using the various applications within SAP SCM, including SAP DP, SNP, SNC, and SPP. SAP Demand Planning (DP) can improve the quality of your forecast, ensuring that your "targets" are being planned to as high a likelihood of being consumed by demand as possible.

Supply Network Planning (SNP) takes inventory positions throughout the entire network into account when making procurement, movement, and sometimes production decisions. Its safety stock functionality can help protect the in-stock position with minimal inventory that adjusts with the supply chain.

SAP SCM provides many applications for improving inventory

In addition, SAP Supplier Network Collaboration (SAP SNC) reduces inventory by improving the visibility of the system between supply chain partners. This transparency results in fewer inventory mistakes. And Service Parts Planning (SPP) can redistribute parts in the field; while this increases the costs of planned transportation, it decreases the costs of expedited transportation and increases the use of inventory.

Generally, SAP SCM helps establish realistic schedules for production procurement and consistent priorities, so that everyone knows the most important job to work on at all times. Visibility of future requirements helps production and procurement prepare for high-level capacity problems, and also helps suppliers anticipate and meet these needs. As changes to demands or supplies occur, SAP SCM helps identify the impact on production and purchasing.

Labor Costs

In the area of warehousing, SAP Extended Warehouse Management (EWM) can increase the use of labor, reduce the need to put away material through the use of cross docking, and better balance work levels to mean less overtime and a higher use of the labor in the ware-

Better planning and efficient use of labor keep costs in line

house. Better visibility and more powerful tools for planning result in fewer planners and less time spent expediting orders. Additionally, Production Planning and Detailed Scheduling (PP/DS) improves the use of production personnel by allocating them to make products that have a high likelihood of being consumed quickly and not sitting in inventory.

SAP SCM's overall planning functionality can improve the likelihood that employees and contractors will be working on the right things. In terms of the groups performing the planning, controlling, and monitoring, SAP SCM can improve the efficiency of these groups, freeing up resources for other tasks.

Transportation Costs

The improvements in transportation can be direct and indirect. Indirectly, SNP better manages the network, resulting in fewer expedited shipments and a more effective management of material in the fields. SAP TM means more efficiently scheduled and loaded trucks, resulting in fewer loads and lower direct transportation costs. Effective bid and carrier management can also result in lower indirect transportation costs through the selection of better alternatives. And analyzing transportation history can help reduce costs through outsourcing geographic areas that aren't serviced in a cost effective manner internally.

Using SAP EWM to improve warehouse efficiency and productivity

SAP Extended Warehouse Management (SAP EWM) can improve the productivity of the warehouse, which allows for a more efficient processing of vehicles and improves their turnaround times. SAP EWM's yard management functionality also allows it to better manage the yard and reduce the amount of time that vehicles sit in the yard. In addition, SAP Event Management (SAP EM) keeps planners up to date on materials in various stages of transportation throughout the supply network. This allows them to see if material is going to arrive on time, or whether they need to expedite other material or perform other adjustments to meet the schedule.

Key Financial Ratios

Ratio analysis provides another way to look at the impact of an SAP ERP system. Three ratios illustrate the effect — two related to liquidity and one to operating performance:

> **Inventory turnover** (Cost of Sales/Inventory). Low inventory turnover can indicate possible overstocking and obsolescence. It may also indicate deeper problems of too much of the wrong kind of inventory, which can create shortages of needed inventory for production and sales. High turnover indicates better liquidity and superior materials management and merchandising.

> **Ex** Example
>
> Let's say for a $10 million company, the current number of inventory turns is 2.5. With a 20% inventory reduction, the number of inventory turns increases to 3.1. It's important to be wary of inventory turnover increase without at least maintaining the existing level of customer service. Should your service level go down, an increase in inventory turnover would signify your increase in out-of-stock situations.

> **Days of Receivables** (365 * 1/(Sales/Receivables)). This ratio expresses the average time in days that receivables are outstanding. It's a measure of the management of credit and collections. Generally, the greater the number of days outstanding, the greater the probability of delinquencies in accounts receivable. The lower the number of days, the greater the cash availability. With an 18% reduction in receivables, the current days of receivable of 73 days can be reduced to 60. This means $356,200 is available for other purposes.

> **Return on Assets** (Profit Before Taxes/Total Assets). This ratio measures the effectiveness of management in employing the resources available to it. Several calculations are necessary to determine the return on assets.

Obviously, many other benefits can result from a successful SAP SCM implementation as we mentioned earlier. But each implementation is different, so each company will benefit differently. Regardless of the benefits you reap, however, you'll need a solid method for calculating the ROI from these benefits.

ROI Estimation Recommendations

In this section, we'll look at some recommendations for you to consider when addressing the complexity and ambiguity of ROI calculations for major SAP SCM implementations:

1. Determine the most likely areas for operational improvement.

2. Ascertain the way to translate operational improvements into financial results.

3. Validate projected operational improvement ranges with high level but comprehensive analysis.

4. Calculate the relevant financial bottom-line impact by value area.

5. Adjust calculations made in number 4 to reflect:

   – Company's competitive situation

   – Company's specific situation for a given value area

   – Company's size

   – Company's operational and distribution model

6. Address the time phasing of the benefits.

7. Separate one-time impacts from recurring benefits. Be careful not to double count.

8. Address the sustainability of benefits.

9. Execute benefit sensitivity analysis, including sensitivity to macroeconomic factors.

10. Optionally disregard certain benefits based on anticipated financial impact and complexity of execution.

11. Finalize the solution footprint and implementation cost. Make sure that you allow for contingencies in both labor and time.

 Note: Differences in ROI

How is the ROI for SAP SCM different from ROI for SAP ERP or other supply chain software? Well, there are some similarities in the ROI within SAP ERP, SAP SCM, and non-SAP solutions because three of the four SAP ERP applications directly impact the supply chain. But because SAP SCM has more advanced functionality, there are opportunities for more benefits. However, one of the major benefits from SAP ERP is the integrated nature of the data that the applications provide between financial information and supply chain information. These are not factors added to the ROI of SAP SCM.

ROI Estimation: Managing the Process

Knowing the right categories of costs and benefits to look for is only one part of the process. This is the content portion of the endeavor, but there's a lot more to it. Just as important as what is looked at is how it's looked at and who is looking. Now let's point out some important considerations that, if followed, can greatly improve the quality of the SAP SCM implementation value estimate.

Getting the Right Input

When calculating ROI, it's important to include significant detail in your assumptions. ROI should not be estimated using only financial resources or using only implementation resources. Rather, members from the business, IT, and finance teams, as well as those with expertise in SAP SCM, should be involved in the evaluation. ROI development is multidisciplinary, and only an informed team can develop a realistic ROI value that has high predicative capability.

Selecting the Right People

Finally, while it's not an industry practice currently, the ROI estimation should not be developed by the firm that would receive the implementation work, or by the software company (in this case SAP), due to conflicts of interests. Rather, the financial analysis should be performed either by the company itself or by a consulting company that isn't in line to receive the implementation work. This issue is often passed over as unimportant, but the need to prevent bias from entering the ROI analysis should be rather obvious.

Be careful to have the right people perform your ROI analysis to ensure the integrity of your results

Many companies may tout their experience in performing these types of analysis, and it's true that both software companies and consulting companies have groups that specialize in this type of analysis. However, in this case, experience is inferior to objectivity. When the consulting or software company leads the analysis, the estimate will almost always be too high. Secondly, there's no reason these skills can't be leveraged by having the company lead the analysis, with the support of the software or consulting resources.

Optimally, the final decision making on the value estimate needs to reside with the company and not the consulting or software company. The lead selected for this role must be sufficiently experienced, capable, and preferably have significant exposure to consulting and software companies, and may even have worked for them. If this type of person can't be made available, plenty of independent contractors will jump at the opportunity to take on this role. Preferably, this contractor won't have preexisting personal relationships with either the software or consulting resources on the team.

To borrow an analogy from the SAP SCM application, good value estimation is a bit like collaborative forecasting. The more groups that are actually on the team, the more realistic the value estimate will generally be. Software and consulting companies want to dominate the process, but as it's the company making the purchase decision, the company needs to control the estimation process. The best way to do this is to control the team member assignments and set strict rules governing the contributory role and the final decision-making role (Figure 16.1).

Estimates are more realistic when there is good collaboration between the team groups

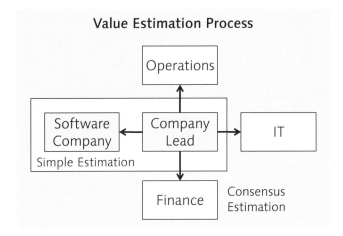

Figure 16.1 Value Estimation

Allowing Enough Time

Based on past experience, the amount of time needed varies depending on whether the team is predominantly internal or external, or whether it's a mix. This is particularly true if the entire estimation team is external to the company. Here the consultants need to get up to speed on the company before they can effectively work on the value estimate. These duration projects are typically filled with many unexamined assumptions.

Don't Overemphasize Finance

Finance professionals are integral to developing value estimations because they quantify both costs and benefits. However, there's a tendency in value estimation projects for finance to begin developing models before assumptions are checked. Benefits that may be readily accepted by a finance resource may not be considered valid by a representative from the business. This is one of the reasons for the multidisciplinary team. It can be frustrating for finance: When asked whether a particular functionality will increase benefits or reduce costs a certain amount, the response of the person from the business will often be, "It depends." But while this may be frustrating, reality is often complicated.

Don't over-
emphasize finance
and have a data
expert on your
evaluation team

The entire value estimation is based on assumptions. It's really the job of the business to doublecheck the assumptions that end up being quantified, particularly with regards to benefits. IT normally evaluates the assumptions regarding hardware and maintenance costs. The software company provides licensing and consulting costs, and the consulting partner is on the hook for implementation costs. Finance can't evaluate these assumptions by themselves because they lack the content knowledge.

Assign a Data Expert to the Team

Value assessments require data pulled from production systems to provide the support for the final ROI number. This is one very good reason why they can't be completed in two weeks. The data requests should be submitted far in advance of need because they aren't mission critical, and thus tend to fall down in the queue as more urgent data requests supersede them.

For this reason, a resource who knows the ins and outs of the data infrastructure organizations in the company should be assigned part time to the team. This person's responsibilities are primarily at the beginning of the project, although it's helpful to have them at the final presentation, as questions of assumptions often lead to questions of data, which can often be answered by this resource.

Consider a Range or Sensitivity Analysis

The issue with providing a single ROI value is that it gives a bit of a false impression regarding the certainty of the value. As a value assessment progresses, the team gradually selects some assumptions over others. The combination of all of the selected assumptions ends up being the ROI. However, providing different values based on different assumptions can help bring a higher level of reality to the process. It can also help bring in people who were not part of the value estimation process into the discussion during presentation. Meeting participants can then begin to understand the analysis more fully and agree or disagree with it. If the presentation were just about presenting one ROI value, it could be accomplished by email. The presentation should be focused on presenting the analysis, and this means the different considered options.

Make the Assumptions Transparent

The following are two sentences that you don't want to hear during a value estimation presentation:

> "We think these estimates are conservative."
> "Everything you're asking about is in the appendix."

Both of these statements give a strong indication that information isn't being shared freely. We've been in many presentations, and on the presenting side, when these exact statements have been made, and there has never been a legitimate reason for it.

These statements are designed to prevent questioners from going where the presenters don't want the questioner to go. When these types of statements are made, they can quickly be put to a stop if the most senior person in the room declares, *"That isn't the way we're conducting this meeting."* If the company lead is giving the presentation, there is far less likelihood of this happening in the first place.

The Calculations

Get the particpants involved in the evaluation

Building on the point of transparency in the previous section, something we haven't seen but think should be done is to provide copies of the actual ROI spreadsheet to the meeting participants. Letting the participants manipulate the values themselves brings them into the process, makes the variable nature of the analysis more transparent, and helps enhance understanding.

How to Set Up and Run the Value Presentation Meeting

In our experience, the value estimation presentation is far too formal. The presenters, who often are consulting or software company reps, are intent on making a big impression. Theater doesn't have a role in logical decision making. This is where having the company lead managing the presentation really pays off. For someone who has a stable job at the company and who isn't being compensated on whether software is implemented, they probably won't much care what the value estimate ends up being. That is exactly who you want to lead the presentation.

It's not necessary for anyone but the lead to present because he has made the final determination of the value. Allowing the software or consulting company reps to stand up and present during this meeting can — and often will — lead to dilution of the company lead's message. Smart companies will not send the lead mixed messages; they will give them the authority to manage the process from beginning to end, which means the final presentation as well.

After the presentation is complete, a general question-and-answer session usually follows. Now is the time for other team members to offer their views. However, no assumption should be off the table from review or analysis, and the team members need to show up with all of their supporting data and conclusions. If they are not ready to do this, the meeting must be postponed. Also, difficult questions shouldn't be pushed off or evaluated in private. This means a sufficient amount of time needs to be scheduled for the meeting. Two hours is fine; even three hours is warranted for complex software decisions and is perfectly acceptable given the importance of the decisions to the company. There is some debate as to whether people can stay at a high level of engagement for more than three hours, so that seems like a good upper limit for a meeting like this. The goal should be to come out of the meeting with a decision on whether to recommend that the implementation go forward. In our experience, if the assumptions are not evaluated in that meeting, they generally won't be.

> The goal of the meeting should be to make a decision

ROI Presentations in Different Countries

The process just described will lead to the minimization of bias and the most objective results for the ROI estimation. We don't think that every company will necessarily attain this state because it's not the way most ROI analyses are done, and it takes more than one book to make people aware that a practice has logical errors in it. Additionally, different cultures will have different interests in implementing this process. The more hierarchical the culture, the less likely this model will be implemented. We can't know how every company within every country will respond to the process we have described; we have simply described a process that will result in a high quality output.

Conclusion

ROI is a critical method for companies selecting from a number of competing projects. ROI can be used to select not only applications within SAP SCM but also the functionality to be implemented within the application.

Surprisingly, ROI is still not completely accepted as a method for software selection. This may have something to do with the assumptions that are used during the ROI analysis. However, to do this requires a very focused approach to investigating the underlying assumptions of what can best improve the company. Questioning these assumptions is critical. It's not necessary to assume that the stated company need or current planning shortcoming is the actual one. As with anything, the really interesting discoveries are made when the most basic and elementary assumptions are questioned. We have seen value estimation projects that have used overly optimistic assumptions, and this may have to do with the incentives of the team performing the value estimation. However, done correctly, ROI is a very rational way to evaluate the benefits of software projects.

17

Conclusion

We hope this book has met its objectives of serving as a primer to SAP SCM and of providing a jumping off point to other areas of research in the different applications. Instead of simply recapping the previous chapters, this final chapter provides observations from our research into SAP SCM and our implementation experience. We want to include the most important concepts that help improve the implementations of SAP SCM and other advanced planning software. These concepts range from the relationship between implementations complexity and implementation success to "real life" supply chain modeling.

Secondly, we think it's important to describe some broad trends that are affecting SAP SCM and that we project will continue to affect SAP SCM, although the degree of the effect isn't entirely predictable. These trends range from likely increases in energy prices in the future to collaborative planning in companies.

Real-Life Supply Chain Modeling

As we provided an overview of the functionality of each of the applications throughout the book, we briefly touched on implementation issues of planning. As a general observation, implementability tends to take a back seat to functionality in discussions regarding planning systems. This method of interpretation isn't unique to planning software or even to software in general. For example, the consumer electronics and automobile markets also have this predisposition. Periodicals that cover new products in these industries primarily focus on initial impressions and functionality, with an emphasis on sophisticated features and capability, rather than actual usage and long-term maintainability.

Implementation planning should include evaluation of functionality, implementation time, and maintenance requirements

Because this line of discussion is so infrequently covered, we don't want to overlook the real-life issues and limitations of advanced planning software. Any solution design eventually approved for implementation has implications not only for software functionality but also for the effort required to keep the solution working properly. This is true of any system implemented, but is especially true of planning systems because they are complex to install and to maintain.

 Note: Complexity Versus Maintainability

Across SAP SCM, more specific and detailed planning configurations can provide higher accuracy, which can result in higher supply chain efficiency and lower overall costs. However, the more complex the solution that is developed, the more maintenance it requires. This is because a finer level of detail varies more than a lower level of detail, and setting up and changing the configuration at a finer level of detail makes more work. Anyone who has tried to update a very detailed project plan can appreciate this. So, a company must be committed to both the upfront effort and expenses of the design and implementation, as well as the effort and expense of the long-term maintenance costs. Too often, these long-term maintenance costs are not properly considered, and a company ends up with a less effective solution than it could have had because the more complex solution the company designed isn't properly maintained.

As an example, let's look at one SAP SCM application and differentiate the maintenance effort required based on the configuration selected. Table 17.1 provides a short synopsis of the maintenance effort generally required for each solution as it relates to SNP; however, the table generalizes to other areas of SAP SCM as well.

SNP Method	Effort in Maintenance
Heuristic	Easier to set up, and also easier to maintain.
Capable to Match (CTM)	CTM can be a moderate maintenance solution, but this depends on the implementation complexity regarding level of detail modeled. The tendency is to make too many profiles, each of which requires maintenance.
Optimization	The highest maintenance solution. A client must be willing to perform both the upfront work to obtain costing information as well as maintain this data. Also, optimization is bound by constraints that must be updated as the business changes.

Table 17.1 SNP Maintenance Plan

Figure 17.1 displays how different SNP methods of planning rank in terms of data quality and the type of effort required to support the implementation.

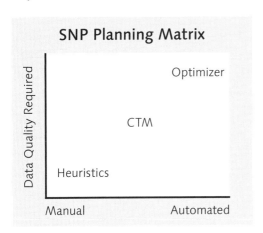

Figure 17.1 SNP Planning Matrix

Changing Constraints

Companies often create constraints for their models without first considering that constraints change as time passes. In the area of manufacturing planning, process manufacturing constraints are typically the most variable, and discrete manufacturing constraints tend to be the most stable. However, both require significant maintenance. There simply needs to be a constant investment in updating constraint information.

For Production Planning and Detailed Scheduling (PP/DS), this means updating the production process models (PPMs) and production data structures (PDSs) to reflect the new realities of the manufacturing floor. For SAP Transportation Management (SAP TM), this means updating the vehicle resources and the delivery constraints on the locations.

The same rules that apply to constraint maintenance apply to other applications that don't use constraints. For instance, for SAP Event Management (SAP EM), resources constraints are not the issue, but messages are. When deciding which events to track, you should consider that they must be detailed enough to provide the necessary level of feedback to planners for track and trace but not so detailed that the solution becomes difficult to maintain. This way, the same trade off between complexity and maintainability exists across the applications.

We've frequently observed at different clients that insufficient consideration has been given to the long-term changes in the business and the long-term maintenance of planning solutions. It's important to consider that while software may be implemented to meet an immediate need, successful implementations continue in operation for years and need to be designed with this perspective in mind from the very beginning.

Missed Opportunities

In the application chapters, we provided an overview of each application. In this chapter, we take a broader view of the entire suite to see which applications have received the greatest market acceptance and why, as well as consider which applications may have been overlooked by companies. In this section, we'll focus on two applications that are underappreciated and underused in the market, and we'll explain why.

Looking at SAP Transportation Management More Broadly

SAP Transportation Management (SAP TM) is one of the oldest and most straightforward of the SAP SCM applications to implement. However, of the older applications (DP, SNP, PP/DS, GATP, SAP TM), it's the least widely installed. From our experience with SAP TM, we can see no functionality-based reason for this. We consider SAP TM to be a stable and fully featured product and one of the easier applications to install.

SAP TM Functionality Covers Both Shipper Owned and Outsourced Transportation

SAP TM can be used to perform the actual vehicle scheduling if the company actually owns the transportation vehicles. If the transportation is outsourced, SAP TM can be used to manage the carriers. If a carrier such as UPS or FedEx is selected as an outsourced supply chain partner, it's not necessary or even possible to perform routing or delivery window management for them. They include various shippers' freight and perform the navigation and routing themselves.

SAP TM is stable, easier to install, and effective at improving operations

However, even when outsourced transportation is used, it's still necessary to manage these carriers. There is functionality in SAP TM that can flex no matter how the company has set up its transportation relationships. Also, it's very uncommon for transportation to be completely in-house or completely outsourced. For instance, SAP TM could be used by the same shipping to schedule an internal less than truckload fleet, while managing the outsourced long haul trucking, air, and ocean carriage components of the company's transportation.

 Note: The Opportunity in Transportation

Making transportation a focus at companies is a serious challenge for firms that spend most of their supply chain IT budgets on demand planning or ATP functionality. Transportation costs represent a high percentage of the nonmanufacturing supply chain costs. And, because of corporate neglect, there is significant value to be unlocked in transportation planning.

The flexibility and straightforward implementability of SAP TM, along with the significant sub-optimization of the transportation management at many companies, leads us to recommend SAP TM for evaluation for many companies that are looking to use SAP SCM to improve areas of their supply chain that may currently be underserved by systems.

SPP and the Industry Need for Service Parts Planning

Until the mid-1990s, off-the-shelf service parts planning applications did not exist, so you had to perform custom development on a service parts planning project

SAP has desired to break into the service parts planning market that, even up to the time of this writing, has been a small market dominated by just a few niche players. SAP Service Parts Planning (SPP) packages have been sold into accounts, but the sales have been more limited than the market need for service parts planning. This market is smaller than it should be for a number of reasons, some political and others technological.

SAP, along with the other vendors in this market, is waging a battle to educate resistant corporations on the importance of service parts planning. As SAP's customers become more saturated with SAP SCM functionality, SAP naturally searches for new markets in which to sell SAP SCM. As of yet, this has not translated into many new implementations. Part of the reason is the inherent lack of interest in service management on the part of corporate America. This is, in our opinion, because few companies place the same emphasis on service management as they do on the production side of their business. This isn't simply hyperbole; in addition to service parts not being a business, there's an actual movement away from service generally. For example, there's ample evidence that products are becoming less, not more, serviceable. Companies also often miss the counter-cyclical benefits to service parts. During economic downturns, a strong service parts capability and sales flow can help reduce the reduction in sales as consumers and businesses opt to repair instead of replace items.

 Tip: Service Parts Planning

> There is no production planning in service parts planning. Production planning is performed by companies that produce the item as a finished good. If a company produces its own service parts, the parts produced are part of a separate finished goods process and not part of the service parts process. So, the output of SPP can be sent directly to SAP EWM or to MM. SPP is similar to SNP in that it also can interact with GATP so that a company can provide ATP for both finished goods and service parts.

We believe that many companies are missing out on the benefits provided by these applications because they are unaware of how suboptimal their transportation and service parts operations actually are. It's the job of strategy consultants, in both SAP and in other consultancies, to highlight the ROI of these products, and for some reason they have either not made this a point of emphasis, or their clients have not been accepting of the message. Part of this has to do with the fact that not many consulting companies have service parts planning experience, and this is very important for helping to guide a client in an SPP evaluation.

ROI estimation for SAP SCM is discussed in Chapter 16

SAP SCM and Larger Supply Chain Trends

SAP SCM is responding to individual customer requests as well as larger industry-wide and even environmental pressures. We thought it important to explain what these trends are so that SAP SCM can be understood from the broadest view. A few of these trends affecting SAP SCM are listed here:

> Energy issues

> The increased rapidity of inventory turnover

> Increased supply chain monitoring

> Collaborative planning trends

Energy Issues

These trends of globalized manufacturing may be incompatible with increased energy prices. If you look at current supply chain networks, it's apparent that they were based on assumptions of cheap energy, which will likely not hold up in the future.

It's generally agreed by scientists that the period of cheap energy is coming to an end. The movie *A Crude Awakening* explains in detail what it defines as the term "peak oil" and its implications for civilization generally. Peak oil is the point in time at which half the world's oil reserves have been consumed, and at that point every subsequent barrel of oil becomes more difficult and more costly to retrieve. Unfortunately, we appear to be getting close to this point at the time of this writing.

This means that our present transportation methods and networks, which are based on assumptions of long-term cheap energy, have to change. There are many pieces to the solution, including alternative fuels and lighter vehicles that are often discussed and well known. Most people are familiar with the concept of hybrid vehicles, but for some reason, commercial vehicles tend to get left out of this discussion. Even less frequently discussed is the energy saving benefits from intelligent transportation planning, navigation, and vehicle scheduling. Many companies still consider transportation an afterthought. But as transportation costs begin to rise, reflecting higher fuel costs, companies will have to take notice.

The SAP SCM suite in its entirety implicitly addresses energy efficiency. This isn't unique to SAP SCM, however. Advanced planning in general is dedicated to making and moving the right material to the right location so that energy-intensive activities such as reordering and repositioning are minimized. So, planning systems are naturally "green." However, several applications explicitly address energy efficiency as listed in Table 17.2.

We expect these applications to grow in prominence as the costs of energy continue to rise

Application	Energy Impact
SAP TM	SAP TM promotes the optimal use of freight within container, as well as optimizing the route of the vehicle. Both of these actions help reduce unnecessary movement and reduce the numbers of vehicles, and thus engines, that must be deployed.
SAP Service Parts Planning	SPP improves the geographic positioning of service parts. Positioning is very important for service parts because if incorrectly positioned, normal demand won't necessarily consume the part before it becomes obsolete. SPP can help reduce the repositioning of parts, reduce the need for new parts to be transported, and help determine which parts should be repaired and when. All of these are transportation saving and thus energy saving activities.
SAP Event Management	SAP EM provides visibility in the supply chain. This can help in the reduction of expedited orders, which are very energy intensive because they often use more energy consumptive methods of transportation. SAP EM is an important tool in reducing the lack of coordination between supply chain partners that result in excess product movement.

Table 17.2 Energy Efficient SAP SCM Applications

As energy costs rise, the high energy consuming supply chains that have been designed up to this point will need to be re-evaluated, and SAP SCM offers you many possible improvements in energy consumptions in a variety of areas.

Increased Rapidity of Inventory Turnover

At the most basic level, having inventory sit in a warehouse costs you money. It costs money in terms of capital, inventory obsolescence, spoilage, shrinkage, and so on. And there are costs in the warehouse related to putaway and picking. Based on this, some believe that traditional warehousing is being replaced by cross docking, which is the unloading of inbound materials directly into an outbound truck, train, and so on, without physically taking the material into inventory.

Slotting and rearrangement, as described in Chapter 11, help improve the efficiency of removing and shipping materials from a warehouse

Fortunately, SAP EWM offers a number of advanced warehousing capabilities such as cross docking, slotting, and rearrangement, along with the supporting functionalities of labor management and yard management. These are all direct factors that are important for increasing the rapidity of inventory turnover. Most of the other applications address inventory turnover as well, though in an indirect fashion. As we'll see later in this chapter, this rapidity of inventory movement is changing inbound material management at factories as well.

4PLs are non-asset-based supply chain intermediaries that use information systems to enhance coordination or management of 3PLs

Increased Supply Chain Monitoring

The number of partners in the supply chain has been increasing rapidly over the past decade, and it doesn't appear to be abating. These partners include the following:

> Contract manufacturers

> Third-party logistics (3PLs) providers

> Fourth-party logistics (4PLs) providers

> Pure transportation companies

> Subcontractors

While the number of supply chain partners has increased, the information systems to manage the interactions between them haven't kept pace. The inability of 3PLs to integrate with one another has lead to the rise of a concept called fourth-party logistics (4PL). This is a configuration and business arrangement that is really just getting started.

To tie these partners together, supply chain monitoring systems have come front and center as the logical mechanism to accomplish a more integrated supply chain. SAP EM is designed to address this need in the supply chain. SAP EM can monitor activities within SAP SCM and SAP ERP, as well as any number of systems that supply chain partners use. It does this by having a messaging infrastructure that can accept messages from a variety of formats. For instance, the ASN, which was previously used for EDI communication, can be read by SAP EM. This is just one example, but there are many others. In this way, SAP EM can allow the monitoring of material movements and supply chain activities that are performed at partners and in non-SAP systems.

3PLs move and store material for shippers and are an important part of the supply chain environment

Collaborative Planning Trends

Collaboration is one of the strongest trends in supply chain management currently. SAP Supplier Network Collaboration (SAP SNC) is the SAP SCM application that most directly addresses this need. SAP SNC supports myriad collaborations and not just supplier collaboration (Figure 17.2).

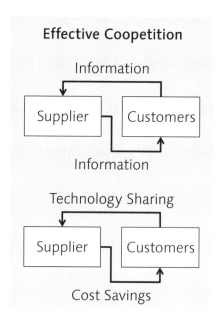

Figure 17.2 Figure Cooperation Beyond Information Sharing

➕ Tip: Advanced Collaboration

Exchanging information is ideally just the beginning of the collaborative relationship. Many of the Japanese manufacturers have become successful, partially by enabling their suppliers with information and guidance, which leads to richer relationships in other ways.

SAP SNC is attractive to companies attempting to improve their coordination and planning along their current processes; however, SAP SNC may be even more appropriate if your company is altering the way you manage its operations. This is symptomatic of a change in how companies across industries are taking a fresh look at how they source and manufacture items. Here's an example from the automobile industry, but the trend discussed generalizes across many industries. According to the book *Why Your World Is About to Get a Lot Smaller* by Jeff Rubin, original equipment manufacturers are increasingly managing the brand, letting suppliers do more value-added activities, and then integrating with them. It could be that success in many industries will be increasingly based on who can best integrate and manage their supplier base to provide a cohesive output.

This builds on a long-term trend of production and sourcing becoming increasingly separated from design and brand management as well as product servicing and maintenance. This model requires visibility and free-flowing information to work. SAP SNC and SAP EM both support this.

Product lifecycle management is how design changes are incorporated from OEMs to suppliers; SAP PLM capability is sprinkled throughout various applications

Collaborative Aspects of SAP SCM Applications Besides SAP SNC

It's important to consider that while SAP SNC is the conduit for collaboration, the data is eventually sent through SAP SNC to a specific SAP SCM or SAP ERP application. For instance, demand collaboration involves both SAP SNC and DP with the potential of improving the quality of the demand plan. So it's important to consider that through SAP SNC, the entire SAP SCM and SAP ERP suite is becoming more collaborative. Many of the types of collaboration have an explicit workflow designed around them in SAP SNC and include collaborations such as the following:

> Demand

> Inventory

> Procurement

> Capacity

> Transportation

These are standard workflows in SNP and were described in detail in Chapter 12, SAP Supplier Network Collaboration (SNC). However, there is a more holistic collaboration that isn't necessarily based around a specific SAP SCM workflow. It's not well known, which is why we want to take this opportunity to describe it.

Example: Retail Collaboration

Depending on how SAP Forecasting and Replenishment (F&R) is implemented, there can also be collaboration management issues. That is, F&R has the ability to share in-store stock information with manufacturers/suppliers. However, allowing for some notable exceptions, retailers for whatever reason are often less than enthusiastic about sharing this information with their suppliers. We can't prove this, but this cultural predisposition may be a contributing factor to the lack of F&R implementations.

Manufacturing Signals

As described in Chapter 12, capacity collaboration allows a customer to see the work orders within the factories of contact manufacturers. This information allows a company to monitor work performed at factories located anywhere globally. This is one popular method of production collaboration. However, things are changing in manufacturing in a way which extends past the conventional conception of collaboration.

What this new method of collaborative manufacturing will end up being called seems to be between the alternatives of integrated "collaborative manufacturing," or a "collaborative manufacturing environment." However, these terms are so loosely defined and so under defined that they could be related to almost any factory collaboration. Whatever it's called, what began as simply JIT (delivering parts and subassemblies as needed, just in time) has evolved to SIT (sequence in time), which is the delivery of the parts and subassemblies both at the right time and in the right sequence to match the production sequence of the receiving plant.

JIT — just in time — has evolved to SIT — sequence in time

Taking a step back from any single plant-to-plant interaction, the degree of integration between multiple plants in terms of components and timing means that the overall system can be interpreted to be evolving into a "super factory," where individual factories serve as integrated subunits to a larger factory that spans geography. This isn't the easiest concept to visualize, so hopefully Figures 17.3 and 17.4 explain what has changed.

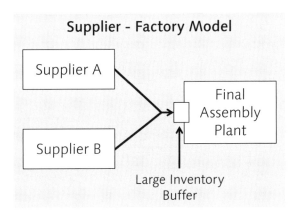

Figure 17.3 This is the Model That Has Persisted Since the Beginning of Industrial Manufacturing

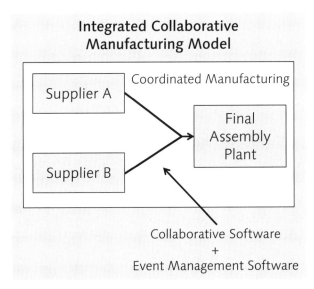

Figure 17.4 This Is the Model That Is Possible with Collaborative and Monitoring Technologies

The end result of this extensive collaboration is that even more advanced supply chain planning and management systems are required to manage it. Companies in this type of environment don't have the option to not collaborate: They must collaborate to execute this design.

Conclusion

The best way of understanding SAP SCM is to interpret it as a series of mature core planning applications, which is combined with new applications that are reacting to rapidly changing supply chain needs. Some of these supply chain needs are beginning to focus outside of the organization, rather than simply improving the internal planning of the company. SAP's investment in constantly bringing out new functionality in SAP SCM has been significant.

The Pareto rule, that only a small percentage of the effects come from a large number of causes, applies to SAP SCM in that, a large number of companies implement a relatively small percentage of the SAP SCM functionality

Keeping the SAP SCM implementation as simple as possible, while still meeting many of the business objectives, is one of the most important lessons you can take away from exposure to many SAP SCM projects. It's also one of the least followed observations because there's a natural inclination to try to take advantage of as much of the SAP SCM functionality as possible to give your business users the tools they need or at least the ones they say they need. The Pareto rule applies to SAP SCM because most business users won't use the majority of functionality they are given. Implementations that do well tend to cover the basics, but they cover those basics thoroughly. Implementations that are less successful get overly wrapped up in the complexity of SAP SCM and try to do too much.

A good indicator of how ready your company is to implement an advanced planning solvution is how the company is presently maintaining the more simplified supply chain management software you're using. If your company is running SAP ERP, it's worthwhile to check into how safety stock is currently being managed in Materials

Management (MM). If this value is being overwritten by different groups within the company and generally not being managed properly, this will most likely be a problem for the SAP SCM implementation. Safety stock is a fast and clearly visible indicator of how the system is being maintained as a whole. Another area to check is supplier lead times in MM. How accurate are the lead times in MM versus the lead times in reality? Have they been kept up to date, and are they constantly checked and maintained? SAP SCM can only provide a quality answer given quality input. Generally, an SAP SCM implementation doesn't necessarily lead to an improvement in the discipline with which system parameters are maintained. If these types of areas are not well maintained, an investment in improving their maintenance is a better investment than attempting to implement advanced planning software. This is true of SAP SCM or any other software package. In addition, SAP SCM will create more data that will have to be maintained (e.g., the system constraints). But after this area has been brought up to standard, your company will be in a much stronger position to realize gains from SAP SCM.

MM is responsible for stock transport orders that move material between facilities as well as purchase orders, which bring in new material from suppliers into the system

A number of broad trends have affected the development of SAP SCM and will likely affect how SAP SCM is developed and implemented in the future. These are important considerations to include in your long-term planning around SAP SCM. The broad trends are listed here:

> Energy issues

> The increased rapidity of inventory turnover

> Increased supply chain monitoring

> Collaborative planning trends

As you learned in Chapter 1, SAP SCM has developed rapidly since its initial introduction in 1998. SAP has navigated the product through a very dynamic period in the history of software. Many of the original projections for software in this space did not come true and don't appear likely to become true. SAP SCM and advanced planning generally are marked by complexity and variability. There is a sea of functionality to choose from in SAP SCM; however, every company has a specific budget and number of personnel resources that can be applied to supply chain planning. Your company should choose what is needed carefully and then apply a very high standard to those applications and functions. A full understanding of SAP SCM means being able to select those applications and subsets of functionality that most substantially affect your company's performance and then configuring them at the appropriate level of detail to create long-term sustainable planning solutions.

Knowing and understanding the history of SAP SCM development and implementation, along with the knowledge of your company's internal capabilities, will allow you to make the best decisions regarding SAP SCM.

We hope you've found this knowledge and understanding within the pages of this book.

Appendices

A Glossary

Activity Areas A section of the warehouse where storage bins are defined in SAP EWM.

Advanced Shipment Notification (ASN) An electronically formatted notification of pending deliveries. Also known as an EDI 856 document.

Alert Monitor Functionality in SAP SCM that allows for the configuration of customized notifications that can direct planners to focus on the highest priority item.

Application When used in reference to SAP SCM/SAP APO, refers to one of the applications such as DP, SNP, PP/DS, and so on.

ATP (Available to Promise) The ability to commit back on customers with high confidence as to whether their requirements can be met. ATP capability can be provided by a number of different ways in GATP.

ATP Quantity Calculated based on storage stock, planned receipts (production orders, purchase orders, planned orders, etc.), and planned issues (sales orders, deliveries, reservations, etc.).

BAPI (Business Application Programming Interface) A precisely defined interface providing access to processes and data in business applications.

Bill of Distribution (BOD) A subnetwork of the overall supply network that is valid for a product or a group of products. The BOD controls the flow parts through the supply network.

Calendar The multiple calendars in SAP SCM include shipping, warehouse, and production. Calendars declare when planned activities can be scheduled.

Capable to Match (CTM) One of the three methods for running SNP. CTM creates allocations by pegging supply and demand in successive runs, with the higher priority customers being allocated the supply over lower priority customers.

Capable to Promise (CTP) Brings capacity into the availability check process.

Capacity Leveling Performed to move loads off of over-capacity periods and resources and into periods where resources are under-capacity. Capacity leveling can be performed either manually or by the system.

Carrier Tendering   The process of the shipper putting freight out to bid and receiving confirmations on prospective freight movements from carriers.

Causals   The independent values on which the causal or leading indicator forecast is based. A common causal is the number of items to be serviced that are in the field.

Characteristics   The names of the descriptions that are represented by key figures.

CIF (Core Interface) Variant
A saved version of an integration model. Variants are particularly important in CIF because they are the main way of saving different integration models.

Collaborative Planning, Fore-casting, and Replenishment (CPFR)   A method of tightly coupling suppliers and buyers in a relationship marked by high amounts of forecast and data sharing.

Cross Docking   The function of moving material through a ware-house without putting the material away. Cross docking is enabled by temporary storage locations in the warehouse that allow the material to be staged without being put away. The emphasis of cross docking is on timing and material flow.

Cross Enterprise Supply Chain Integration   The concept of systems that integrate supplier and buyer supply chains. SAP Event Management and SAP Supplier Network Collaboration are key enabling technologies for cross en-terprise supply chain integration.

DRP Matrix   A main user inter-face into the SPP module, which shows both a forecast graphic as well as parameters that can be altered, all on the same screen.

Event Discreet   Activities in the supply that can be tracked.

Freight Units   A physical unit that includes packaging materials and the materials contained with them. Freight units control the material to be moved through SAP TM.

Handling Units   Controls the materials moved in the warehouse and in SAP EWM.

Heuristics   Rules of thumb that are used in planning to control things such as the movement of material. It's a nonoptimal but rapid method of arriving at a solution. Heuristics are used in SNP and PP/DS.

InfoCubes The objects that are ultimately queried in DP.

InfoObjects A superset of key figures and characteristics.

Integration Model A selection of data that is set up in CIF and used to move information between SAP ERP and SAP SCM.

Inventory Optimization The use of service levels to set inventory levels.

iPPE (Integrated Product and Process Model) A structure that supports engineering change management by enabling PP/DS to collect all of the data for an entire product lifecycle in one integrated model. It's appropriate for repetitive manufactured products with many variants.

Key Figures The numerical values that are used in the system.

Kit A grouping of materials that are sold together but don't result in a discrete finished good. That is, the individual items are used in conjunction with one another to accomplish a task. Examples of kits

are common in service parts and in the medical supplies field.

Labor Management The management of labor in the warehouse in a way that maximizes throughput while minimizing costs.

Leading Indicator Forecasting SAP nomenclature for causal forecasting, where the forecast is based not on history but on "causals," such as installed base, or the material or equipment that is in the field.

liveCache A combination of hardware memory and memory management software that allows the planning calculation to be performed to meet the performance needs to SAP SCM.

Mass Maintenance How large amounts of data is altered in SAP SCM at once.

MCA Morris Cohen and Associates, a software company specializing in service parts planning and whose SIO product is an approved xApp.

Models Create different data setups that allow the existence of an active version, which sends results back to SAP ERP for execution, along with inactive versions that are primarily used for simulation.

Multi Echelon Inventory Optimization   The ability to make planning decisions that move inventory up the supply chain network as well as down, and the ability to flexibly repositioning inventory to meet service level objectives. The factors in the decision to reposition inventory in SPP are move costs, inventory savings, service benefits, and warehouse space savings.

Multi Echelon   Where the distribution center isn't directly replenished from suppliers, but instead there's an intermediate regional distribution center (RDC).

Optimizer   A cost-driven method of running SNP, PP/DS, and SAP TM. The concept is to set up costs for different activities and to allow the optimizer to run against constraints to arrive at an optimal solution.

Party Entitled to Dispose   The business partner at a location that holds the title. Used in SAP EWM.

PDS (production data structures)   PDSs are, like PPMs, structures that hold resources, routing, and bills of material. The difference between the two is that PDSs were developed after PPMs, they provide better performance, and they have more capabilities with regards to engineering change

management. They also are created in SAP ERP, and unlike PPMs, cannot be altered in SAP SCM.

Pegging   The action of connecting a supply element (e.g., inventory) to a demand element (e.g., an order). Pegging can be either static (which means that the initial pegging isn't changed), or dynamic, where the pegging changes or can change per run.

Picking Waves   Picking waves refers to a premeditated way of performing picking in a warehouse.

Planned Dependent Requirements (PDR)   A requirement based on either a sales order or a component based on the demand of the bill of material that it's a part of.

Planned Independent Requirements (PIR)   A requirement for material that isn't driven by a sales order but is based on a forecast.

Planning Areas   The central data structure of DP and SNP. It's a container for key figures. The planning area feeds the planning book.

Planning Book   The primary planner or user interface to SAP SCM. Provides a method of saving different views into the data and ultimately represents bucketed data in a spreadsheet format.

Planning Object Structures (POSs)   The central data structure of DP and SNP that serves as a container for characteristics. The POS stores every unique combination of characteristics.

Planning Version   A setup of data that is available for use in SAP SCM. Planning versions are a variation of the planning models.

Poisson Distribution   A probability distribution used, among other things, for the management of low turning and or service parts.

PPM (Production Process Models)   The structures that hold the resources, routings, and bills of material.

Process Integration   The integration product from SAP that connects SAP to non-SAP systems, and SAP to SAP systems.

Product Allocation   The amount of supply set aside for a customer or for a category of customer. Allocation is a way of protecting supply from lower priority customers.

Product Allocation Quantity   The available quantity of the product to be allocated for a period. The incoming order quantity reduces the product allocation quantity.

Product Availability Check   The function of checking the availability of a product based on the ATP quantity.

Product Location Master   This is the combination of physical location and product record, which is where a great deal of master data used to manage the planning process is located.

Product View   Similar to the stock requirements list in SAP ERP, shows inbound and outbound activity at location.

Promotion Forecasting   The alternation of the forecast in anticipation of product promotions.

PSM (Planning Service Manager)   A transaction for accessing functionality that is distributed across SAP SCM. Currently it's generally focused on running SPP services (i.e., functionality).

Purchase Requisition (PReq)   A planned purchase order. Purchase requisitions are created in both SAP ERP and SAP SCM; however, they can only be converted in SAP ERP.

Purchasing Info Records   A mechanism in SAP ERP for connecting the material to the vendor.

Quota Arrangement A mechanism that allows the determination of applicable sources of supply for a purchase requisition at a point in time. The quota arrangement is the data that includes the source, validity period, and quota amount.

Realignment The process of adjusting the characteristic value combinations to match the reality of the business.

Repair Planning In SPP, the ability to plan a repair in lieu of bringing in new material to cover an expected demand.

Reservations A request to the warehouse or stores to keep a material ready for issue at a future date for a specific purpose.

Resource The object that allows SAP SCM to represent the reality of constrains in the supply chain. Resources can represent work centers in factories and trucks, among many other items that are used by the supply chain and restrict the throughput of the supply chain.

RFID (Radio Frequency Identification) A technology that provides serialized tracking of material in a warehouse but eventually throughout the supply chain.

SAP Business Objects Supply Chain Management An application that allows companies to track important metrics and to perform root-cause diagnostics of your supply chain. This will likely replace the approach on at least some projects where the metrics that are run out to BW.

SAP for Retail An industry solution for SAP ERP that allows the system to better manage the requirements of the retail industry. SAP F&R is used in conjunction with SAP for Retail.

SAP NetWeaver BW The SAP NetWeaver Business Warehouse.

Scheduling Agreement Outline purchase agreements against which materials are procured on specific dates within a time period. Scheduling agreements can be planned by SAP APO or be generated by SAP ERP.

Serialization The function of tracking individual items in a warehouse.

Service Level Planning The concept and functionality that allows planning decisions to work backwards from a stipulated service level.

Slotting The determination and use of the best locations in the warehouse for receiving items to be placed to maximize the efficiency of future picking.

Stock Transport Requisition (STR) A planned stock transport order. Stock transport orders are created in SAP SCM and converted in SAP ERP.

Storage Bin The lowest level of organization within SAP EWM.

Storage Section A subdivision of a storage type. Used in SAP EWM.

Storage Type Defines the physical storage areas that are assigned per warehouse number. Used in SAP EWM.

Subcontracting Where one company performs value added services, most often manufacturing, with materials provided by the company that is the customer to the principle.

Supersession The planned replacement of one service part for another service part. Often, this is to account for a new version of the part. Supersession can be one to one or one to many and can be one way, or two way (meaning

that the parts can serve as substitutes for one another).

Supply Chain Network The combination of locations and transportation lanes. Planning the supply chain network is considered the functionality area of SNP.

Supply Chain Unit A location in SAP EWM.

Time Horizon An important element of planning that basically states how far out a planning system looks in making decisions that affect the plan. The planning horizon changes per planning area.

Transportation Lanes The connection between locations that represents how materials flow through a supply chain network.

Unserviceable Service parts that are waiting to be repaired.

VAS (Value Added Services) Activities outside the traditional tasks of warehousing, including activities such as kitting, packing, labeling, and light assembly.

WM (Warehouse Management) A module in SAP ERP that performs a number of the functions of SAP EWM. The differences between WM and

SAP EWM are that SAP EWM is integrated into the SAP SCM planning system (as it's part of it) and has more advanced functionality.

Work Center   In SAP ERP, where work is performed in a factory. Work centers convert to resources in CIF when brought into SAP SCM.

xApp   A software application resulting from a partnership between SAP and a best of breed software company.

Yard   The parking area for trucks outside of the warehouse.

Yard Management   The effective management of the yard in a way that supports the objectives of the warehouse.

B   Bibliography

Chapter 4

http://sapplanning.wordpress.com/2008/05/08/capacity-leveling-in-detail-in-snp/

Chapter 6

Jorg Dickersbach, *Supply Chain Management with SAP APO* (New York: Springer Press, 2009).

Chapter 7

http://fourthpartylogistics.wordpress.com/2009/06/21/tendering-and-freight-marketplaces/

http://help.sap.com/saphelp_tm60/helpdata/en/d0/d3018b3f3d401eac867b287e8172c1/frameset.htm

Chapter 8

Konzepte, Prozesse, Erfolgsfaktoren, Praxisbeispiele, *Supply Chain Event Management* (Heidelberg: Physica-Verlag, 2006).

SAP Training Material: SCM663.

http://sapplanning.wordpress.com/2009/05/24/event-handlers-in-event-management/

http://sapplanning.wordpress.com/2009/07/12/collaborative-database-for-event-management-events/

Chapter 9

http://sapplanning.wordpress.com/2008/05/21/introduction-to-the-cif-for-scm-to-ecc-integration/

http://sapplanning.org/2008/05/21/cif/

SAP Training Manual: SCM 212 - SCM Integrated SCM Model.

Chapter 10

http://spplan.wordpress.com/2009/06/10/the-real-service-parts-question/

http://sapplanning.wordpress.com/2009/04/23/inventory-balancing-in-spp/

http://sapplanning.wordpress.com/2009/04/03/spp-forecast-profile/

http://sapplanning.wordpress.com/2009/04/22/spp-operating-parameters-and-repair-vs-buy/

Chapter 11

http://sapplanning.wordpress.com/2009/06/19/product-postponement-in-scm/

http://sapplanning.wordpress.com/2008/10/30/ewm-stock-replenishment/

www.redprairie.com/upload/resources/files/Auto_Best_Practices.pdf

http://cdcsoftwareinc.com/documents/cdcglobalservices/CDCGS_Catalyst_WP_Closing_The_Gap_Docking.pdf

www.ciber.com/downloads/whitepapers/CIBER_SAP_SupplyChain.pdf?CFID=12837792&CFTOKEN=67924036

Chapter 12

Chi-Kin Chan, Heung Win J, *Successful Strategies in Supply Chain Management* (Pennsylvania: Idea Group Inc., 2005).

Daniel Sorenson, *The Automotive Development Process* (New York: Springer Press, 2000).

Chapter 13

SAP Retail to SAP F&R integration manual: *https://websmp207.sap-ag.de/~sapidb/011000358700001758372008E.*

Chapter 14

http://spplan.wordpress.com/2008/01/13/performance-based-logistics/

http://spplan.wordpress.com/2008/10/03/is-performance-based-logistics-for-real/

http://spplan.wordpress.com/2008/01/01/service-parts-and-pbl/

www.ecis2009.it/papers/ecis2009-0482.pdf

www.oppapers.com/essays/Evolution-Amazon-S-Supply-Chain-Distribution-Systems/175681

http://sapplanning.wordpress.com/2009/05/07/gatp-atp-trees-and-amazon-com/

www.pbcentral.com/columns/hildreth_leo/070711b_Sony-MacBook_or_Apple-VAIO.shtml

http://hbswk.hbs.edu/item/2862.html

Chapter 17

http://sapplanning.org/2009/04/24/plm-and-lifecycle-planning-in-scm-dp-2/

"Change Drivers: Navigating the New Auto Supply Chain," *Inbound Logistics* (February, 2007).

Jeff Rubin, *Why Your World Is About to Get A Whole Lot Smaller* (Random House, 2009).

Thomas Klier, James Rubenstein, *Who Really Made Your Car* (UpJohn Institute, 2008).

Index